Hanas
Jonas
The Concept of
Responsibility

HERODOTUS

ON THE WAR FOR
GREEK FREEDOM

HERODOTUS

ON THE WAR FOR GREEK FREEDOM

Selections from the *Histories*

Translations by
SAMUEL SHIRLEY

Edited, with Introduction and Notes, by
JAMES ROMM

Hackett Publishing Company, Inc.
Indianapolis/Cambridge

For further information, please address:

Hackett Publishing Company, Inc.
P.O. Box 44937
Indianapolis, IN 46244-0937

www.hackettpublishing.com

Cover art: *Audience Scene from Treasury. King with Crown Prince and Attendants behind Him.* Persepolis, South Portico, Courtyard 17, c. 522–486. Courtesy of the Oriental Institute of the University of Chicago.

Cover design by Abigail Coyle
Text design by Meera Dash
Maps on pages xxii–xxv, xxvii by Bill Nelson
Composition by Agnew's, Inc.
Printed at Sheridan Books, Inc.

Library of Congress Cataloging-in-Publication Data

Herodotus.
    [Historiae. English. Selections]
    On the war for Greek freedom : selections from the Histories / translations by Samuel Shirley ; edited, with introduction and notes, by James Romm.
      p. cm.
    Includes index.
    ISBN 0-87220-668-8 (cloth) — ISBN 0-87220-667-X (paper)
    1. Greece—History—Persian Wars, 500–449 B.C.   2. Iran—History—To 640.   I. Shirley, Samuel, 1912–   II. Romm, James S.   III. Title.

DF225 .H3913 2003
938′.03—dc21

                                  2002038791

Contents

Introduction   vii
Chronology of the Archaic Age   xx
Maps   xxii

Herodotus, *On the War for Greek Freedom*

    I. Herodotus' Introduction   1
   II. Prologue: The Reign of Croesus of Lydia
       (c. 560–46 B.C.E.)   4
  III. The Growth of Persia: Cyrus Conquers Asia
       (c. 550–30 B.C.E.)   28
  IV. The Growth of Persia: Cambyses Conquers
       North Africa (c. 530–22 B.C.E.)   51
   V. The Growth of Persia: Darius Enters
       Europe (521–499 B.C.E.)   75
  VI. The Greek Revolt from Persia (499–94 B.C.E.)   90
 VII. Persia versus Greece: Darius' Wars (494–90 B.C.E.)   99
VIII. Persia versus Greece: Xerxes' War (484–80 B.C.E.)   119
  IX. Persia versus Greece: Mardonius' War and After
       (480–79 B.C.E.)   165

Historical Epilogue   188
Main Characters and Places   190
Index of Proper Names   197

Introduction

"Those cities that were formerly great are now diminished, while those that are now great were once small." If a single sentence can be said to sound the keynote of Herodotus' *Histories*, surely it is this one, privileged by its position at the end of the work's introductory segment. Change is the greatest of Herodotus' many themes and the one that, like the sun in Plato's famous metaphor, sheds illumination on all the others. A particular kind of change interested him most, moreover: Not mere instability or flux, but the movement that results in a leveling of extremes, like the reversal of a pendulum that has swung too far in one direction. Such changes reveal the hand of divinity at work in the world, for the gods dislike extremes and everywhere favor balance, proportion, and the mean. Human attempts to attain extremes—of power and wealth, for example—are doomed to fail in the long run; just as with the oscillation of boom and bust in finance, a "correction" must inevitably take its course.

The long run, however, may be very long indeed. While the ups and downs of economic cycles can be plotted on monthly charts, the rises and falls of nation-states occur over decades or even centuries, often too slowly to be perceived in the span of any one lifetime. Hence the need for historians, who can remind us of the larger perspective when we feel we have attained a stasis or a control of our destiny ("the end of history," as the triumph of liberal democracy was famously dubbed at the end of the twentieth century). Herodotus was the first writer in the Western tradition to examine the ebb and flow of political power over such a vast time span, to capture not just a single war (as Homer had done) but the rise of a great empire, the cresting of its influence and might, and the beginnings of its inevitable lapse into decline. Although he has been called the father of history, he might be better hailed as the discoverer of the historical time scale, a breakthrough as significant for his era as the invention of the telescope was to the Renaissance.

The Scope of the *Histories*

Herodotus claims at 1.5 that he will begin his story with the rise of Croesus of Lydia (c. 560)[1], but this claim quickly turns out to be disin-

---

1. All dates in this volume are B.C.E. unless otherwise indicated.

genuous. No sooner has Croesus been introduced in 1.6 than Herodotus leaps back in time five generations, to relate how Croesus' ancestor Gyges seized the Lydian throne from Candaules; and he even pauses to take a further look backward at the origin of Candaules' dynasty among the offspring of the god Heracles, over five hundred years earlier. Much the same back-leaping movement occurs in the narratives of the Medes, the Egyptians, and the Greeks, tracing a continuous line of development over about three thousand years (in the case of Egypt, one of the world's two oldest peoples). But even such vastitudes of historical time are dwarfed by the slow evolution of the earth's surface, as in the formation of the land of Egypt out of Nile silt "in the vast stretch of time before my birth" (2.11)—an expanse marked off by Herodotus in increments of ten thousand years. Here his time scale approaches the geological, easily surpassing the biblical scheme, which, up until the eighteenth century C.E., circumscribed all terrestrial events within a span of six thousand years.

Of course, this reach back into the distant past had a benefit for Herodotus, as Thucydides was quick to point out some years later: With no surviving evidence to gainsay him, Herodotus had a free hand in embellishing, altering, or perhaps even inventing the events he records as history. Readers who are accustomed to the empirical bias of modern-day historiography will feel at sea in the first few books of the *Histories*, no longer sure where the boundary lies between fact and fiction, memory and invention; indeed, the most accomplished experts are often unsure (as was, on some occasions at least, Herodotus himself). In most cases, a solid grounding of recoverable facts underlies the narrative, but many layers of imaginative material have been added, including speeches and dialogues, omens and portents, folktales and myths. Some readers will adapt easily to this Herodotean farrago and come to savor it as one of the text's principal delights; others will remain uneasy and mistrustful of the author's intentions. In this regard I think it worth quoting at length what Robert Alter has recently written of the historiographical method of the biblical books of Samuel:

> The known general contours of the historical event are not tampered with, but the writer brings to bear the resources of literary art in order to imagine deeply, and critically, the concrete moral and emotional predicaments of living in history, in the political realm. To this end, the writer feels free to invent an inner language for the characters with a fine mesh of recurrent motifs and phrases and analogies of incident, and to define the meaning of events through allusion, metaphor and symbol.

The writer does all this not to fabricate history but in order to understand it.[2]

This description, it seems to me, eloquently defines the technique Herodotus uses in the first book of the *Histories*, where he often looks back as many centuries into the past as did the chroniclers who composed the historical books of the Hebrew Bible.

The length of Herodotus' chronology is matched by the breadth of his geography. His predecessor Hecataeus had composed a kind of world tour in prose, probably entitled *Periodos Gēs* (circuit of the earth). The surviving fragments show that this was an ambitious catalogue of the lands and peoples known to the archaic Ionian Greeks, who, with their exposure to the intellectual crosscurrents of the Asian mainland, had learned more about such matters than their European kinsmen. Herodotus shared Hecataeus' goal of depicting the entire known world and, quite possibly, borrowed some of his information as well, but unlike his predecessor he housed his verbal world atlas within a connected narrative framework. His is not a mere "circuit of the earth" but a study of how power advances, stage by stage, across the globe, until it threatens to encompass under one regime all that the globe contains. And this includes all the richly varied cultures of the earth's peoples, ranging from the Stone Age primitives of its least developed regions to the masters of its great urban centers, the Egyptians, Babylonians, and the Greeks themselves, whom Herodotus never describes explicitly but whose culture often stands as the norm against which others are evaluated.

The Persians

The framework that allows Herodotus to survey so much of the earth's surface is the story of Medo-Persian imperial expansion, from roughly 650 to 480. In these 170 years the map of the ancient world underwent as much change as it had in perhaps the preceding millennium. The Medes, a nomadic people skilled in horsemanship and archery, first entered the historical record as tribute-paying subjects of the Assyrians in the ninth century. By the seventh century they had begun to chafe under the overlordship of the ancient Assyrian empire, and around 650 they actually dared to attack it, with the help of their own subjects, the Persians. Only a few decades more sufficed to make

2. Robert Alter, *The David Story: A Translation with Commentary of 1 and 2 Samuel* (New York: W. W. Norton, 1999), xvii–xviii.

the Medes strong enough to overcome the Assyrians and destroy the imperial capital, Nineveh, in 612. In the next century the Persians under Cyrus overthrew the Medes and took over the territory won from Assyria, and the Achaemenid empire was born.

World history offers few parallels to the aggressiveness and drive of this new Persian entity; only perhaps the Mongols in the thirteenth century C.E. and the Aztecs in the fifteenth had similarly meteoric rises to superpower status. In the thirty years following Cyrus' accession, the Persians subdued the kingdoms of Lydia, Chaldaea (Babylon), and Egypt, along with numerous other less prominent realms (including the Greek cities of Ionia). A departmental system of taxation was quickly put in place, with tribute payments collected by twenty regional satraps, or governors, being funneled to the imperial capitals of Susa, Persepolis, and Pasargadae; all the precious metals of Asia were drained into these coffers. Highways were built, sea routes charted, and lines of communication laid across the length and breadth of the empire. Lands stretching from North Africa to the banks of the Indus River were united in a single contiguous state, by far the biggest the ancient world had yet seen.

The Jews, who have left us the most complete record of how these events were perceived by contemporary observers, attest in many of their scriptures to a sense of awe at the rapidity of the changes around them—changes that, from their perspective, could only have been guided by a divine hand. They chose to interpret the rise of Cyrus as part of a plan for their own redemption: For unlike the now-fallen empires of Babylon and Assyria, the Persians were tolerant masters who did not interfere with the religious practices of their subjects. Indeed, Cyrus' capture of Babylon and freeing of the captive Jewish population earned him the epithet *messiah* (the anointed one) in the later sections of the book of Isaiah. Conversely, the dramatic collapses of the former overlords of the Near East were viewed as punishments for their arrogance, over-confidence, material decadence, and mistreatment of the Jews.

To the Greeks, by contrast, who had had very little experience of imperial subjugation prior to the coming of Cyrus, this new Persian state looked far less benign. The Greek cities on the coast of Asia felt the most immediate threat. Granted, they had been paying tribute to the kings of Lydia for decades, but these were hellenized monarchs from a culture resembling their own (1.95); the Greeks even fought on Croesus' side in his war against Cyrus, rather than supporting the Persians as liberators. As a result, Cyrus bore them a grudge from the time of his first arrival in western Asia Minor, and most of them sought, in vain, to build defensive walls to resist him. These new Persian overlords, moreover, neither knew nor respected the Greek way of life, as illustrated in the anecdote Herodotus relates (1.153) concerning the first encounter between Persians and mainland Greeks. The prospect of paying tribute to such a distant and unrecognizable master rankled more deeply than subjection to Lydia, and Herodotus uses the word "enslavement" to describe the new relationship (1.169, not in this volume), though its terms could hardly have been as harsh as that would imply.

Politically, the Persian state was organized as a strong, centralized monarchy, a system Herodotus believed had been chosen by the Persians themselves over oligarchy or democracy (3.80–83). The imperial leader was known to the Greeks as "the King" or "the Great King"; his supremacy over the barbarian world was so overwhelming that the qualifier "of Persia" was not needed. The semidivine stature of this monarch meant that all subjects had to prostrate themselves before him, a custom abhorred by the Greeks as a blurring of the boundaries between mortals and gods. The solemn, reverent stone reliefs from the royal palaces at Persepolis, still visible today in the deserts of Iran, attest to the awe inspired by the king's presence. By contrast, Herodotus' portraits of the four kings of Persia who ruled in the empire's first century—Cyrus, Cambyses, Darius, and Xerxes—are drawn on a human scale and at times reveal deep flaws, though as personifications of supreme power they remain majestic.

The Greeks

Whereas monarchy thrived in Asia in the sixth century, the institution had mostly been eliminated from the Greek world well before that time. Of the major Greek city-states, only Sparta retained a monarchy during the period Herodotus records—or perhaps "dyarchy" would be a better term, since, by a curious development (explained by Herodotus in legendary terms at 6.52), two kings reigned there at any one time. Other cities were governed by loosely formed oligarchies in which most powers rested with a council of wealthy estate owners, and only token privileges were extended to the assemblies constituted by the great mass of poorer citizens. In many cases, strife between these two economic strata, or factionalism within the aristocracy, became severe enough in the sixth century to allow a self-appointed strongman, or *tyrannos*, to come to power and govern the city as a kind of private corporation. These *tyrannoi*, or "rulers"— the English derivative "tyrant" is inaccurate since it implies a harsh or despotic regime—often did great good for their populations, especially the more disadvantaged elements who had no other champions. But without any constitutional checks on their power, they were also capable of great abuses, and the sons who succeeded them were often harsher and more rapacious still. By about 500, the *tyrannoi*, like the kings before them, had been mostly swept out of the city-states of mainland Greece, though in Ionia the Persians found it useful to retain them as puppet rulers of their Hellenic subjects.

At Athens, the ejection of the ruling *tyrannos* Hippias in 510 created a political upheaval that led, two years later, to the enactment of a radically progressive, antiaristocratic set of reforms. The newly organized regime can be called the world's first working democracy, though it was hardly democratic by today's standards; the great majority of residents, including all women, had few civil rights. Nevertheless the popular assembly at Athens was now given unprecedented control of the city's affairs, and high offices were thrown open to all but the poorest adult male citizens. Herodotus referred to this new experiment as *isonomia* (equality under the law), or *isēgoriē* (equal rights of [political] speech); on only one occasion does he use the more modern term, *demokratia*, to refer to similar assembly-based governments set up by the Persians in Ionia as a way to win popular support. His interest in its development at Athens, especially its relationship to military strength, attests to the remarkable success the regime had enjoyed in his own lifetime, as it became both increasingly democratic and increasingly powerful during much of the course of the fifth century (more on this below).

While divided internally by factionalism and class tensions, the archaic Greek cities were also divided from one another by territorial disputes, rivalries for power and trade, and ethnic distinctions. Though all Greeks of the age acknowledged a shared culture that set them apart from non-Greeks, they also had few collective institutions in which that shared culture was made manifest, the shrine of the Delphic oracle being one early and prominent exception. Herodotus is in fact the earliest Greek author we know of to use a single name, Hellas, to refer to all the lands inhabited by Greek peoples, or to use the adjective Hellenic to refer to the gods, language, and customs that characterized them. In his work, especially the three last books with their account of an allied Greek resistance to Persian domination, we see the first halting steps taken by the Greeks toward establishing a national identity that would transcend the bounds of the city-state. But at the outset of his narrative such steps were still a long way off, and cooperation or even consultation between the fiercely independent *poleis* took place only rarely. The tension between this fractious diversity of the Greek world and the collective action needed to fight the Persians forms one of the central themes of the *Histories*.

Among the features of Greek life that distinguished it from that of the barbarians was the use of a particular military strategy developed in the seventh and sixth centuries. Hoplites, metal-clad foot soldiers, were organized into cohesive blocks called phalanxes, such that the shields of those in the front lines joined together to form a wall of armor. Used against less organized armies or against soldiers not protected by metal, the hoplite phalanx was devastatingly effective. Already by the mid-seventh century, Egyptian pharaohs had begun using Greek hoplites as mercenaries to support their regimes and defeat their enemies, a development noted by Herodotus at 2.152 (not included in this volume). Eventually the Greek way of war would prove so superior to that of the barbarian world as to enable a largely Hellenic army, led by Alexander the Great, to conquer not only Egypt but most of Asia as well. But in the period covered by the *Histories*, this tactical advantage was as yet still inchoate and was offset by the many weaknesses in Greek military organization, principally by the amateurishness of armies who were assembled by each state on an occasional basis from its untrained and self-equipped citizens.

Only one Greek city of this era had established a truly professional standing army, by devoting almost the whole of public life toward the goal of training its offspring to become soldiers. As in its political institutions, so in its military, Sparta had evolved along totally unique lines during the age of city-state formation. With its tiny population, and its need to dominate the much more populous neighboring region of Messenia, which supplied most of its food crops, the Spartans early on became a warrior race, devoting all civic resources to the perfection of hoplite tactics. Constant drill and exercise made each Spartan citizen or "Spartiate" a kind of superman, greatly feared by both Greek and barbarian foes. Relying on its superiority in hoplite warfare, Sparta had by about 600 established a hegemony over its own region, the Peloponnese, and a much looser and less formalized leadership of the Greek world generally. But its military supremacy came at a steep price: Culturally and economically, the city remained frozen in time and resistant to the innovations that marked other Greek societies of the age, in particular Athens.

Herodotus

The author of the *Histories* belonged to neither Athens nor Sparta by birth, nor even to the Greek world exclusively. He was born in Halicarnassus, a mixed Greek and Carian city on the western coast of modern Turkey, and his own family tree contains both Greek and Carian names. The date of his birth can only be inferred from his writings and a few other slender bits of biographical data, and it probably should be placed around 485. Thus, he might have been just old enough to witness and recollect the events he describes in the last third of his *Histories*, though his mature understanding of them could only have come from secondhand stories passed on by his elders. Halicarnassus, it should be noted, appears in the *Histories* as a city fighting perforce on the Persian side against the Greeks, led by an enthusiastic supporter of Xerxes, the colorful Carian queen Artemisia.

At some point in his youth, as we are told by an ancient but not always reliable biography, the *Suda*, Herodotus clashed with a ruler of Halicarnassus named Lygdamis, one of Artemisia's descendants, and was forced into exile on Samos (the information squares with Herodotus' detailed knowledge of Samian history and monuments). Thereafter, the course of his life remains almost totally opaque to us. He is said to have lived at Thurii, a Greek colony founded in Italy around 443, and to have died either there or in Macedonia. The date of his death is usually given as circa 425, but this, too, like his birth date, is purely inferential (the latest events mentioned in his text occurred around 430).

From his one surviving work, the *Histories*, we know that Herodotus traveled widely throughout the ancient world, visiting (by his own account) much of Egypt, the coast of the Black Sea, the Levantine coast, northern Africa, southern Italy, and perhaps Babylon as well. Such far-flung journeys would not have been easy to undertake in that time, and some scholars have supposed that he sailed as a merchant seaman to these various ports of call. Others, more cynically, have suggested that he cribbed much of his foreign material from other writers and then lied in claiming that he had gathered it himself. Such a view would call Herodotus' credibility into question on many fronts, but it is not generally accepted. Assuming he is not one of history's great hoaxers, then, Herodotus must be ranked as one of its great inquiring travelers, anticipating Ibn-Battuta and Marco Polo in his penetration of distant lands and peoples.

Herodotus' personality is sketched on every page of his text, even though he tells us almost nothing about his own thoughts and emotions. He was a keen observer of the world around him, whose interests were engaged by almost every field of knowledge, from geology to politics to moral philosophy. He delights in sharing choice bits of information to which he alone is privy, or in collecting the great rarities of human experience one finds today in "strange but true" newspaper items. In his portraits of historical characters he shows a great capacity for clemency and understanding; his sympathies go out even to the lunatic Cambyses (3.33), and the Persians who led the assault on Greece in 480, Xerxes and Mardonius, are often treated with respect and even admiration. Indeed, the whole narrative of the *Histories* reads more like a tragic portrait of the defeat of Persia than a celebration of Greek victory (though both strains are present); like the playwright Aeschylus before him, Herodotus refrained from demonizing the invaders of Greece or glorying in their downfall. His lack of pro-Hellenic bias, not only in his account of the Persian Wars but in his descriptions of foreign lands and peoples, earned him the epithet *philobarbaros* (barbarian-lover), in a later era of Greek antiquity.

This lack of bias also extended to his evenhanded treatment of the two principal Greek cities involved in the war, Athens and Sparta—also the two superpowers that were wrestling for dominance during much of Herodotus' own life. As a writer and thinker, Herodotus would naturally be attracted to Athens as "the school of Hellas," and, indeed, a poem supposedly written by Sophocles is addressed to him, suggesting he had made friends among the Athenian intelligentsia. But the *Histories* also contains glowing portraits of Spartan military valor, especially in the episode of Thermopylae and the commentary by Demaratus that surrounds it. Herodotus seems almost studiously evenhanded in recording the heroism first of one city, then of the other, though in an important passage (7.139) he argues that credit for the victory belongs primarily to Athens. It is an opinion he thinks will be unpopular among the majority of his readers, a sign of how much had changed in Greece since the end of the Persian Wars.

The *Histories* in Its Time

No matter when we suppose Herodotus wrote the *Histories*—and he may have worked on it over decades, with final publication at some point in the 420s—he addressed a Greek audience who knew a very different world than the one he describes. Persia had ceased to be a threat to European Greece and had even been decisively beaten in Asia during the 460s; after 449 not even the Ionian cities that had always been Persia's prey had anything left to fear from it. However a new master had arisen to take its place as ruler of the Aegean: Athens, whose supreme naval power enabled it to dictate to any island or coastal city, whether Greek or barbarian. The coalition of Aegean states formed by Athens in 479 (see 9.106) evolved gradually from an anti-Persian alliance into a tributary empire, and after 454 Athens began treating her subjects' contributions as her own personal treasury rather than a common defense fund. Cities that regarded this arrangement as an infringement of sovereignty and tried to exit the alliance now discovered that they were unable to; Athens would use naval blockades to force them back in. Eventually this empire grew so powerful and expansive that Sparta, the traditional military superpower of Greece, felt compelled to check it, and the disastrous twenty-seven–year Peloponnesian War began in 431.

Herodotus only rarely makes explicit reference to these post–Persian-War developments. Yet they formed the essential context in which he expected his *Histories* to be read, and we modern readers must always bear them in mind. The actions of Miltiades after the battle of Marathon, or of Themistocles after that of Salamis (8.111–12), closely anticipate the tactics of the mature Athenian empire, while the speeches of Artabanus to Xerxes about the uncertain chances of war (7.10, 7.49–51) are similar to arguments that were advanced at both Athens and Sparta in the years leading up to their great conflict. We do not know how much of that conflict Herodotus lived to see, but conceivably he already knew, at the time he gave his work final shape, that neither side was succeeding in its war goals and that Athens had suffered a devastating plague that had undermined its stability and strength. Just conceivably, he had witnessed the great Sicilian invasion mounted by Athens in 415, in which many of the Persian errors of 480 and 479 were repeated, with disastrous consequences. However that may be, he certainly knew that any intelligent reader would draw lessons from the past regarding events in the present, and that Athens' attempts to build and defend a Greek empire would be compared with those of Persia to do likewise some fifty years earlier.

That is not to say that Herodotus means us to see Athens as the new Persia, for he was aware of vast differences between the goals and characters of the two nations. But the remarks he puts into the mouths of his wisest speakers over and over again, concerning the perils of big enterprises, the inevitability of change, and the jealous opposition of the gods to any human quest for greatness, were meant to be heeded by imperial powers in all cultures at all times. Herodotus would be gratified, certainly, to learn that they are being studied in America during the twenty-first century, at a time when a latter-day hegemon debates where the limits of its power should be fixed.

In addition to the political and military changes he witnessed, Herodotus also lived through a period of unprecedented intellectual ferment in the Greek world. Radically modern ideas and teachings, including the moral philosophy of Socrates, were gaining adherents at Athens and elsewhere, sometimes to the detriment of traditional religious practices and conceptions of the gods. Indeed, an exact contemporary of Herodotus, Protagoras of Abdera, publicly proclaimed his agnosticism about the gods, a risky move in a society that was capable of prosecuting and even executing the impious. Herodotus takes a certain interest in these new schools of thought but holds them at a great distance; his text constantly reaffirms the power of the divine, the forethought taken by the gods for maintaining an orderly and balanced world, and even the intervention of divine forces in recent human history. The episode of Xerxes' and Artabanus' dreams concerning the invasion of Greece (7.15–18) forms a good case in point. Herodotus allows the two men to hold a discussion over the origin of dreams, in which Artabanus advances a purely psychological explanation and dismisses the role of the gods. But after giving an airing to this modern, quasi-scientific view, Herodotus shows Artabanus proven wrong; it was the divine, after all, that willed the Persian attack.

Even in matters as deeply personal as religion, however, it is difficult to say with certainty what Herodotus believed or what view his text expresses. Though in general, for example, he reveres the sacred authority of the Delphic oracle, he also shows how the Priestess of that shrine can be bribed or manipulated into giving a desired answer (6.66), or can even *change* an answer under pressure (7.141, not in this volume). In other matters too, even the essential contrast between Asian and Greek political systems, Herodotus does not sketch out a single doctrine or conviction but shows his readers a wealth of stories and anecdotes that point sometimes in one direction, sometimes in another. The *Histories* invites questions and explorations more than it gives answers; it seeks to capture the complexities and contingencies of the world it records without reducing them to neat formulas. It remains an enigmatic text for readers of today, as it presumably was in Herodotus' own time; now, as then, it provides an invigorating model of one man's keen observation of the world, open-minded inquiry, and humane, unbiased analysis of historical figures and events.

About This Edition

The title of this collection of excerpts, *On the War for Greek Freedom*, is intended to highlight the main story line of the *Histories*, though in doing so it eclipses a great number of other subjects Herodotus addresses in the text. The same can be said of the excerpts themselves: They have been chosen so as to give a reduced version of the text's central thread, with only a passing glance at its many tangents, digressions, and subplots. We have tried to capture the main thrust of the *Histories* without entirely losing a sense of its vastness, diversity, and breadth.

Most of the passages presented here were translated by Samuel Shirley and then edited and revised by James Romm. The editor takes responsibility for whatever inaccuracies or infelicities the translations may contain. Several passages were also added by the editor, in his own translation, to those prepared by the translator; these have been identified in the notes as the work of the editor.

Each paragraph of the translation has been marked with the book and chapter numbers in brackets, but the correlation with the same numbers in standard editions of Herodotus is not exact. In some cases there is a small discrepancy where a sentence ending a story or marking the transition to a new topic has been assimilated into the preceding chapter. The bracketed numbers serve not only as a referencing system but as indicators of where excisions have been made within a single story or episode; nonconsecutive chapter numbers, rather than ellipses at the ends of paragraphs, reveal these cuts. Ellipses have been used only to show excisions within a single chapter. Italicized summaries, which bridge the selections, are the work of the editor. Herodotean book divisions have been superseded by the editor's section headings denoting political events in the story; it is only happenstance that there are nine of these, as there are nine books in the conventional division of the *Histories*.

I wish to thank Leslie Clockel for helping to prepare the manuscript; Deborah Wilkes and the rest at Hackett Publishing for their constant support and encouragement; Carolyn Dewald and Walter

Blanco for collegial consultations and conversations (Carolyn in particular suggested the title of the volume); and, above all, my wife, Tanya Marcuse, without whose love and patience nothing would flourish, including this book.

James Romm

Chronology
of the Archaic Age
(All dates are B.C.E.)

GREECE	EGYPT	NEAR EAST
Early history		
1400–1200 Mycenaean age	c. 3400 Union of upper and lower Egypt	9th–7th c. Assyrian domination of Near East
c. 1150 Trojan War	2700–2200 Building of pyramids	8th c. Invasions of Asia by Scythians, Cimmerians from North and East; rise of Median kingdom
1200–750 Dark Ages		
c. 750 Homeric poems composed		
8th c. Age of colonization		
700		
Beginnings of Greek literacy	c. 711–664 Egypt ruled by Ethiopians (25th dynasty)	701 Invasions of Egypt and Judea by Assyrians under Sennacherib
7th c. Establishment of Spartan constitution (perhaps by Lycurgus)	664 Conquest of Egypt by Assyrians	c. 660 Rise of Lydian kingdom
	663 Founding of Saite or 26th dynasty by Psammetichus	668–27 Reign of Ashurbanipal in Assyria
		664 Assyrians conquer Egypt
650		
625–585 Periander tyrant in Corinth	604 Egyptians under Necho defeated in Asia by Babylonians (Battle of Carchemish)	612 Fall of Nineveh (Assyrian capital) to Medes, Scythians, and Babylonians
Late 6th c. Thales of Miletus; beginnings of Ionian philosophy and natural science		605–562 Nebuchadnezzar king of Babylonians
600		
594 (?) Archonship of Solon at Athens	Early 6th c. Egypt begins using Greek mercenaries	598 Babylonian conquest of Judea
560–56 First tyranny of Pisistratus at Athens	593–88 Reign of Psammis (Psammetichus II)	585 Battle of Medes and Lydians (inconclusive)
	588–69 Reign of Apries	c. 560 Croesus king in Lydia
	570–25 Reign of Amasis	

GREECE	EGYPT	NEAR EAST
550		
c. 550 Ionia subject to Croesus	Mid-6th c. Alliance of Amasis with Croesus of Lydia against Persians	549 Cyrus defeats Astyages
540–22 Polycrates tyrant in Samos		546 (?) Cyrus defeats Croesus
510 Fall of Pisistratid tyranny at Athens; democratic reforms	525 Cambyses of Persia conquers Egypt	539 Cyrus conquers Babylon
		530 Death of Cyrus
		525 Cambyses conquers Egypt
		522 Death of Cambyses, accession of Darius
500		
499–94 Ionian rebellion	459 Amyrtaeus' unsuccessful rebellion against Persia; Athenian troops called in for support	492 Darius' first attempt on Greece
490 Darius invades Greece		490 Darius' second attempt on Greece
485 (?) Birth of Herodotus		486 Death of Darius
480 Xerxes invades Greece		480 Xerxes invades Greece
479 Final defeat of Persians		465 Death of Xerxes
450		
454–32 Height of Athenian empire; age of Pericles	Late 5th c. Egyptians expel Persians, regain independence	448 Peace treaty between Persians and Greeks
431–04 Peloponnesian War		
425 (?) Death of Herodotus		

INDIA

Caspapyrus

Indus R.

Arimaspians

Issedones

Massagetae

Sogdians

Bactrians

Argippaei

Thyssagetae

CAUCASUS

CASPIAN SEA

Araxes R.

Colchians

Saspires

MEDES

ASIA

PERSIANS

Susa

RED SEA

Tanais R.

Geloni

Budini

Oarus

Lycus

Hypanis

LAKE MAEOTIS

Phasis R.

Tigris R.

Babylon

Euphrates R.

ARABIA

ARABIAN GULF

Melanchloeni

Gerrhus R.

Androphagi

SCYTHIANS

BLACK SEA

Tyras R.

Olbia

Sinope

Cyprus

Nile Delta

Memphis

Thebes

Elephantine

Meroe

Macrobians

Neuri

Agathyrsi

Maris R.

Ister

Getae

THRACIANS

Crete

Cyrene

Syrtis

Augila

Ammonium

SIGYNNAE

Agathyrsi

EUROPE

Carpis R.

Alpis R.

ILLYRIANS

Adrias

Ombri

Eneti

Tertheni

Taras

Lotophagi

Atarantes

Garamantes

LIBYA

Automoli

ETHIOPIANS

Ister

Pyrene

Lygyes

Massalia

Cyrnus

Sardo

Carthage

Atlantes

Mt. Atlas

Nile R.

CELTS

Iberes

Cynetes

Tartessus

Gadeira

Pillars of Heracles

Soloeis Pr.

ATLANTIC SEA

The Persian Empire at Its Height

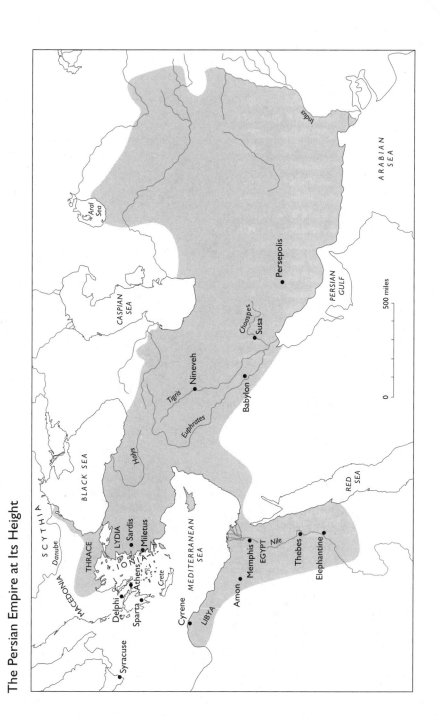

Greece and Asia Minor

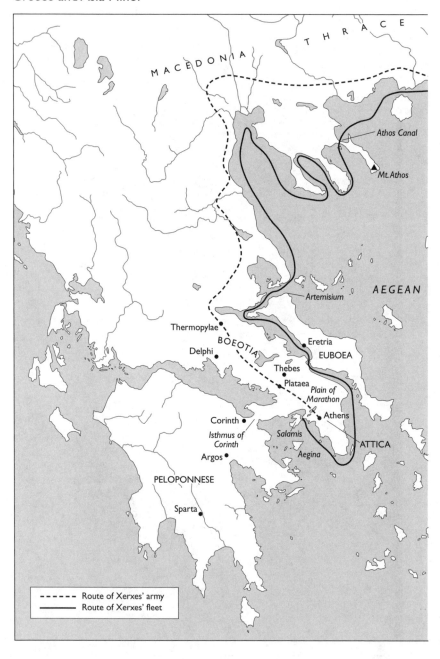

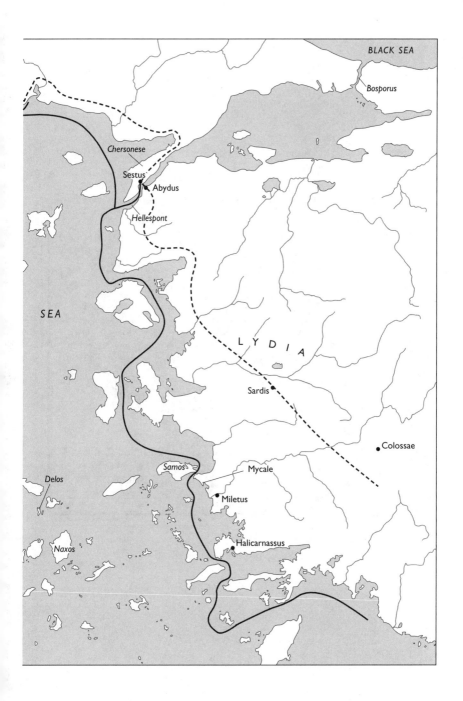

BLACK SEA

Bosporus

Chersonese

Sestus

Abydus

Hellespont

SEA

L Y D I A

Sardis

Colossae

Samos

Mycale

Delos

Miletus

Naxos

Halicarnassus

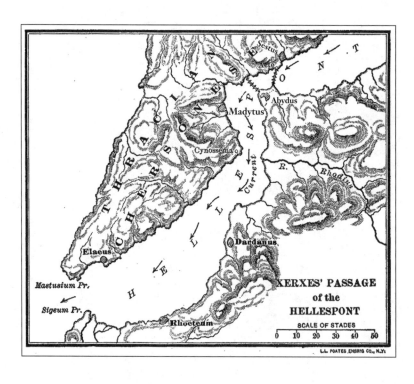

XERXES' PASSAGE
of the
HELLESPONT

SCALE OF STADES

0   10   20   30   40   50

L.L. POATES ENGR'G CO., N.Y.

Salamis, the Night before the Battle

OOOOO Greek fleet
XXXXX Persian fleet, original station
XXXXXX Persian fleet, night before battle

Athens

Phalerum

Bay of
Phalerum

Munychia

Piraeus

PSYTTALEIA

Mt. Aegaleos

Thriasian Plain

Eleusis

BAY OF ELEUSIS

Salamis

SARONIC GULF

SALAMIS

Megara

3 miles

0

xxvii

I

Herodotus' Introduction

Herodotus of Halicarnassus here gives the results of his researches,[1] so that the events of human history may not fade with time and the notable achievements both of Greeks and of foreigners may not lack their due fame; and, among other things, to show why these peoples came to make war on one another.

[1.1] Persian storytellers place the responsibility for the quarrel on the Phoenicians, a people who came to the Mediterranean from the so-called Red Sea region and settled in the country where they now dwell.[2] They at once began to make long trading voyages with cargoes of Egyptian and Assyrian goods, and one of the places they called at was Argos, at that time the most eminent of the places in what is now called Hellas. Here on one occasion they were displaying their goods, and for five or six days after their arrival, when they had sold almost all their goods, there came down to the shore a considerable number of women. Among these was the king's daughter, whose name was Io, daughter of Inachus (and on this point the Greeks are in agreement).[3] These women were standing about the vessel's stern, buying what they most fancied, when the Phoenicians, at a signal, made a rush at them. The greater number of the women escaped, but Io was seized along with some others. They were thrust on board, after which the ship made off for Egypt.

1. The word here translated as "researches" is *historiē*, literally "inquiry," which later evolved (largely due to Herodotus' prominent use of it here) into our word *history*. It also became commonly used as the title for Herodotus' work, the *History* or *Histories*, but these are modern contrivances; authors in Herodotus' day did not yet have a convention of titling their works.
2. Herodotus uses the term "Red Sea" to mean the Persian Gulf and/or Indian Ocean; thus the Phoenicians are imagined to have migrated roughly from what is now Iran or India to what is now Lebanon. See the map of "Herodotus' world" for all questions involving global geography and ancient place names.
3. Note how, in the very first story he records, Herodotus begins his usual practice of mentioning conflicting or supporting versions he has heard from other informants. The story of Io was a myth well known to the Greeks; Io appears as a character in Aeschylus' tragedy *Prometheus Bound*.

Conflicting people are abducting kings' daughters for revenge on one another.

women to be as offended when their were taken

Asia didn't seem to

[1.2] This is the Persian account of how Io came to Egypt—the Greeks have a different account—and how the series of wrongs began.

Some time later, they say that certain Greeks—their name is not given, but they were probably Cretans—put into the Phoenician port of Tyre and carried off the king's daughter, Europa. So far it had been a case of an eye for an eye, but the Persians say that the Greeks were responsible for the next outrage. They sailed in a warship to Aea in Colchis on the river Phasis, and then, when they had finished the business for which they had come, they seized the king's daughter, Medea.[4] The king sent an envoy to Greece to demand reparation for the abduction and to request the return of his daughter. The Greeks replied that, since they had received no reparation for the abduction of Io from Argos, they in turn refused to give one.

[1.3] The Persians say that it was two generations later when Paris, son of Priam, influenced by these stories, resolved to use abduction to get a wife from Greece, being confident that he would get away with this unpunished, just as the Greeks had done; so he carried off Helen. The Greeks decided to send messengers to demand the return of Helen, together with reparations for her abduction. But they were answered with a rebuke about the seizure of Medea, for which the Greeks had made no reparations, nor had they returned the woman. So how could they now expect reparations from others?

[1.4] Up to this point there had been nothing worse than the abduction of women on both sides, but thereafter, say the Persians, the Greeks were much to blame; for before the Persians had made any assault on Europe the Greeks mounted a military expedition against Asia.[5] The abduction of women is, of course, quite wrong, but only fools make a great fuss about it, while wise men pay little heed; for it's obvious that women would not be carried off unless they themselves were willing. The Persians say that the peoples of Asia paid little regard to the seizure of their women, whereas the Greeks, merely for the sake of a Spartan woman, gathered a great army, invaded Asia, and destroyed the kingdom of Priam. Thereafter they have always regarded Greece as an enemy, for the Persians consider Asia, and the

---

4. The voyage here referred to is one of the most famous Greek quest-myths, the journey of Jason and the Argonauts in pursuit of the Golden Fleece. Colchis was in what is now Armenia.

5. The reference is to the Trojan War—that great struggle portrayed in Homer's *Iliad* and countless other Greek works.

disagreements *really* *happened? what*

peoples dwelling there, as their concern, while Europe and the Greeks are something apart.[6]

[1.5] Such, then, is the Persian account; the destruction of Troy, they say, was the origin of their hostility to Greece. As to Io, the Phoenicians disagree with the Persian account, and they deny that it was by abduction that they brought her to Egypt. They say that while in Argos she had an affair with the ship's captain, and finding herself pregnant she voluntarily accompanied the Phoenicians to escape the shame of exposure.

Well, believe what you please; I will pass no judgment. Rather, by indicating the man whom I myself know to have begun the outrages against the Greeks,[7] I shall proceed with my history, which will be no less concerned with unimportant cities than with the great. For those that were formerly great are now diminished, while those which are now great were once small.[8] Being well aware that human prosperity never long endures, I shall deal with both alike.

6. This bold division of the continents ignores the fact that the Greeks, through their settlements on the coast of Asia Minor, had come to inhabit both Europe and Asia—a geopolitical anomaly that would lead to innumerable conflicts.
7. Croesus, King of Lydia starting about 560, is meant. Herodotus chooses to begin his narrative with events that preceded him by about a century; these, he suggests, are subject to investigation and confirmation ("I myself know"), whereas the earlier episodes of the mythic tradition are not, and are therefore summarily dismissed.
8. Herodotus here first states his greatest single theme, that of the divine balance governing both human and natural affairs.

II

Prologue:
The Reign of Croesus of Lydia
(c. 560–46 B.C.E.)

[1.6] Croesus, king of Lydia, reigned over the peoples west of the river Halys, which flows from the south between the Syrians and the Paphlagonians, and runs northward into the Black Sea.[1] He was the first foreigner, as far as we know, to have contact with the Greeks, subjugating some by forcing payment of tribute and forming friendships with others. He subjugated the Ionians, Aeolians, and Dorians who dwell on the Asian seaboard and made a treaty of friendship with the Lacedaemonians.[2] Before the time of Croesus' reign, all the Greeks were free.

[1.7] Now sovereignty over Lydia had once belonged to the descendants of Heracles, and I shall describe how it came to pass into the hands of the Mermnads, the ancestors of Croesus. . . . The Heraclids[3] had held power for 22 generations, or 505 years, each son succeeding his father in turn, until the throne came down to Candaules, son of Myrsus.

---

1. That is, Croesus ruled over the western portion of the Anatolian or Turkish peninsula.
2. The Lacedaemonians were the people of Lacedaemon in the Peloponnese, the region that included, principally, the city of Sparta. They were the military superpower of the Greek world and hence valuable allies for Croesus; Herodotus explains at 1.69, a passage not included in this volume, that the Spartans had been won over to friendship with Croesus by a gift of Lydian gold. The "Ionians, Aeolians, and Dorians" referred to here are the Greek colonists who had settled the coast of Turkey (often called "Asia" by Herodotus), who, being far less powerful and also near neighbors of the Lydians, were easy prey. Though all Greeks ultimately shared the same language and culture, they also divided into smaller ethnic subgroups (e.g., Ionians, Dorians), much as the modern British divide into Scots, Welsh, Cornish, etc.
3. The suffix "-ids" means "descendants of," hence "Heraclids" = "descendants of Heracles." Herodotus believed that the god Heracles had sired children by a Lydian slave-girl and had thus begotten a line of kings.

4

[1.8] This Candaules was utterly devoted to his wife, whom he considered to be by far the most beautiful woman on earth. Among his bodyguard was a man named Gyges, who was the king's particular confidant, and Candaules not only discussed state matters with this man but expounded to him many praises of his wife's beauty. One day the king, who was destined to come to a bad end, spoke to Gyges thus: "Gyges, I am not sure that you fully believe me when I speak of my wife's beauty. Well then, since a man is inclined to trust his eyes more than his ears, I will arrange for you to see her naked." Gyges gave a cry of horror. "Master," he said, "what a shocking idea. Do you bid me look on my queen when she is naked? When a woman puts off her clothes, she puts off her modesty. We should obey the rules of morality devised for mankind ages ago, and one of these rules requires us to look only on what is our own. I am convinced that she is the fairest of women, and I beg you not to ask me to do what is wrong."

[1.9] Thus did he try to resist the king, dreading what harm might ensue for himself. But the king replied: "Be of good cheer, Gyges, and have no fear that I am making a trial of you, or that any injury will befall you from my wife. I will surely contrive that she won't know that you have seen her. I will station you in our bedroom behind the door as it opens. When I have entered, my wife too will follow me to bed. Near the door is a chair. On this she will lay her garments one by one as she takes them off. You will have plenty of opportunity to see her. Then, when she walks to the bed with her back to you, take care to slip through the door without her seeing you."

[1.10] Gyges made ready to do what he could not avoid. Candaules brought him into the bedroom and was soon followed by the queen. Gyges watched her enter and place her clothes on the chair, and when she turned her back to him and moved toward the bed, he quietly slipped out. But the queen caught sight of him. Realizing what her husband had done, she neither gave vent to her shame by screaming nor gave any other indication that there was anything amiss, but she resolved to take revenge on Candaules. For with the Lydians, as with almost all foreign peoples, it is reckoned a shameful thing even for a man to be seen naked.

[1.11] For the time being she gave no sign and kept quiet. But as soon as morning came, she made ready those of her servants whom she knew to be most devoted to her and summoned Gyges. Not suspecting that she knew anything of what had happened, he came at her bidding, for it was quite usual for him to be called to attend on the queen. "Gyges," she said, "I offer you the choice of two courses that are open to you, and you may choose whichever you please. Either kill Candaules and take the throne, with me as your wife, or you must die on the spot, so that never again will you give such unquestioning obedience to Candaules as to see what is forbidden. Either he who plotted this must die, or you, who have broken our laws by beholding me naked."

Gyges was at first astounded and fell to begging the queen not to force him to make such a dreadful choice. But his pleadings were in vain, and he realized that he was, in truth, faced with the necessity either of slaying his master or of losing his own life. He chose to live. "Since you compel me against my will to kill the king," he said, "come, tell me how we are to attack him." "The assault will come from the very place where he displayed my nakedness," she said, "and you will strike while he is asleep."

[1.12] There was no escape possible for Gyges; either he or Candaules must perish. When night fell, he followed the queen into the bedroom. She gave him a dagger and concealed him behind the very same door. Then, when Candaules was asleep, Gyges slipped out of his hiding place, struck, and took possession of both queen and kingdom.

[1.13] His hold on the throne was confirmed by the oracle at Delphi. For when the Lydians, angered at the fate of Candaules, took up arms, and when civil strife seemed inevitable between Gyges' partisans and the rest of the population, they agreed to consult the oracle and abide by its decision as to whether Gyges should rule or the throne be restored to the Heraclids. The answer favored Gyges, but the Priestess[4] also added this: that the Heraclids would be avenged in the fifth generation from Gyges. This prophecy was disregarded by the Lydians and their kings until it was fulfilled.

Once in power, Gyges begins to make forays against his Greek neighbors to the west, especially the Ionian city of Miletus, the principal Greek settlement in Asia Minor. After his death his son Ardys and grandson Sadyattes continue to harass Miletus and other Greek cities until the throne at last comes to Alyattes, father of Croesus, about 600 B.C.E.

[1.17] Alyattes used to make annual inroads into Milesian territory in the following way. He made his invasions when the crops were ripe, accompanied by the sound of pipes, harps, and flutes. He never destroyed the farmhouses or burned them or tore off their doors but left

---

4. Oracles at Delphi were thought to originate from Apollo but were actually spoken by a Priestess, sometimes called the Pythia.

them undamaged, destroying only the trees and crops before withdrawing. It was pointless to lay siege to the city because the Milesians commanded the sea. Now the reason why he refrained from demolishing the dwellings was this, so that the Milesians would be encouraged to sow seed and work the land, thereby providing a source of plunder for his future invasions.

[1.18–19] This went on for eleven years, in the course of which the Milesians were twice defeated in battle. . . . But in the twelfth year the burning of the crops had an unusual sequel. As soon as the crops were set on fire, a strong wind drove the flames onto the temple of Athena at Assesus, which burned down to the ground. At the time this caused little stir, but when the army returned to Sardis, Alyattes fell ill. As his illness continued, he sent messengers to the Delphic oracle to inquire about it, either on somebody's advice or on his own initiative. The Priestess refused to make any reply to the messengers until the Lydians should rebuild the temple of Athena of Assesus in Milesian territory. This is what I myself have gathered from the Delphians, but the Milesians add the following details to the story: They say that Periander of Corinth, a close friend of Thrasybulus who at that time was ruler over Miletus, got to know of the oracle's reply and sent a message giving Thrasybulus prior information, so that he could take appropriate measures.

[1.21] Alyattes, on receiving the oracle's reply, sent a messenger to Miletus, proposing a truce that would last until he could rebuild the temple. Anticipating through his foreknowledge what Alyattes was likely to do, Thrasybulus adopted the following plan: Gathering together in the public square all the grain in the city from both public and private sources, he instructed everyone at a given signal, to start drinking and holding parties. His purpose was this, to induce the messenger reporting to Alyattes to make mention of the immense pile of grain and the high spirits of the populace. And this, indeed, was what came about. The messenger marked what was going on, delivered his message, and returned to Sardis. A peace treaty was then signed, and it was for this reason alone, as I judge, that Alyattes, expecting to find the Milesians oppressed by famine and the populace reduced to extreme suffering, was informed by the messenger that the situation was quite the reverse of what he had thought.

Thereafter peace was established, the two sides becoming friends and allies. Alyattes built two temples instead of one to Athena of Assesus and recovered from his illness. This was the way that Alyattes concluded his war with the Milesians and their leader Thrasybulus.

[1.23–24] This Periander, the one who gave information about the oracle to Thrasybulus, was the son of Cypselus, and ruler over Corinth.[5] During his lifetime there occurred a very great wonder, as the Corinthians say (and the Lesbians agree with them): Arion of Methymna, by far the foremost lyre-player of his period—the man who first, as far as we know, composed the dithyramb, gave it its name, and taught it at Corinth[6]—was carried on a dolphin's back to Taenarum. Arion, they say, after spending a great part of his life at Periander's court, felt an urge to sail to Italy and Sicily. There he amassed a great fortune and eventually decided to return to Corinth. Having faith in Corinthians above all others, he hired a Corinthian vessel to sail from Tarentum. But when they were at sea, the crew formed a conspiracy to throw Arion overboard and seize his wealth. Realizing what they were about, he gave them his money and begged for his life. But the sailors, unmoved, ordered him to take his own life if he wished to be buried on land, or else to leap overboard forthwith. Faced with this painful dilemma, Arion asked the crew to allow him to stand on the quarterdeck, dressed in his full musician's robes, and to sing for the last time, after which he undertook to do away with himself. The sailors, pleased at the prospect of hearing a performance by the best musician in the world, gathered amidships, and Arion, donning his full attire, took up his lyre, stood on the quarterdeck, sang a stirring air, and then flung himself into the sea, fully robed just as he was.

The sailors continued their voyage to Corinth, but the story goes that a dolphin swam up, took Arion on his back, and carried him to Taenarum. Arion reached land, made his way to Corinth in his musician's attire, and related what had befallen him. The incredulous Periander would not release him but kept him under strict guard while he watched for the crew's arrival. When at last they did arrive, he sum-

5. Here and elsewhere in this volume, the word "ruler" translates the Greek *tyrannos*, a term that has no good English equivalent. A *tyrannos* holds absolute power in a Greek city, but his authority is not grounded either in tradition or in constitutional legitimacy, as is that of a king. Usually a *tyrannos* wields power and hands it on to his sons only because he has enough armed support to defend himself against any challenges. But that does not make him a despot, as the English word "tyrant," derived from *tyrannos*, might imply. Indeed many such "rulers" were beloved by their fellow citizens, especially the lower classes whose cause they often championed. Periander of Corinth is the first of several Greek *tyrannoi* we meet in Herodotus' work; Polycrates of Samos is another (see 3.39 ff.).
6. The dithyramb is a kind of choral poetry especially used for hymns in honor of the god Dionysus.

moned them and asked them if they had any news of Arion. "Yes," they replied, "he is in Italy; we left him safe and well at Tarentum." Thereupon Arion made his appearance, attired just as he had been when he leapt overboard. The sailors were dumbfounded and could make no further denial. This is the story as told by the people of Corinth and Lesbos, and there is at Taenarum an offering made by Arion, a small bronze figure of a man riding a dolphin.

Alyattes having died, Croesus now comes to the throne of Lydia, the man who, as Herodotus has claimed (1.5), was "the first . . . to harm the Greeks." We must understand this to mean "harm seriously," for Lydian kings had already been making sallies againt Miletus, and other Greek cities in Asia, for four generations before this. Croesus is said to be thirty-five years old at the time of his accession.

[1.28–30] Under Croesus' rule nearly all the peoples west of the river Halys were added to the Lydian empire, except the Cilicians and Lycians. . . .When Croesus had subjugated all these and added them to his empire, there came to his capital, Sardis, then at the height of its wealth, all the most distinguished teachers of that period throughout the length and breadth of Greece, and one of these was Solon of Athens. The Athenians had entrusted to him the task of drawing up a code of laws for them, having bound themselves with mighty oaths to make no change in it for a period of ten years without his permission. Solon carried out this task and then went abroad, so as not to be compelled to alter any of his laws—but giving out as a pretext that he wanted to see something of the world. First he visited the court of Amasis, ruler of Egypt, and then the court of Croesus at Sardis.[7]

He was welcomed and hospitably entertained at Croesus' palace, and in three or four days' time, at Croesus' bidding, servants escorted Solon around the royal treasuries to display the magnificence of Croesus' wealth. When Solon had had the opportunity to view and examine all that was there, Croesus said to him, "My Athenian friend,

---

7. Solon is a historical figure who did indeed draw up new laws for Athens, probably in 594, and who might well have traveled the world thereafter. That he actually met with Croesus though, who came to power around 560, is doubted. The scene that follows should therefore be read not as a record of fact, even though it involves two historical figures, but as a kind of philosophic dialogue, exploring the different ethical perspectives of a Greek wise man and a barbarian king.

much talk of you has reached us, both in respect of your wisdom and of your extensive travels in search of knowledge. Now I have a great desire to put this question to you: Who is the happiest man you have ever seen?" He was, of course, expecting to be named the happiest of humankind, but Solon was no flatterer. With strict regard for the truth he replied, "O king, it was Tellus the Athenian." Croesus, amazed at that reply, asked with some sharpness, "And how do you arrive at this judgment?" "In the first place," said Solon, "living at a time when his native city was flourishing, he had fine, handsome children and got to see children born to *them*, all of whom survived. Secondly, after enjoying a prosperous life, as we judge of prosperity, he came to a most glorious end. In a battle between the Athenians and their neighbors of Eleusis, he played his part in the battle, put the enemy to flight, and died most nobly. The Athenians granted him a state funeral at the very place where he fell, and paid him great honor."

[1.31] Solon's account of the many blessings of Tellus spurred Croesus on to ask who it was whom Solon judged the happiest of men after Tellus, doubtless expecting that he, Croesus, would at least be placed second. But Solon replied, "Two young men of Argos, Cleobis and Biton. Their means were quite sufficient for their needs, and they were blessed with remarkable physical strength. They were both prizewinners in athletic contests, and the following tale is told of them. When the Argives were holding the festival of Hera, it was an urgent religious duty for the mother of these men to be conveyed to the temple in a special carriage, but the oxen had not returned from the fields in time to pull it. In this emergency the two sons got into the harnesses and pulled the wagon themselves, with their mother aboard, a distance of almost six miles to the temple. After this remarkable feat, witnessed as it was by the entire assembly, their lives came to a most wonderful close, whereby the deity revealed how much better for humankind is death than life. The Argives were crowding around the two young men, congratulating them on their strength, and the women were rejoicing with their mother on having such sons. Overjoyed at the public recognition of their achievement, their mother stood before the statue of the goddess and prayed to her to grant Cleobis and Biton, the sons who had brought her such honor, the greatest blessing that can befall mortals. After her prayer, when they had sacrificed and feasted, the two sons lay down to sleep in the temple and never rose again. They were finished. The Argives had statues made of them and set them up at Delphi—to show that they honored them first among humankind."

[1.32] To these, then, did Solon award second place for happiness. In his exasperation Croesus said, "My Athenian friend, do you so despise my happy state that you rank me beneath common folk?"

To this Solon replied, "Croesus, you are questioning one who understands how the divine power is envious of human good fortune, and never leaves it long undisturbed. Over a lengthy period of time one sees much that one would wish not to see and undergoes much one would wish not to. Let us take 70 years as the space of a man's life. This period, if you disregard the intercalary months, contains 25,200 days. If you add a month every other year so as to make the seasons come around at their due time, you have 35 extra months, that is, 1,050 days. So the full total comes to 26,250 days.[8] Of these days not a single one is like another in what it brings forth. So you see, Croesus, the extent to which people are at the mercy of chance. I hold you to be exceedingly rich and the ruler over many peoples. But I will not answer your question until I learn that you have reached the end of your life in the same state of happiness. The man who is immensely rich is no better off than the man who just makes ends meet, unless he has the good fortune to reach the end of his life in the same happy state. Many wealthy men are unlucky, while many in moderate circumstances are blessed by fortune. The man who is very rich but unlucky has only two advantages over the man who is merely lucky, but the latter has many advantages over the former: The rich man is better able to fulfill his desires and to cope with disaster when it befalls him, but the poor and lucky trumps him: Though he cannot manage desires and disasters as easily, his good luck dispels the need to do so, for he avoids injury, disease, and calamity and is blessed in children and good-looking. If, beyond these boons, he also comes to a good end of life, then this is the man you are seeking, the man who merits the title 'happy.' But until his death you should withhold the title 'happy'; he is merely temporarily fortunate.

"No human being can possess all blessings, just as no single country can produce all that it needs; it will possess one thing and lack another. Similarly, no man is entirely self-sufficient; he will surely lack something. But whoever possesses the greatest number of blessings and retains them until he reaches the end, and then dies happily, he is the one, in my opinion, who should be awarded the title. In every mat-

---

8. Intercalary months were inserted by the Greeks to realign their lunar calendar with the solar, though they did not occur quite as often as Herodotus (or Solon) here supposes.

ter you should look to the ending. To many men the god grants but a glimpse of blessedness, only to bring them to utter ruin."

[1.33] This view found no favor with Croesus, and he contemptuously dismissed Solon, regarding as a fool a man who urged him to look to the ending of every matter and who paid no heed to present prosperity.

[1.34] After Solon's departure, terrible punishment, sent by god, fell upon Croesus, probably because he considered himself the happiest of men. It began with a dream that seemed to indicate that disaster was about to befall his son. Croesus had two sons, of whom one was a cripple, being deaf and mute, while the other, named Atys, surpassed all other young men of his time. Croesus dreamed that Atys would be killed by a blow from an iron weapon. When he awoke and reflected on his terrifying dream, he took action. He arranged a marriage for his son and no longer permitted him to take the field with the Lydian soldiers whom he used to command. He banished all warlike weapons—javelins, spears, and so on—from the men's quarters and had them gathered together in the women's apartments, lest any weapon hanging on the wall should chance to fall on his son.

[1.35] While he was busy with arrangements for the marriage, there came to Sardis a man in the grip of misfortune, with blood on his hands, a Phrygian by birth and of royal lineage. Presenting himself before Croesus, this man begged the king to cleanse him from the blood-guilt according to the laws of the land, and this Croesus did. (The Lydian method of purification is very similar to that of the Greeks.)[9] After the ceremony, Croesus questioned the man. "Stranger, who are you? From what part of Phrygia do you come to seek my protection? What man or woman have you slain?" "Sire," replied the man, "I am the son of Gordias, whose father was Midas, and my name is Adrastus.[10] I accidentally slew my own brother, and I have been driven into exile, destitute." "You are descended from a family with friendly relations to mine," said Croesus, "and you have come among friends, where you shall lack for nothing. I urge you to bear your misfortune as best you can." Thus did Adrastus come to reside with Croesus.

---

9. According to ancient religious practices, a murderer, especially one who kills his own kin, becomes stained with pollution or blood-guilt and cannot take part in normal social relations until he is ritually cleansed or "purified." Note the parenthetic sentence in which Herodotus opportunely inserts an anthropological note concerning Lydian purification rites.

10. The name Adrastus is significant; one possible meaning of it is "he who cannot be escaped."

[1.36] At about this time there was a monstrous wild boar on Mount Olympus in Mysia. Issuing forth from its mountain lair it used to ravage the Mysians' crops. Many an expedition did the Mysians make against it, but inflicted no injury on it while themselves sustaining many injuries. Finally their messengers sought audience with Croesus and spoke as follows: "Sire, a monster of a boar has appeared in our land, destroying our crops. Our efforts to catch it have all been in vain. Now we beg you to send us your son with a chosen band of young men and hunting dogs, so that we may drive it out of our land." Bearing in mind his dream, Croesus answered with these words: "Let there be no more mention of our son. I could not send him because he is newly married and has much to occupy him. However, I will send you a select band of men with hunting equipment, and I will urge them to show the utmost zeal in ridding your land of this beast."

[1.37] The Mysians were all satisfied with this answer, but then Atys, who had heard of the Mysians' request, came in. Seeing that Croesus declined to send him, Atys spoke to him as follows: "Father, it was once thought most noble and most honorable for me to win renown in war and hunting. Now you have cut me off from both these pursuits, although you have seen no cowardice or lack of spirit in me. What will people think of me when I appear in public? How will the citizens regard me, how will my bride regard me? What kind of man will she think she has married? Either let me take part in the hunt or give me reason for your refusal."

[1.38] "My son," said Croesus, "it is not because I have seen cowardice or any other fault in you that I act in this way. It is because of a dream I had that you had not long to live, and that you would perish by an iron weapon. It was that dream that made me hasten your wedding and makes me reluctant to send you off on this enterprise. I am taking these precautions so I may keep you out of death's reach during my lifetime. You are my only son, for I cannot look on that other one, with his defect, as my son."

[1.39–40] "It is understandable, Father," replied Atys, "that you should take precautions after being visited by such a dream. But there is a point in that dream that has escaped your notice, and it is not improper for me to mention it. You say that the dream indicated that I would be killed by an iron weapon. But what sort of hands does a boar have? How can it use an iron weapon? Had the dream foretold that I would be killed by a boar's tusk or the like, you would be doing your duty. But it is a *weapon* that is in question, and since I shall not be fighting against men, let me go." "My son," replied Croesus, "I own myself vanquished in the matter of the dream's interpretation, and, being vanquished, I change my decision and permit you to go to the hunt."

[1.41–43] Thereupon the king sent for Adrastus the Phrygian and said to him, "When you came to me, Adrastus, smitten by dire disaster—for which I do not reproach you—I cleansed you, received you into my household, and provided for all your needs. Now I call upon you to requite good with good. I charge you to be my son's guardian when he goes forth to this hunt, to protect him against robbers or evildoers who may come upon you. Furthermore, you too have the duty of going where you may win distinction by your deeds. That is your heritage, and you do not lack strength." "Sire," replied Adrastus, "I would not normally wish to go on this expedition. It is not proper for one who is smitten with misfortune to seek the company of more fortunate young men, nor do I desire it, and I would hold back on many accounts. But since you ask me to do so and it is my duty to please you—for I owe you a great debt of gratitude—I am ready. Your son, whom you bid me protect, shall be unharmed as far as his protector can ensure it, and you may look for his safe return." Such was Adrastus' answer, after which the party set out with a chosen band of men and dogs. They came to Olympus, sought out the boar, surrounded it, and hurled their spears. It was then that the stranger named Adrastus, the man who had been purified from blood-guilt, hurling his spear missed his mark and hit Croesus' son; struck by an iron blade, Atys fulfilled the prophecy of the dream.

[1.44] A messenger hastened to tell the father of his son's fate. The shock of his son's death was dreadful but was made more horrible by the fact that he had been killed by one whom Croesus himself had purified of blood-guilt. In the excess of his grief Croesus called upon Zeus as the god of purification, asking him to bear witness to his sufferings at the hands of the stranger whom he had purified; he called upon Zeus as the god of the hearth, because in welcoming the stranger into his home he had unwittingly entertained the slayer of his son; he called upon Zeus as the god of comradeship, in that the man whom he had charged to guard his son had been found to be his greatest enemy.

[1.45] Soon the Lydians arrived, bearing the body and followed by the slayer. Standing before the body he submitted himself to Croesus, stretching forth his hands and bidding Croesus to slaughter him on top of the corpse. To crown his previous trouble, he said, he had ruined the man who had cleansed him, and he could no longer bear to live.

At these words, in spite of his own domestic sorrow, Croesus took pity on Adrastus. "Since you condemn yourself to death," he said, "justice makes no further demands on you. You are not to blame for this calamity, except that your unwitting hand did the deed. No, it was some god, who long ago gave me warning of what was to be."

So Croesus buried his son with fitting ceremony. But when all was quiet about the grave, Adrastus, son of Gordias, and grandson of Midas, the man who had destroyed his own brother and then had destroyed him who had granted him purification, knowing himself to be the most ill-fated of humankind, slew himself upon the tomb.

[1.46–47] For two years Croesus continued in deep mourning for his son and was roused from grief only by the rapidly increasing power of the Persians on his eastern border, a power founded by Astyages, son of Cyaxares, and greatly increased by Cyrus, son of Cambyses.[11] It occurred to Croesus to take the initiative by attacking the Persians before they could grow even stronger; in pursuit of this plan, Croesus contrived to make trial of the various oracles in both Greece and Libya. To this end, he dispatched messengers to the oracles at Delphi, at Abae in Phocis, at Dodona, to the oracles of Amphiaraus and Trophonius, to the oracle of Branchidae in Milesia, and, not content with Greek oracles, to the oracle of Ammon in Libya. He sent these messengers as a test of the knowledge of the oracles: If one oracle was found to know the truth, then he would send a second time to ask if he should undertake a campaign against the Persians. These messengers were instructed to consult the different oracles on the hundredth day after leaving Sardis and to inquire what Croesus, king of Lydia, was doing at that moment. They were to write down the reply and bring it straight back to Croesus. What the rest of the oracles replied is not told by any of my sources, but at Delphi, as soon as the Lydians arrived in the enclosure and put their question to the god, the Pythia said as follows, speaking in hexameter verse:

I can count the grains of sand on the beach, and I can measure
  the sea.
I understand the speech of the dumb, and I hear the voiceless.
There has come to my nostrils the odor of the hard-shelled
  tortoise
Boiling together with lamb's flesh in a brazen cauldron,
With a base of bronze and a bronze cover.

11. The Persians at last enter the narrative; soon they will become its primary characters. The war between Croesus of Lydia and Cyrus of Persia is here described as an episode of Lydian history, but later in Book 1 (108 ff.)

[1.48–50] These words the Lydians recorded and carried back to Sardis. At last all the replies came back to Croesus, who opened and read them, and it was the Delphic reply that he accepted with deep reverence, declaring that it was the only true oracle in the world. For after dispatching his messengers Croesus had devised an action least open to guesswork. On the appointed day he had cut up a tortoise and a lamb and boiled them together in a brazen cauldron with a brazen lid. . . . Croesus now proceeded to offer the most sumptuous sacrifices to Apollo of Delphi.

[1.53–54]¹² The messengers who conveyed these gifts were to put the following question to the oracle: "Croesus, king of Lydia and other nations, convinced that you are the only true oracle in the world, has sent you these gifts and asks you if he should march against the Persians, and also whether he should make allies of some other army." In reply the oracle prophesied that if Croesus marched against the Persians he would destroy a great empire. As to an alliance, he should seek friendship of the most powerful of the Greeks. Croesus was overjoyed at this reply, confident that he would destroy the power of Cyrus. He bestowed further presents on Delphi, two gold staters for every citizen, having first inquired how many there were. In return the Delphians granted to Croesus and to all Lydians, in perpetuity, the right to become citizens of Delphi, exemption from taxes, priority in access to the oracle, and front seats at all state functions.

[1.55–56] Being now eager to extract full value from an oracle of whose genuineness he was firmly convinced, Croesus sent one more question—would his reign be a long one? The Priestess made the following reply:

> When a mule shall sit on the Median throne, then stay not,
> Tender-footed Lydian, but flee by the many-pebbled stream
> Of Hermus, and think no shame of being a coward.

This reply gave Croesus more satisfaction than any other. Was it likely that a mule would become king of the Medes?

Herodotus will deal in more detail with Cyrus, treated this time as the founder of the Persian empire.

12. The sections are not consecutive because a lengthy catalogue of Croesus' offerings at Delphi has been omitted.

[1.71] Croesus, having missed the meaning of the oracle, now prepared to invade Cappadocia,[13] confident that he could destroy the power of Cyrus and his Persians. While he was making these preparations a certain Lydian named Sandanis, already renowned for his wisdom, gave him the following advice, thereby greatly increasing his reputation with the Lydians. "Sire," he said, "you are preparing to fight against men who are so poor that they dress in leather, breeches and all. Their country is so rough that they eat what they can manage to get, never as much as they want. They have no wine to drink, only water. They have no luxuries, not even figs for dessert. If you conquer them, what will you take from them, seeing that they have nothing? If they conquer you, think what you will lose. Once they have tasted our good things, they will hold onto them and will not ever let go. Indeed, as it is, I am grateful to the gods for not putting it into the minds of the Persians to attack the Lydians."[14] Croesus rejected this advice, yet Sandanis was right on one point. The Persians had no luxuries of any sort before they conquered Lydia.

[1.73–74] Croesus made the invasion of Cappadocia because he wanted to extend his territories and, more importantly, because he trusted the oracle. But there was this further reason—he wanted to take revenge on Cyrus on behalf of Astyages. Astyages, formerly king of Media, had been conquered and held in subjugation by Cyrus.[15] Astyages was Croesus' brother-in-law, and the marriage connection came about in this strange way. A band of Scythians, a nomadic people, left their country as a result of internal strife and emigrated to Media. They were at first welcomed by Cyaxares, at that time ruler over Media, who treated them kindly as suppliants. He even entrusted to them the education of some boys, whom they were to teach their language and the use of the bow. As time went on, the Scythians, who continually went out hunting and returned with game, on one occasion returned empty-handed. Cyaxares, a man of quick temper, re-

13. Cappadocia is the eastern portion of the Anatolian peninsula, across the river Halys from Croesus' realm. It was at this time part of Persian territory.
14. Another thematic keynote of the text is sounded here: The contrast between wealthy, advanced, luxury-loving aggressors and the poorer, tougher, hardier nations they attack. Though the Persians here fall into the latter category, they will shortly develop the attributes of the former, as Sandanis here predicts.
15. The story of Cyrus' overthrow of Astyages will be told at length by Herodotus further on in Book 1 (see below 1.107 ff.).

ceived them with harsh words and abuse. Resenting this undeserved ill-treatment, the Scythians resolved to kill one of their pupils, chop him up, prepare the pieces like game, serve them to Cyaxares as a side dish, and then make their escape to the court of Alyattes at Sardis. And that is indeed what happened. Cyaxares and his guests ate some of the meat. The Scythians escaped to Alyattes and sought his protection. Cyaxares demanded their return. Alyattes refused, and war broke out between Lydia and Media. It lasted five years, with victory going first to one side, then to the other. After all this indecisive fighting, in the sixth year, there was a battle during which day suddenly turned into night. (This change from daylight to darkness had been foretold to the Ionian Greeks by Thales of Miletus, who even fixed the year in which it did in fact occur.)[16] When the Lydians and the Medes saw day turn into night, they became awestruck and broke off the engagement, and both sides became anxious to make peace. Certain mediators (Syennesis the Cilician and Labynetus the Babylonian) were responsible for bringing about a reconciliation and for making a peace treaty reinforced by a marriage connection. These men persuaded Alyattes, king of Lydia and father to Croesus, to give his daughter in marriage to Astyages, Cyaxares' son; for agreements do not usually remain strong unless backed up by strong assurances. (These nations have the same form of oathtaking as the Greeks, but in addition they make an incision in the skin of their arms and lick each other's blood.)

[1.75] I will explain further on why Cyrus had overthrown, and now was holding prisoner, his grandfather Astyages. But it was this insult that Croesus held against Cyrus, leading him to ask the oracle whether he should attack the Persians; and when he received a double-edged answer, he assumed the oracle was on his side and invaded Persian territory.

When Croesus reached the river Halys, he crossed it, in my opinion, by the existing bridges. But there is a version widespread in Greece that it was Thales of Miletus who took the army across. They say that the bridges did not exist at this time, and that Thales, who was present in Croesus' camp, solved the difficulty by splitting the river into two channels. This he did by digging a deep, crescent-shaped channel from a point above the camp around to the rear of the

---

16. Modern astronomers have fixed two possible dates for this eclipse, one in May 585 and the other in September 582. The idea that a Greek scientist had enough skill to predict a solar eclipse, at this early stage, is remarkable but not unthinkable. Thales was a legendary wise man of Greek lore, like Solon; another anecdote about his cleverness is related below.

camp, so that the river ran for a space in two channels, each of which could be forded. Some even say that the river was entirely rerouted and the old channel left dry. But this I cannot accept; for how would the army have crossed again on their return journey?[17]

[1.76] Be that as it may, Croesus crossed the river with his army and reached the district called Pteria in Cappadocia. He ravaged the properties of the Syrians who lived there, captured the town of the Pterians, enslaved the inhabitants, seized the outlying settlements, and drove out the Syrians, though they were uninvolved in the quarrel.

Cyrus meanwhile had assembled his army and marched to meet Croesus, recruiting more men on his way. Before marching out he had already sent messages in an attempt to persuade the Ionians to throw off their allegiance to Croesus, but the Ionians had not heeded him. When he had encamped opposite Croesus, the two armies met in a sharp struggle. There were heavy losses on both sides, but the result was indecisive, and night broke off the engagement.

[1.77–78] Croesus' army was somewhat inferior in number to Cyrus' forces, and it was to this that he attributed his lack of success. When Cyrus did not advance to attack on the following day, Croesus decided to withdraw to Sardis. He intended to reinforce his army by calling on his allies, the Egyptians (for he had made an alliance with Amasis, king of Egypt),[18] and also the Babylonians (for he had made an alliance with these too, who were at this time ruled by Labynetus), and the Spartans. These were to join him at an appointed time, and then he proposed to wait until the winter was over and attack Cyrus in the following spring. So he sent out messengers, requesting his allies to assemble at Sardis in four months' time, and meanwhile he disbanded his mercenaries, for he did not imagine that Cyrus would venture to march on Sardis after the even fortunes of the recent battle.

At this time an unusual incident occurred. Snakes swarmed in the suburbs of Sardis, and horses, leaving their customary pastures, came and devoured them. Croesus regarded this as an omen, as indeed it was, and he sent messengers to Telmessus where there were seers

---

17. The logic behind this objection is obscure; perhaps Herodotus assumed that the army's return would be in the rainy winter, when rivers would run much higher. In any case it is noteworthy that he retells a story, in some detail, which he himself deems incredible.

18. Amasis will become an important character in Books 2 and 3 (see below 2.162–74 and 3.39–43). The alliance between him and Croesus demonstrates that the rapid growth of Cyrus' power had scared all the other Near Eastern powers into aligning their interests against him.

skilled in interpretation. These messengers were told the significance of the omen, but they had no opportunity to report back to Croesus, who became a prisoner before they could complete the return voyage to Sardis. The interpretation of the Telmessian seers, which they gave before knowing that Croesus was captured, was as follows: Snakes were natives of the soil, horses were beasts of war and foreigners. Croesus must expect the coming of a foreign army that would subdue the natives of Sardis.

[1.79] When Croesus retired toward Sardis after the battle of Pteria, Cyrus found out that he was going to disband his army. So he took counsel and resolved that his best plan was to march on Sardis as swiftly as possible before the Lydian forces could gather again. No sooner said than done, and Cyrus made such good speed that he reached Sardis as his own messenger.[19] This unexpected development put Croesus in a dilemma, but he nevertheless led out his Lydians to battle, for at this time there were no braver or stouter warriors than the Lydians, or better horsemen.

[1.80] The armies met on a level plain before Sardis. . . . When Cyrus viewed the battle-array, he was very apprehensive of the Lydian cavalry, and he adopted the suggestion made to him by a certain Mede named Harpagus. He gathered together all his camels that were used as pack animals to carry stores and provisions, unloaded them, and mounted men on their backs to act as cavalry. These he ordered to advance against Croesus' cavalry, to be followed by the infantry, while his own cavalry brought up the rear. The reason for this maneuver was the instinctive fear that camels inspire in horses, who cannot endure the sight or smell of them. In this way the Lydians' cavalry, their greatest source of confidence, would be rendered useless. Having made these dispositions, Cyrus gave a general order to his army to kill all the Lydians they encountered except Croesus, whom he wanted taken alive even if he offered resistance.

When battle was joined, as soon as the Lydian horses smelled and saw the camels, they turned and fled, and Croesus found his hopes dashed to the ground. But there was no cowardice on the part of the Lydians. Seeing what was happening they leapt from the saddle and fought as infantry. There were heavy losses on both sides, but finally the Lydians were forced to give way and retreat within their walls, where they were besieged by the Persians.

19. A colorful phrase, meaning that he arrived so swiftly that no advance report had preceded him.

[1.81] Thus began the siege of Sardis, and Croesus, believing it would be a lengthy affair, sent messages from the besieged city to his allies, this time begging for assistance not in four months' time but immediately, to relieve the siege. He applied to all his allies, among them the Spartans.

[1.82] The Spartans were at this time engaged in a quarrel with Argos over some border territory called Thyreae, which had belonged to Argos but had been cut off and seized by the Spartans. The Argives marched out to recover it, and a conference was held at which it was decided that the fighting should be restricted to three hundred men on each side, and Thyreae should belong to the victors. The main body of each army should not stay to watch the fighting, but retire each to its own homeland, so as to avoid the temptation of coming to the assistance of their own men if they were being defeated. On these terms they retired, and the chosen three hundred on either side joined the battle.

So equally balanced was the contest that out of six hundred men only three were left alive—two Argives, Alcenor and Chromius, and one Spartan, Othryades; and these survived only because night fell. The two Argives hastened back to Argos, claiming victory, but the Spartan Othryades remained on the field of battle, stripping the dead and carrying back their spoils to the Spartan camp.

On the following day both sides returned to discuss the outcome. For a while both sides claimed victory, the Argives because they had the greater number of survivors, and the Spartans because, while the Argives had run away, their own man had remained on the battlefield and stripped the dead. The argument led to blows, and then to a general engagement in which both sides suffered heavy losses, with the Spartans finally victorious. From that day onward the Argives, who were previously required to wear their hair long, began cutting it short and made a vow that no Argive man should wear long hair, nor any Argive woman wear gold jewelry, until Thyreae was reclaimed. Meanwhile the Spartans did the opposite: They began wearing their hair long, which had not been their custom before. It is said that the single Spartan survivor of the three hundred, being ashamed to return to Sparta after the death of his companions, killed himself there at Thyreae.

[1.83] Such were the circumstances in which the Spartans found themselves when the messenger from Sardis arrived, seeking assistance for the besieged Croesus.[20] Nevertheless, when the Spartans

20. Having completed his digression on the Spartan-Argive war, Herodotus now returns us to the main story, the fall of King Croesus.

heard his message, they were eager to send help. But by the time they had completed their preparations and the ships were ready to sail, a second message brought news that the city had fallen and that Croesus was taken prisoner. The Spartans were greatly distressed, but there was nothing they could do.

[1.84] This was how the city of Sardis was taken: On the fourteenth day of the siege, Cyrus sent cavalrymen to ride through his army, proclaiming a rich reward to whomever should be the first to scale the walls. This was followed by a concerted assault, which met with no success. While the others were resting, a Mardian named Hyroeades resolved to make an attempt at a point in the fortifications that was left unguarded because there appeared to be no danger of its ever being scaled. There was a sheer drop there, which made it inaccessible. (Many years before these events a former king of Sardis, named Meles, had a concubine who gave birth to a lion. The seers of Telmessus declared that if the lion were carried around the walls of Sardis, the fortress would be impregnable. Meles followed their advice and carried the lion around the entire circuit of the walls except for this part, which he considered impossible to scale.) This Hyroeades had observed one of the Lydians climbing down the precipice to retrieve a helmet that had rolled down. This put the idea into his head. He made the ascent himself, was followed by many others and finally by a great mass of the Persians. Thus was Sardis taken, and the city was sacked.

[1.85] What was Croesus' fate? I have already mentioned[21] that he had a son, a fine enough young fellow except for being mute from birth. In the days of his prosperity Croesus had spared no effort to help the lad and had consulted the Delphic oracle. The Priestess replied,

> O Lydian, king over many peoples, thou foolish Croesus,
> Seek not to hear the longed-for sound of thy son's voice
> In thy palace. Far better were it otherwise,
> For his first words will be spoken on a day of great sorrow.

When the city was taken, a Persian soldier advanced on Croesus to slay him, not knowing who he was. Croesus saw him. But, sunk in mis-

---

21. The mute son will be recalled from the story of the death of Atys (1.34). Cross-references like this one reveal the care Herodotus took to tie together the many originally separate stories that went into his work; but it is worth noting also that he sometimes errs, referring ahead to stories that are not in fact found in his text.

ery, he paid no heed, not caring whether he lived or died. But this son, the mute one, was so appalled by the danger that he gained speech and cried, "Fellow, do not kill Croesus." These were the first words that he uttered, and he retained the power of speech for the rest of his life.

[1.86] So Croesus was captured alive after a reign of fourteen years and a siege of fourteen days. He had indeed fulfilled the oracle by destroying a great kingdom—his own. He was brought before Cyrus, who had him put in chains and placed on a pyre which he had constructed, and with him fourteen Lydian boys.[22] Perhaps he intended making an offering to some god, perhaps he was fulfilling some vow, or perhaps he had heard tell that Croesus was a pious man, and he wanted to find out if some divine power would save him from being burned alive. As Croesus stood upon the pyre, in spite of his miserable condition he remembered the saying of Solon, surely divinely inspired, that no man could be called happy during his lifetime. Remembering this, he sighed bitterly, and breaking a long silence, he uttered a deep groan and thrice called Solon's name: "Solon, Solon, Solon."

On hearing this, Cyrus bade his interpreters ask Croesus upon whom he was calling. For some time Croesus maintained an obstinate silence, but when they forced him to speak he replied, "One who should speak with every ruler in the world—if only my riches could buy this." As this answer seemed mysterious and they continued to question him, pressing him hard and giving him no rest, he told how Solon the Athenian came to Sardis and was unimpressed by all the magnificence he saw there, and how everything he said, meant generally for all humankind but especially for those who deemed themselves happy, had come true in his case exactly as Solon had said.

While Croesus was still speaking, the fire had been kindled and was burning around the sides. Then Cyrus, listening to the interpreters, had a sudden change of heart. He reflected that he himself, a mere mortal, was burning alive another man who had once been

---

22. Well before Herodotus wrote, the Greeks were already captivated by the idea of Croesus ending his reign on a flaming pyre: A vase painting from about 500 B.C.E., and an ode of Bacchylides, from a few decades later, depict the very same event. In Bacchylides however, Croesus had climbed the pyre himself to commit suicide, and the same is likely true of the figure in the vase painting. Whether this remarkable confluence of traditions reflects some historical reality is not known; we have no independent evidence of what became of Croesus after the fall of Sardis.

equally as prosperous as he. This thought, and the thought of retribution, and the realization of the instability of the human condition, persuaded him to order his men to extinguish the fire as quickly as possible and to bring Croesus and those with him safely down. But the fire had got a hold, and in vain did his men try to extinguish it.

[1.87] Now the Lydians tell[23] that, when Croesus realized that Cyrus had had this change of heart, and when he saw that every man was engaged in a vain attempt to extinguish the fire, he called loudly upon Apollo. "If any of my gifts have found favor in thy sight, come to my aid, rescue me from this present peril." Thus did he, with tears, call upon the god, and although the day had been clear with hardly a breeze, the sky was suddenly darkened with clouds, and a storm broke with such a violent downpour of rain that the flames were extinguished.[24]

In this way Cyrus learned that Croesus was a good man and a friend to the gods, and when he had brought him down from the pyre he questioned him. "Croesus, who of humankind induced you to march against my country and become my enemy rather than my friend?" Croesus made answer, "O king, what I did has proved to be for your good fortune and for my own ill fortune. The fault lies with the god of the Greeks who encouraged me to embark on this campaign. No one is so foolish as to choose war instead of peace. In peacetime children bury their fathers, in wartime fathers bury their children. It must be by divine will that this has come upon me." Cyrus set him free, seated him at his side and treated him kindly, gazing at him in wonder, as did all his attendants.

[1.88–89] Croesus sat deep in thought; then, turning around and seeing the Persians sacking the city, "O king," he said, "shall I tell you what is in my mind or ought I to keep silence?" Cyrus bade him speak frankly without fear. "This vast crowd of men," said Croesus, "what are they so busily doing?" "Why, they are plundering your city and carrying off your treasures," said Cyrus. "Not my city, nor my treasures," was the reply. "They are no longer mine. It is you they are robbing." These words gave Cyrus food for thought, and dismissing his

23. It is typical of Herodotus to cite a source when his stories become implausible or fantastic, as if to shore up their credibility. Whether these source citations are merely convenient fictions, as has been charged, is difficult to know.

24. This miraculous redemption is closely echoed by the Bacchylides poem on the subject of Croesus' pyre, where Apollo whisks the king away from the flames and gives him a happy immortality among the mythical Hyperboreans.

attendants, he asked Croesus what was his advice under these circumstances. "Since the gods have made me your slave," said Croesus, "it is right for me to advise you for your good. Persians are proud by nature, and poor. If you suffer them to accumulate great wealth from sacking the city, you can expect that whoever gets the most will rebel against you. If you will be advised by me, you will station men of your personal guard at every gate, and let them take all the valuables as men bring them out, saying that a tenth part of the spoil must be given to Zeus. They will not resent this act of piety and will willingly surrender their spoil."

[1.90] Cyrus was highly pleased at what seemed to him good advice, and after giving the orders Croesus had recommended, he said to Croesus, "I see that you are willing to do me service. Ask me for any gift you please in return." "The greatest boon you can bestow on me," said Croesus, "is to allow me to send these chains to the god of the Greeks whom I have most honored, and to ask him if it is his custom thus to reward those who serve him." And he explained to Cyrus how he had come to trust the oracle, the magnificent gifts he had sent, and the oracle's reply. Cyrus laughed. "This request is granted, and anything else you may ask." So Croesus sent to Delphi, and instructed his messengers to lay the chains on the floor of the temple and ask the god if he was not ashamed of having encouraged Croesus to make war against the Persian empire, in the belief that he would end the power of Cyrus, from which venture had come such "rewards" (here he bid them point to the chains). Was it usual (he bid them ask) for Greek gods to be so ungrateful?

[1.91] It is said that the Priestess replied to these reproaches as follows: "Even the gods cannot escape allotted destiny. In the fifth generation Croesus expiated the crime of his ancestor, a soldier in the bodyguard of the Heraclids, who succumbed to a woman's treachery, slew his master, and seized a throne that was not his.²⁵ Nevertheless Apollo wanted the fall of Sardis to be postponed to the time of Croesus' son but failed to persuade the Fates. They did, however, make some concession to him: They put off the fall of Sardis for three years, and Croesus should understand that his fate caught up to him three years late. Then again, Apollo came to his rescue when he was on the pyre. As to the oracle, Croesus does wrong to blame it, for Apollo foretold only this, that if he took the field against the Persians, he would destroy a great empire. Croesus should have made a further inquiry as to whether the empire was that of the Persians or his own.

25. Referring to Gyges' murder of Candaules (1.8 ff.).

But he failed to understand the reply, made no further inquiry, and was himself to blame. Again, when he consulted the oracle on the last occasion and Apollo's answer made reference to a mule, this too Croesus misunderstood. The mule meant Cyrus, for he is the offspring of parents of different races,[26]an aristocratic mother and a baseborn father. His mother was a Mede, daughter of Astyages, king of Media, while his father was a Persian, at that time subject to the rule of the Medes, and in every way inferior to his wife." When the Lydian messengers returned with this reply, Croesus had to admit that the fault was his, not the god's.

Throughout the first half of his work, Herodotus gives brief descriptions of the lands and cities his account has dealt with, and the customs of the peoples who dwell there. These ethnographies, as they are called, can be as short as a few sentences or very, very long; indeed, most of Book 2, one of the longest of the nine books of the Histories, *consists of a detailed ethnography of Egypt. This volume presents excerpts from a few of the more important ethnographies, and that of the Lydians is included in its entirety below.*

[1.93] The country of the Lydians has few remarkable features in comparison with other countries, except for the gold dust carried down by the river from Tmolus. It does, however, show the greatest work of human hands except for those wrought by the Egyptians and Babylonians. I refer to the tomb of Croesus' father, Alyattes, the base of which is built of huge stone blocks surmounted by a huge mound of earth. It was constructed by the joint efforts of three classes: tradesmen, craftsmen, and prostitutes. Five stone pillars stood on the summit even up to my own days, with inscriptions engraved on them showing the contributions of each class; calculations reveal that the prostitutes' share was the largest. The daughters of the common people of Lydia all ply the trade of prostitute to collect money for their dowries, and they continue to do so until they marry, choosing their own husbands. The tomb is nearly three-quarters of a mile in circumference and about a quarter-mile wide; there is a large lake near it called Gyges' Lake, which the Lydians say is never depleted.[27] And that's what the tomb is like.

[1.94] The Lydians' way of life is not unlike our own, except for the prostitution of their daughters. They were the first people we

---

26. A mule being the offspring of a horse and a donkey.
27. Both the tomb and the lake have been located by modern archaeologists.

know of to adopt silver and gold coinage[28] and to engage in trade, and they also claim to have invented the games now played by them and the Greeks. This invention they date back to the time when they colonized Tyrrhenia in Italy. In the time of King Atys the whole of Lydia suffered a terrible famine, which they endured as best they could. But as the famine continued, they devised various ways to alleviate their misery, including games of dice, knucklebones, and ball games. In fact, they claim to have invented all games except checkers. On one day they would play all day long, hoping to banish all thought of food, and the next day they would eat and not play. This mode of life continued for eighteen years. Finally, as their sufferings went on unabated and even grew worse, the king divided the population into two groups and decided by lot which group should emigrate and which should remain. He himself took charge of the group chosen to stay where they were, while the emigrants were commanded by his son Tyrrhenus. After the lots had been drawn, the departing group went down to the coast at Smyrna and fashioned boats and, after loading on all the equipment needed for the voyage, sailed away in search of land and livelihood. They passed by many peoples and finally settled in Umbria in northern Italy, where they remain to this day. But they have changed their name from Lydians to Tyrrhenians, after their great leader Tyrrhenus.[29]

28. Archaeology again bears out Herodotus' information here.
29. "Tyrrhenians" are known to us as Etruscans, a mysterious people who ended up in central Italy but whose origins are widely debated.

III

The Growth of Persia:
Cyrus Conquers Asia
(c. 550–30 B.C.E.)

[1.95] And now to Cyrus. Who was this man who destroyed the empire of Croesus, and how did the Persians gain the mastery of Asia? I shall base my account on the Persian authorities, who seem to tell the simple truth about Cyrus' achievements without exaggeration, and I shall ignore three other versions.

Going back in history to the time when the Assyrian empire had ruled upper Asia for 520 years, it was the Medes who began the revolt against them, fighting for their freedom with such bravery that they shook off the Assyrian yoke. Other nations followed their example until every nation in that part of the continent had won their freedom. But once again they fell under autocratic rule, in the following manner:

[1.96–97] Among the Medes was a wise man named Deioces, who, in his lust for power, did the following: The Medes at this time dwelled in small villages, and Deioces, already a man of note in his own village, during a period when lawlessness was rampant throughout Media, displayed ever-increasing zeal in the practice of just dealing, understanding that justice and crime are opposing forces. In view of the character he acquired, the men of his own village chose him to judge disputes among themselves. This function he performed with absolute integrity. The considerable reputation he gained among the villagers spread to other villages, the inhabitants of which had suffered much from corrupt judgments. Gladly they submitted their disputes to Deioces for arbitration, and finally they would turn to nobody else. As people came to recognize the impartiality of his judgments, they resorted to him in increasing numbers, and Deioces saw that he was becoming indispensable. Thereupon he refused to sit in the judge's seat any longer. "It is no profit to me," he said, "to neglect my own affairs in order to render judgment all day for my neighbors." Robbery and lawlessness spread among the villages even more than before, and the Medes gathered together in a meeting to discuss this. (I imagine that Deioces' friends spoke loudest.) "We cannot go on like

28

this," they said. "Let us appoint one of our number as king, so that the country can be well governed and we can turn our attention to our own affairs without danger of disorder." Thus they were persuaded to set up a monarchy, and when candidates were nominated Deioces was by far the most popular choice. They agreed to appoint him king.

[1.98–99] Deioces' first action was to order them to build a palace worthy of a king and to give him a bodyguard. This they did, building him a great strong palace on the site he chose and allowing him to select his bodyguard from all the Medes. When he was first in firm control, he compelled the Medes to build one capital city that would excel in importance all other settlements. His wishes were met, and a mighty fortress was built that they called Ecbatana, fortified with concentric walls, each circle standing above its outer neighbor by the heights of its battlements. There are seven circular walls, the innermost containing the palace and the treasury; the outermost and largest is about the size of the walls of Athens. The battlements of the outermost circle are colored white, the next black, the third crimson, the fourth blue, the fifth orange, and the next two silver and gold. In this way Deioces walled in himself and his own palace, while ordering the people to dwell outside the inner wall.

When the work of construction was completed, Deioces introduced for the first time the following protocol. Nobody was admitted to his presence, all business being conducted through messengers. Nobody was allowed to see the king, and it was an offense to laugh or spit in his presence. The purpose of all this pomp was to debar his contemporaries from setting eyes on him, for having been brought up with him, themselves of no inferior stock and as good men as he, they might resent him and plot against him. But if nobody saw him they would regard him as different from ordinary men.

[1.100] These arrangements being established and his power confirmed, he was stern in the administration of justice. All applications for judgments were conveyed to him by written documents and his decisions similarly sent out. He punished arrogant offenders, and his spies and listeners were active throughout his realm.[1]

[1.101–02][2] Deioces unified all the different tribes of Media, but in his reign of fifty-three years he did not extend his empire. (These

---

1. This portrait of how Deioces used awe, secrecy, and repression to achieve absolute power over Media is entirely convincing to those familiar with modern autocracies.

2. The following two chapters were translated by the editor.

are the tribes of the Medians: the Bousae, Paretaceni, Strouchates, Anzanti, Budii, Magi.) It was his son Phraortes, succeeding his father, who, not content to rule the Medes alone, carried arms beyond the borders of Media. The first country he conquered and attacked and subdued was Persia. With these two powerful peoples under his control he reduced one nation after another throughout Asia until he attacked the Assyrians who held Nineveh.[3] This nation had formerly been masters of Asia but were now isolated through the defection of their allies, though still thriving within their own borders. Phraortes was slain, after a reign of twenty-two years, and most of his army was destroyed.

[1.103] With Phraortes dead, Cyaxares, son of Phraortes and grandson of Deioces, succeeded to the throne. He is said to have been a more powerful warrior than his ancestors; he was the first to divide up the Asians into separate contingents according to their weaponry, separating the spearmen, archers, and cavalry that had formerly been mixed together. (It was he who had been battling the Lydians at the time when day turned into night.)[4] He gathered under his rule all the peoples of Asia east of the Halys River, and with this coalition of subjects he attacked Nineveh, avenging his father and hoping to destroy the city.

Cyaxares' campaign against Assyria is interrupted when an army of Scythians suddenly bursts on the scene, marauding through Asia and causing a total breakdown of order. After twenty-eight years of this rampage, Cyaxares finally dispatches the Scythian warriors by getting them drunk at a banquet and killing them. At that point he completes his conquest of Nineveh and makes the Assyrians slaves of the Medes. The fall of Nineveh, dated by modern historians to 612 B.C.E., was indeed a great turning point for the ancient Near East, marking the end of many centuries of Semitic domination and the emergence of a new continental superpower, the Medes. Sometime after subjugating the Assyrians, Cyaxares died.

[1.107] Astyages, son of Cyaxares, then inherited the throne. Astyages had a daughter named Mandane, and one night he had a strange dream about her. He dreamed that she urinated to such an extent as to fill the whole city and flood the whole of Asia. He told his

---

3. The more familiar biblical name of the Assyrian capital city is used here, in place of the name Herodotus uses, "Ninos."
4. This battle has been described as part of Lydian history, above 1.73–74.

dream to the dream-interpreters of the Magi,[5] and their interpretation filled him with alarm. When Mandane came of age, instead of marrying her to some high-ranking Mede, in fear of the dream he gave to her a Persian named Cambyses, a man of decent family and quiet disposition, whose rank was considered far inferior to that of a Mede even of the middle class.[6]

[1.108] Before Mandane and Cambyses had been married a year, Astyages had another dream. He dreamed that a vine grew from his daughter's genitals and overshadowed the whole of Asia. Again he submitted the dream to the interpreters and then sent to Persia for his daughter, who was now pregnant. When she arrived, he kept her under guard, intending to destroy the child, for the Magi had told him that his daughter's child would displace him from the throne. When the child was born, Astyages summoned his kinsman Harpagus, the most trustworthy of the Medes and controller of all his property. "Harpagus," he said, "the task I am assigning you is one that you must carry out most faithfully. Do not shirk it; if you betray me and cast your lot with others, you will pay for it in the end. Take Mandane's child to your own house, kill it, and bury it as you see fit." "Sire," replied Harpagus, "you have never as yet had reason to reproach me for failing in my duty, and I am on guard against letting you down at some future time. If this be your will, it is my duty to obey." Such was the reply of Harpagus.

[1.109] The baby was dressed in grave-clothes and delivered to Harpagus, who went home in tears. When he had told his wife all that had been said, she asked him what he had in mind to do. "I will not obey Astyages," he said, "even if he grows more insane than he is now. I will not consent to it nor take part in so cruel a murder, and that for many reasons. Firstly, the child is my kinsman. Secondly, Astyages is getting on in years and has no son. If he dies and is succeeded by Mandane, whose son I am to have a hand in murdering, will not a perilous future await me? My present safety demands that the child should die, but one of Astyages' servants must do it, not one of mine."

[1.110] So saying, he immediately sent a messenger to one of the king's herdsmen, Mitradates, whom he knew to have suitable pastureland and mountains infested with wild beasts. With him lived a

5. The Magi were the priestly caste of the Persians, who played a major role in politics, even usurping the throne briefly as Herodotus describes in Book 3.
6. Recall that Cyrus, the offspring of this union, was described as a mule by the Delphic oracle because he came from parents of different rank (1.55, 1.91).

female servant, his wife, whose name was Cyno ("Bitch") in Greek, or Spaco in the Median language; for the Medes call a female dog a spaca. . . .[7] The herdsmen hastened to answer the summons, and Harpagus spoke to him as follows: "The king orders you to take this baby and expose it in the most desolate spot you know of among the mountains, where it may the soonest perish. He bade me add this: If you do not kill the child but find some means of preserving it, you will die most horribly. I am appointed to see that this is done."

[1.111–12] The herdsman took the child and returned to his cottage. As fate would have it, his wife, who had daily been expecting her own child, was that day delivered while her husband was away in the city. They had each had their worries, he over his wife's confinement, she because her husband had so unexpectedly been summoned by Harpagus. When the man returned home with unexpected speed, his wife asked him right away why Harpagus had sent for him so eagerly. "Wife," he said, "would that I had never seen what I saw and heard on my visit to the city, and would that such things not befall our masters! The entire household of Harpagus is a scene of sorrow. I entered in dismay. There was a baby lying there, kicking and howling, dressed in gold and brightly colored garments. On seeing me, Harpagus told me to take the child and carry it off in haste and expose it to the wildest part of the mountains. The king has so ordered, he said, and he uttered terrible threats if I should disobey. I took the child and went off with it, thinking that it belonged to one of the servants. Although I was surprised at the gold and expensive clothes and the wailing in Harpagus' household, I should never have guessed whose it was, had I not learned the whole story from the servant who escorted me out of town. It is the child of Mandane, daughter of Astyages, and Astyages commands that it is to be destroyed. Look, here it is." So saying, the herdsman uncovered the child. When she saw what a fine, strong child he was, his wife burst into tears and, throwing herself at his knees, besought him not to expose the child. "But I have no choice," said he, "Harpagus will send his spies to check on me, and I shall perish horribly if I do not obey." Not being able to persuade him, his wife had an alternative suggestion. "Since I have failed to persuade you, and the dead body of the child has to be seen, do as I say. I, too, have given birth, but my boy-child was stillborn. Take our child and

7. There is a small excision here where Herodotus pauses to describe the mountainous country in northern Media. Even in a tightly connected story like the tale of Cyrus' birth, he regularly asks the reader to "pause" the narrative and absorb ethnographic or geographic information.

expose it, and let us rear the child of Astyages' daughter as our own. In this way you will not be discovered disobeying our master, and we shall do well out of it. For our dead child will have a royal burial, and the other child will live."

[1.113] The herdsman was well pleased with his wife's suggestion and at once proceeded to carry it out. He handed over to her the child he had brought condemned to death, and his own dead child he placed in the basket in which he had carried the other. Dressing it in all the raiment that the other child had been wearing, he conveyed it to a most desolate place in the mountains and left it there. When the child had lain exposed for two days, the herdsman went to town, leaving one of his assistants to watch over the body, and told Harpagus he was ready to show him the child's corpse. Harpagus dispatched the most trustworthy of his guards, who confirmed this by eyewitness account, and he had the herdsman's child buried. So the child was buried, and the herdsman's wife took over and reared the child who was one day to be Cyrus but was not yet so called.

[1.114–15] When the boy had reached the age of ten, his identity was revealed in the following manner. In the village where the herdsman's oxen were kept, the lad was playing on the road with the other boys of his age. In their game of pretend, they elected the supposed herdsman's son as their king. He appointed them to various tasks, some to build houses, some to be a bodyguard, one to be the king's "eye,"[8] one to be the king's chamberlain, and so on. But one of the players, son of Artembares, a man of some distinction among the Medes, refused to carry out the task Cyrus had assigned him. Cyrus ordered the other boys to seize him and, when they obeyed, he whipped him savagely. The boy was furious at this humiliating treatment, and when he was released he went home to the city and with loud lamentations related to his father what the herdsman's son had done to him. The indignant Artembares hastened to Astyages with his boy to inform him of his outrageous treatment. "Sire," he said, showing the welts on the lad's shoulders, "see how we have been insulted by your slave, a herdsman's son." Intending to avenge the boy for the sake of his father's honor, Astyages summoned the herdsman and his son and, when they presented themselves, he fixed his gaze on Cyrus and said, "Did you, the son of a man of humble station, have the effrontery to inflict such injuries on the son of one who is my distinguished subject?" "Master," said the boy, "it was with justice that I so treated him. For in our game the boys of the village, of whom he was

8. The "king's eye," as the name implies, was his chief of espionage.

one, made me their king. They thought me the most suitable for that office. The other boys carried out my orders, but he would not listen and paid no heed until he was punished. If for this I deserve to suffer, I am ready."

[1.116] As he was speaking, Astyages began to recognize him. The boy's features seemed to resemble his own, the boy's answer was not that of a slave, and the date of the exposure seemed to fit with the boy's age. Thunderstruck, Astyages was for a time speechless. With difficulty he recovered and, wishing now to get rid of Artembares so that he could question the herdsman alone, he said, "Artembares, I will deal with this matter so that you and your son shall have no cause for complaint." So he dismissed Artembares and ordered his servants to take Cyrus to an inner room.

When the herdsman was left on his own, Astyages questioned him. "Where did you get the boy? Who gave him to you?" "The boy is mine," said the herdsman, "and his mother is still with me." "You are a fool to drive me to extreme measures," said Astyages, signaling to the guards to seize the man. The herdsman was being carried off to be tortured when he revealed the truth. He told all the facts from the beginning and fell to begging the king for mercy.

[1.117] Now that the herdsman had told the truth, the king gave him no further attention, but transferring his anger to Harpagus he ordered his guards to summon him. When he appeared, Astyages said, "Harpagus, when I gave you my daughter's child, how did you dispose of him?" Seeing the herdsman present, Harpagus realized that it was useless to try to lie his way out. "Sire," he said, "when I took charge of the child I debated with myself how I might satisfy your wishes and yet avoid becoming a murderer in your daughter's eyes and in your eyes. So I called this herdsman and handed over the child to him, telling him that it was you who commanded me to kill him. In that there was no lie, for those were your orders. I instructed him to expose the child in some remote mountain spot and to remain with it until it died, threatening him with terrible punishment if he disobeyed. When he had carried out these orders and the child was dead, I sent the most trustworthy of my eunuchs to see for me, and had the child buried. That, sire, was what happened, and that was the fate that befell the child."

[1.118] This was the straightforward story told by Harpagus, and Astyages, concealing his anger, repeated to Harpagus the herdsman's account and ended by saying that the child was alive, and this was all to the good. "I was greatly distressed," he said, "by what had been done to the child and much disturbed by my daughter's enmity toward me. And now, to mark this stroke of good fortune, send your own son to visit our newcomer, and come to a banquet, for I intend to celebrate the deliverance of the boy by sacrificing to the gods, to whom the honor belongs."

[1.119] Harpagus made a low bow and went home in high spirits. His failure in strict obedience had turned out so fortunately that he was even invited to a banquet to celebrate this happy occasion. He told his wife, in great joy, all that had happened and sent his son, an only child of thirteen, to Astyages' palace, bidding him do whatever the king commanded.

But when Harpagus' son came to the palace, Astyages had him butchered and cut into joints. Some of the flesh he boiled, some he roasted, making it ready for the table. When the time came for the banquet, the guests assembled, among them Harpagus. Dishes of mutton were served up to the other guests and to Astyages, but to Harpagus was served the flesh of his son, except for the head, hands, and feet, which had been put aside and covered in a dish. When Harpagus had eaten enough, Astyages asked him whether he had enjoyed the feast. "Very much," replied Harpagus. Then, those who were appointed to do so brought in the boy's head, hands, and feet and bade Harpagus lift the lid and take what he would. Harpagus obeyed and saw the remains of his son. He did not collapse or lose his self-control. "Do you know of what animal's flesh you have eaten?" asked the king. "Yes," said Harpagus, "and whatever the king does is to be accepted." With this reply he gathered the remains and went home. He intended, I imagine, to bury it all together. Such was Harpagus' punishment.

[1.120] Astyages now turned his mind to Cyrus. Summoning those of the Magi who had interpreted his dream, he asked them whether they still attached the same significance to it. They remained firmly of the same opinion; the boy had been destined to displace him from the throne, had he lived and not met with an early death. "The boy is alive and well," said Astyages, "and when he was living in the country, the boys of the village elected him their king. He carried out his duties as real kings do, appointing guards and sentries and messengers and all. What do you think this signifies?" "If the boy is alive and well," said the Magi, "and has been 'king' in this unplanned manner, you can rest assured that he will not rule a second time. Sometimes oracles are fulfilled in trivial ways, and the issue of dreams has often been of slight importance." Astyages replied, "My own opinion agrees with yours. As the boy was named king, the dream has been fulfilled, and he no longer presents any danger to me. Still, consider carefully what is the best course for my house and for yourselves."

"We, too," answered the Magi, "are deeply concerned for the prosperity of your reign. If power should pass into the hands of this boy, a Persian, we who are Medes and of different race will become subservient to the Persians, whereas with you on the throne—one of ours—we receive great power and privilege from you. Thus we always watch out for you and your regime. We would tell you if we apprehended any danger arising from this boy. But we are confident that your dream has had a trivial issue, and we invite you to share our confidence. Send the boy to his parents in Persia where he will be out of sight."

[1.121] Satisfied with this reply, Astyages called Cyrus and said, "My boy, I once did you a wrong because of a misleading dream, but you have been saved by your own good fortune. Be off now to Persia; I will provide an escort. There you will find a father and mother of a very different kind than herdsman Mitradates and his wife."

[1.122] It was with boundless joy that his parents welcomed Cyrus, for they had thought him long since dead. He told them the tale of his survival, saying he had learned his history on the journey thither; he had been entirely in the dark before that, believing himself to be the son of Astyages' cowherd. He explained how he was raised by the cowherd's wife, whom he greatly praised; indeed her name, Cyno ("Bitch"), came up over and over throughout the story. His birth parents, taking their cue from the name, began putting out the rumor that Cyrus, when exposed, had been reared by a dog—this so as to make the survival of their son seem more miraculous to the Persians. So began this well-known rumor.

[1.123] Cyrus grew up to be the bravest and the most popular among all his young companions. Then Harpagus began to court his favor, sending him gifts. For Harpagus longed to take revenge on Astyages, but he realized that he was powerless to do this on his own. As Cyrus came of age, he sought him as an ally, likening his own sufferings to those of Cyrus. Already, prior to this, he had secretly approached each of the great Median nobles, urging the advantages of transferring power from Astyages to Cyrus because of the severity of the former's rule. When he thought the time was ripe, Harpagus had to face the difficulty of sending the message to Cyrus, who dwelled far away in Persia, because all the roads were guarded. Finally, he devised the following plan. He split open a hare without removing its fur, inserted a letter, sewed up the hare, gave it to the most trustworthy of the servants, dressed him as a huntsman complete with hunting net, and sent him off to Persia, ordering him to present the hare to Cyrus and tell him by word of mouth to cut it open with his own hands when nobody else was present.

[1.124] His orders were obeyed. Cyrus received the hare, cut it open, and read the following message: "Son of Cambyses, since the gods have you in their care—as your good fortune shows—take revenge on Astyages, your would-be murderer. If he had had his way, you would have died. To the gods and to me you owe your survival. No doubt you have long ago learned what he did to you and how he punished me because I did not kill you but gave you to the herdsman. If you will now be guided by me, you will become master of the whole of Astyages' kingdom. Persuade the Persians to revolt and take the field against the Medes. If I am appointed to lead Astyages' army against you, you will conquer; and the same is true if any other Mede of high rank is so appointed. For they will be the first to desert and to join you in destroying him. All is ready here. Act, and act quickly."

[1.125–26] After reading this letter, Cyrus began to think how best he might persuade the Persians to revolt, and he hit upon the following device as being most effective. He composed a suitable document and, summoning an assembly of Persians, unrolled the parchment and read it out, declaring that Astyages had appointed him commander of the Persians. "And now," he said, "I command each one of you to appear before me with a scythe." (There are many tribes among the Persians, only some of which Cyrus summoned and persuaded to revolt: These are the Pasargadae, the Maraphi, and the Maspii; of them the Pasargadae rank the highest, and the Achaemenidae, from which the Persian kings derive, are a clan of these. The other tribes, which are dependents of those already mentioned, are the Panthialii, Derousiaei, and Germanii—all farming peoples—and the nomadic tribes Dai, Mardi, Dropici, and Sagartii.) When the Persians had dutifully appeared with their scythes, he ordered them to clear an area of land full of thorns, about two miles square, in the space of a day. This task was accomplished, and then he gave them a second command: They were to appear the following day after having bathed. Meanwhile, Cyrus gathered together all his father's goats, sheep, and oxen, slaughtered them, and prepared to entertain the entire Persian host at a banquet, together with the choicest wine and dainties. When the Persians arrived the following day, he seated them in a meadow and feasted them. Then he asked them, "Which do you prefer, yesterday's tasks or today's good cheer?" They replied that there was a vast difference between them. "Men of Persia," said Cyrus, "your situation is this. If you hearken to me, you will have no servile tasks but will enjoy these and a thousand other pleasures. If you pay no heed to me, you must face countless toils like yesterday's. Listen to me and win your freedom. I know that I am divinely appointed to win your liberation, and I am sure that you are in no way inferior to the Medes in war or in any other way. This being so, I urge you to revolt against Astyages this very day." Now, the Persians had long resented the rule of the Medes and, with their newfound leader, they were eager to seek their freedom.

[1.127–28] When Astyages learned what Cyrus was about, he summoned him by messenger but instead received this reply: That Cyrus would be there much sooner than Astyages would like. Thereupon Astyages put all the Medes under arms and was so deluded[9] as to appoint Harpagus to command them, forgetting the injury he had done him. When the two armies met in battle, some of the Medes who were not privy to the plot fought manfully, while others defected to the Persians, and the greater number played the coward and fled. When news of this disgraceful defeat reached Astyages, he uttered threats against Cyrus: "He will pay for this!" He first impaled the Magi dream-interpreters who had persuaded him to let Cyrus go, then he armed all the Medes who had been left in the capital, above and below military age, and led them out to battle. They were defeated with great loss, and Astyages was taken prisoner.

[1.129] Harpagus now came to taunt the captive, hurling the bitterest insults at him and reminding him of the banquet at which the king had feasted him with his son's flesh. "What does it feel like to be a slave instead of a king?" he asked. Astyages only looked at him and then asked in return, "Was it you who urged Cyrus to revolt?" "Yes," said Harpagus, "I wrote the letter. It is my doing." "Then you are the most stupid and wickedest of men," said Astyages, "the most stupid because, if you were indeed the instigator of the revolt, you could have seized the crown for yourself instead of giving it to another. The most wicked because, on account of that banquet, you have enslaved all the Medes. If you had to confer the crown on somebody other than yourself, it would have been most just to give this prize to a Mede rather than a Persian. Now the Medes, guiltless as they are, will be the slaves of Persian masters—these same Persians who were once slaves of the Medes."

[1.130] After a reign of thirty-five years, Astyages lost his throne in the way I have described. And because of his harsh rule, the Medes, who had ruled Asia west of the Halys for 128 years (not counting the

---

9. The untranslatable inference of the Greek word used here is that the gods were partly responsible for Astyages' delusion.

period of Scythian power),¹⁰ had to bow before Persian domination. Some time later, under Darius, the Medes had a change of heart and mounted a rebellion, but they were defeated in battle and the rebellion was put down. But to return to the time of Astyages: The Persians, led by Cyrus, rebelled from the Medes and became masters of Asia from that day to this. As for Astyages himself, Cyrus did not illtreat his former enemy and kept him at his court until he died.

Thus was Cyrus born and raised and made king, and later conquered Croesus (as I have already related) after Croesus had first wronged him. As a result of this conquest, he came to rule all Asia.

[1.131] A word now about Persian customs, of which I have some personal knowledge. It is not the Persians' practice to set up images and temples and altars; they regard it as foolish to do so because, I think, they do not conceive the gods as having human form, as the Greeks do. They regard Zeus as being the whole circle of the sky, and they sacrifice to him on mountaintops. They worship the sun, the moon, the earth, fire, water, and the winds. In addition to this old-established religion, they have taken over from the Assyrians and the Arabians the worship of Aphrodite, Queen of Heaven. The Assyrians call Aphrodite Mylitta, the Arabs Alilat, and the Persians Mitra.¹¹

[1.133] As regards their deliberations, all important decisions are first discussed when they are drunk. On the next day, the master of the house where they have assembled submits the decision for reconsideration when they are sober. If it is approved, it is ratified; if not, it is abandoned. Conversely, any decision they have reached when they are sober is reconsidered when they are drunk.

[1.134]¹² They honor most after themselves those who inhabit the lands nearest to them, they honor slightly less those who dwell next to those, and so on in that fashion; they give the least honor to those dwelling farthest from themselves, since they hold themselves to be by far the best among the races of humankind, while others have a share of virtue that diminishes over distance, so that the basest are those inhabiting lands farthest from themselves.

10. That is, the period of twenty-eight years in which the Scythians wreaked havoc through Asia (see p. 30).
11. Herodotus assumes that foreign gods are the same as Greek ones, only under different names. In this case, though, he has gotten his names confused, since Mithra (or "Mitra") is a male Persian deity in no way connected with Aphrodite.
12. Chapters 134 and 135 were translated by the editor.

[1.135] The Persians adopt foreign ways more easily than any other people. Since they deemed Median dress more lovely than their own, they now wear it, and they use Egyptian armor in war. They start practicing all sorts of indulgences as soon as they learn of them; thus from the Greeks they have adopted pederasty.[13]

[1.136–37] Every man has several wives and an even greater number of mistresses. A great proof of manliness, second only to prowess in fighting, is to be the father of many boys. The king sends presents every year to the fathers of the greatest number of boys, for it is his belief that his strength lies therein.

Boys are educated from the age of five to the age of twenty, and they are taught three things only: to ride, to shoot the bow, and to tell the truth. Before the age of five, a boy is reared by women only, and his father never sets eyes on him. The purpose of this custom is to avoid distress to the father if the child should die in infancy, and a good custom it is. Another praiseworthy custom is this, that not even the king is allowed to put a man to death for a single offense, nor is the master allowed to inflict irreparable injury on any of his servants.[14] It is only when, on mature consideration, they find that the wrongdoing outweighs good service that they give vent to anger.

[1.138] What they are forbidden to do, they are also forbidden to speak of. They consider lying to be the most shameful thing, and second to that, being in debt, chiefly because being in debt is frequently a cause of lying.

[1.141] To return to where I left off the story: The Ionians and the Aeolians,[15] hearing of the Persian conquest of Lydia, immediately sent their envoys to Cyrus at Sardis, asking for the same terms as had been granted to them by Croesus. Cyrus replied with the following story. A flute-player who saw some fish in the sea played his flute to them, hoping that this would induce them to come ashore. His hopes were in vain, so he took a net, drew a large catch, and hauled them in. Seeing the fish leaping about, he said to them, "You can stop that.

---

13. That is, the Greek pattern of sexual affection between mature men and pubescent boys. It is not clear how Herodotus regarded the practice, but the fact that it is given as an example of the *eupatheiai* adopted by the Persians— "pleasures" or "dalliances"—suggests that the race had by his time come a far way from their rugged, impoverished origins (see 1.71 above).
14. In this instance and in others, the behavior of the Persians depicted by Herodotus elsewhere in his text does not conform to his own ethnographic template.
15. Greeks from the coastal cities of Asia Minor.

When I played my flute for you, you refused to dance, and now it is too late." Cyrus was referring to the time when, besieging Croesus in Sardis, he had invited the Greeks to revolt and they had refused; they were offering their allegiance only now when he was the conqueror. When the Ionians received this reply, they began to see to their defenses, all except the Milesians, to whom Cyrus granted the same terms as they had enjoyed under the Lydians. The other cities met in common council and resolved to send a joint embassy to Sparta, seeking assistance.

[1.152–53]¹⁶ They chose a Phocaean named Pythermus as their spokesman, who, dressed in purple so as to attract a larger audience, made a long speech to the Spartans. The Spartans paid him no heed and rejected the idea of helping the Ionians; they sent the envoys away but were sufficiently stirred as to send a penteconter¹⁷ to the Asiatic coast, no doubt to keep an eye on what was happening. The galley put in at Phocaea, and the most eminent of the crew, a man named Lacrines, was sent to Sardis to warn Cyrus not to injure any Greek city, for the Spartans would not allow it. Cyrus asked some Greek bystanders, "Who are these Spartans, and how many in number?" When he had received their answer, he said to the Spartan spokesman, "I have never yet been afraid of men who have a place specially appointed in the middle of their city where they gather to cheat one another, swearing false oaths. If my fortunes thrive, they will have their own troubles to chat about, never mind those of the Ionians." Cyrus' jibe was directed against the universal Greek practice of having a marketplace for buying and selling, a practice quite unknown to the Persians.

After this, Cyrus put Tabalus in charge of Sardis as governor and appointed a Lydian named Pactyes to deal with the gold of Croesus and his countrymen; he himself marched off toward Ecbatana, bringing Croesus with him; he paid little heed to the Ionians and delegated one of his generals to subdue them, preferring to lead the assaults on the Bactrians, Sacae, and Egyptians.

[1.154–56] Cyrus had marched no great distance when news was brought to him that the Lydians, encouraged by Pactyes, had revolted. Pactyes, he learned, had taken the gold of Sardis down to the coast and used it to hire mercenaries and persuade the coastal peoples to support him; then he had marched on Sardis and was now besieg-

16. A long description of the lands and peoples of Ionia has been omitted here.
17. I.e., a warship.

ing Tabalus in the stronghold of the city. "How can I bring an end to all of this?" said Cyrus to Croesus, who was accompanying him. "It seems that the Lydians will not cease to bring trouble on me and on themselves. My best course, I fear, is to enslave them all. It appears that I have acted like a man who has slain the father and spared the children. For you, who were more than a father to them, I have taken away prisoner, and have restored their city to the Lydians. After that, is it surprising that they have rebelled against me?"

When Croesus heard Cyrus thus speak his mind, he feared that Sardis would be utterly destroyed. "O king," he said, "what you say is fairly said. Yet do not give full vent to your wrath, nor destroy an ancient city that is guiltless alike of former and current misdoings. For former misdoings I am responsible, and I have paid a heavy price. This time the villain is Pactyes, the man to whom you entrusted Sardis, and who alone should be punished. Forgive the Lydians, but take the following measures to ensure their future loyalty and good conduct. Forbid them to possess weapons of war, order them to wear tunics under their cloaks and soft slippers on their feet, and make them teach their sons to play the lute and the harp and to tend shops for a living. You will soon see them turning into women instead of men, and they will never again be a source of trouble to you." Such was Croesus' advice, for it seemed to him preferable to being sold into slavery, and he realized that he could not persuade Cyrus to change his mind unless some drastic alternative was suggested. As it was, Cyrus was delighted with this suggestion and ceased his anger, saying he would do as Croesus suggested.

Cyrus appoints a subordinate, Mazares, to put down the Lydian rebellion by punishing only those in the rebel faction; Pactyes is finally caught after a long chase. Meanwhile Cyrus appoints Harpagus, the man who had helped him defeat Astyages, to deal with the Greek cities of the Asian coast. Using advanced tactics of siege warfare, he forces all of these to become Persian subjects, except for the inhabitants of Phocaea and Teos who sail away en masse with all their valuables and leave Ionia for good.

[1.177] While Harpagus was subduing the western side of Asia Minor, Cyrus himself marched against the north and east, conquering every people and leaving none untouched. I shall pass over his minor conquests and turn my attention to those that required the most effort and that most deserve retelling.

[1.178] Having brought all the continent under his control, Cyrus turned his army against the Assyrians.[18] Assyria contains many great cities, but the most notable and the strongest is Babylon, which became the seat of government after the fall of Nineveh; a vast city of square formation, its sides are nearly fourteen miles long and its circuit fifty-six miles. It is more splendidly adorned than any other city we know of. It is surrounded by a broad, deep moat full of water and further protected by strong outer and inner walls.

[1.183] The great temple of Bel, the Babylonian Zeus,[19] is a square building with gates of bronze, two stades each way, still existing in my time. In the center is a solid tower, a stade in breadth and height; on this is superimposed a second tower, and on this a third, and so on to a total of eight towers. A way of ascent is provided, encircling the towers in spiral form, and about halfway up there is a resting place and seats for those making the ascent. On the summit of the topmost tower is a great shrine containing a magnificent couch with rich coverings and a golden table beside it. No image is to be found there, and no mortal stays the night there except for one native woman all alone, whoever may be chosen by the god—so we are told by the Chaldaeans who are the priests of this god. The Chaldaeans also say—though I do not find this credible—that the god himself comes to the temple and rests on the bed.

[1.184, 187] I shall discuss in my Assyrian account[20] the notable rulers of Babylon who in the past added to its adornment and defenses; among them were two queens, Semiramis and Nitocris, separated by five generations. . . . The latter was responsible for devising a remarkable hoax. Above the main gate of the city she had a tomb built for herself high above the very gates, bearing the following inscription: "If any king of Babylon after me is in need of money, let him open my tomb and take what he wants, but he should in no way do this except in dire need; that would be a bad idea." The tomb remained intact until the time of King Darius. He resented not being

---

18. Not the same people as those conquered by Cyaxares in 612 B.C.E. (1.103, 106 above), though Herodotus calls them by the same name. This second group of "Assyrians" could more properly be called the Chaldaeans.

19. Bel = Ba'al, also known as Marduk, the chief deity of the Babylonians. The building described in what follows has been identified as one of Babylon's great ziggurats or step-pyramids.

20. One of three erroneous cross-references found in the *Histories;* the text as we have it contains no "Assyrian account."

able to use this gate, which would have necessitated driving beneath the corpse of Nitocris, and he also considered that the inscription was an invitation to take the money. But when he opened the tomb, he found no money, just the corpse and an inscription reading: "If you were not a greedy scoundrel, you would not have opened the tomb of the dead." Such is the kind of queen Nitocris is said to have been.

[1.188–89] It was against the son of Nitocris, Labynetus, king of Assyria, that Cyrus was now making war. (When a Persian king takes the field, he is abundantly furnished not only with provisions from his homeland and his own cattle but with water from the river Choaspes, which flows past Susa, his capital city. No Persian king will ever drink from any other stream, and wherever he goes, a supply of this water, readily boiled, is conveyed in silver vessels by a long column of four-wheeled mule-wagons.) On his march, Cyrus reached the river Gyndes, which later joins the Tigris and flows into the Persian Gulf. While Cyrus was preparing to cross the river by boat, one of his sacred white horses, a high-spirited animal, plunged into the river in an attempt to cross on his own and was carried away by the current and drowned. In high wrath with the river that had dared to insult him, Cyrus swore that he would so weaken it that even a woman could cross it with ease without wetting her knees. He suspended his march against Babylon, divided his army into two sections, marked out on either side of the river 180 channels in a straight line in all directions, and ordered his men to dig. Even with this huge labor force, it took the whole summer to complete the task. So Cyrus punished the river Gyndes by dividing it into 360 streams and then resumed his march on Babylon.

[1.190–91] The Babylonians had gone forth in battle-array to await him. Cyrus now arrived and the Babylonians attacked; in the ensuing engagement the Babylonians were defeated and forced to retire within their own walls where they felt secure. They already knew of Cyrus' ceaseless activity and had seen him attacking every nation in turn, and so they had accumulated a vast stock of provisions that would last for several years. The siege became a protracted affair, and Cyrus was beginning to despair of making any impression on the defenses when an ingenious plan was devised, whether by himself or another I do not know. He stationed part of the forces where the Euphrates, flowing under the walls, enters the city, and part where it flows out, with orders to invade through the channel as soon as the waters were shallow enough. When he had given these instructions, he took the nonserviceable part of his army to a point above the city and diverted the river into the adjoining lakes by means of ditches.

When the level of the Euphrates had sunk to thigh level, his forces proceeded silently along the riverbed and entered the town. Had the Babylonians realized what was happening, they could have shut the gates leading to the river, manned the walls on either side of the river, and caught the Persians in a trap. But, as it was, the Persians took them by surprise, and the Babylonians themselves say that their city is so large that the outer suburbs were captured before the people at the center had any idea that there was something amiss. In fact, there was a festival in progress, and they were singing and dancing while the city was being taken.[21]

[1.195] The Babylonian style of dress is as follows: A linen tunic reaches right down to the feet, and over this there is a woolen tunic, with a coverlet on top. Their shoes are of a peculiar native kind, rather like those to be found in Boeotia. They wear their hair long, with a bonnet, and their bodies are perfumed all over. Every man has his own seal and his own staff specially made for him, on top of which is carved an apple or a rose or a lily or an eagle or some other figure. No staff is without some ornament.

[1.196] They used to have a custom that, in my opinion, was most cleverly devised, and that is shared, I believe, with the Eneti of Illyria. Every village practiced it once a year. Girls who had reached marriageable age were gathered together in one place, while the men stood around in a circle. The herald then called upon each girl to stand up in turn, starting with the most beautiful, and offered her for sale. When she had been purchased for a considerable sum of money, he passed on to the next fairest. Marriage was the purpose of the bargaining. The wealthy Babylonian bachelors would bid against each other for the most beautiful brides, while the common folk, for whom beauty in a wife was a luxury they could not afford, were actually paid to take the least prepossessing of the maidens. For when the herald had disposed of all the fairest, he would start on the plainest, perhaps a cripple, and ask who would take the least money to marry her, until she was assigned to the one who demanded the smallest sum. In this way the money accruing from the sale of the most beautiful damsels provided dowries for the ill-favored or cripples. A father was not allowed to marry his daughter to whomever he would, and nobody was permitted to take away a maiden he had bought without pro-

21. The fall of Babylon came in 539 and was jubilantly greeted by the Jews who had been held in "Babylonian captivity" for decades before that. In several books of the Hebrew Bible, notably Second Isaiah, Cyrus' victory over Babylon is hailed as a redemption sent by God.

viding sureties that he would marry her. In case of disagreement between husband and wife, the money would be returned. Men from other villages were also allowed to buy a wife at these sales. This very admirable custom has now fallen into disuse and has been succeeded by a quite different practice. When hardship came to the city after its conquest, the common people resorted to prostituting their daughters as a means of eking out a living.

[1.197] Another of their customs, scarcely less ingenious than their former marriage custom, is concerned with illness. They have no doctors but carry the sufferers out into the marketplace where passersby offer advice and remedies, either having experienced the same sickness themselves or having observed it in other cases. They suggest such remedies as have proved efficacious for themselves or that have been seen to succeed with others. Nobody is allowed to pass by in silence; they must ask the sufferer the nature of his ailment. They bury their dead in honey, and their lamentations are similar to those used in Egypt.

[1.201] After the conquest of Assyria, Cyrus' next ambition was to subjugate the Massagetae. These are said to be a numerous and mighty nation, dwelling eastward beyond the river Araxes;[22] some authorities believe them to be of Scythian descent. It is not clear whether the Araxes is greater or smaller than the Danube. Some say that it contains many large islands as big as Lesbos, and that these are inhabited by men who live on roots that they dig up in the summer, while for their winter supplies they lay in store the fruits of certain trees that they have found to be suitable for food. Other trees they have found to bear fruit of a peculiar kind. Gathering in groups, they sit in a circle around a fire and they cast this fruit into the flames. As it burns, it sends out smoke, the smell of which makes them drunk just as wine does the Greeks. The more fruit they cast into the flames, the more drunk they get, until they jump up and start singing and dancing.[23]

[1.204] There were many motives that impelled Cyrus to make war on the Massagetae. First, there was his belief in his superhuman origin. Secondly, he could reflect on his uninterrupted success in

22. See the map p. xxii for Herodotus' notions about the Araxes; he believed that this river flowed east-west and so divided Europe from Asia in the eastern regions of those continents. Thus the episode that follows represents the first of several Persian invasions of Europe, all of them leading to misfortune. There is no independent evidence concerning this invasion.

23. This "fruit" is of course cannabis or marijuana, still cultivated today in the part of the world where Herodotus locates the Massagetae.

the past; for wherever he campaigned, no nation could withstand his assault.

[1.205–06] At this time the Massagetae were ruled by a queen, Tomyris, who had succeeded to the throne on her husband's death. Cyrus sent a messenger to her on the pretext of asking for her hand in marriage, but Tomyris rejected his overture, knowing well that it was her kingdom, not herself, that he was wooing. Failing in this stratagem, Cyrus now openly embarked on a campaign against the Massagetae. He advanced to the river Araxes and prepared bridges for his army to cross and fortified his ferryboats to force a landing. While he was thus busily engaged, Tomyris sent him this message: "King of the Medes, abandon what you are about. You cannot know if it will turn out as you would like it. Rule over your own people and endure to see me rule over mine. But of course you will not hearken to me, for you cannot bear to live at peace. Well, then, if you are so eager to try the strength of the Massagetae, you need not engage in the toil of bridge-building. We will retire a three days' march from the river, and you may cross over to our territory. But if you prefer to engage us on your own territory, go and withdraw some distance, and we will cross over to your side."

[1.207] On receiving this message, Cyrus summoned his leading counselors to advise him which of the alternatives he should choose. They were unanimous in proposing that Tomyris and her army should cross over to their side. But Croesus the Lydian, who was present at the council of war, took the opposite view, speaking as follows: "O king, I have said before that ever since Zeus gave me into your hands, I will do all I can to avert any danger threatening your house. My own misfortunes have taught me a bitter lesson. If you think that you and your army are immortal, it would be pointless to declare my opinion in this matter. But if you recognize that you are merely human, and your men too, then first learn this, that there is a cycle in human affairs that does not permit the same people to enjoy unbroken good fortune. In this matter I do not agree with your counselors. If we allow the enemy to cross over to our side of the river, in the event of defeat you will lose not only a battle but your entire empire. For it is obvious that the victorious Massagetae would not retreat but would continue to drive on right through your realm. If, on the other hand, victory falls to you, it would not be as decisive as it would be if you were to pursue a defeated enemy into their own land. Then again there is the further consideration that it would be intolerable for Cyrus, son of Cambyses, to retreat before a woman. My advice is to cross over the river and advance as far as the enemy withdraws and then employ this stratagem: I gather that the Massagetae have no experience of the good things that the Persians enjoy and are insensible to life's pleasures. Let us provide for them in our camp a most generous banquet, with huge numbers of sheep slaughtered and dressed for the table, bowls of strong wine on a liberal scale, and all kinds of other dishes. When this has been done, let the greater part of your army retire, leaving behind some inferior troops. Unless I am mistaken, on seeing this attractive banquet, the enemy will fall upon it, and this will afford you the opportunity to deliver a mighty stroke."

[1.208] These were the conflicting counsels presented to Cyrus, who elected to follow Croesus' advice and sent a message to Tomyris bidding her withdraw, as he was about to cross the river. She withdrew in accordance with her undertaking, and Cyrus, placing Croesus in the care of his son Cambyses, whom he named as his successor, with earnest instructions to treat him with honor and respect if he, Cyrus, should meet with disaster, sent them both back to Persia and crossed the river with his army.

[1.209] On the night after the crossing, as Cyrus was asleep in the land of the Massagetae, he had a dream. He dreamed that he saw the eldest son of Hystaspes with wings on his shoulders, one of which overshadowed Asia and the other Europe. Now the eldest son of Hystaspes, of the Achaemenid clan, was Darius, a young man of about twenty at the time, who had been left behind as not yet of military age. When Cyrus awoke, he reflected on the dream and, sending for Hystaspes, he spoke to him in private. "Hystaspes," he said, "I have discovered that your son is plotting against me and my throne, and I will disclose to you the reason for my certainty. The gods have me in their care and warn me of what is to come. Last night in a dream I saw your eldest son with wings on his shoulders, one overshadowing Asia and the other Europe. There can be no doubt of the significance to this—he is plotting against me. Do you therefore return to Persia with the utmost speed and see to it that you produce the young man for trial when I return victorious from this war."

[1.210] So spoke Cyrus, thinking that Darius was plotting against him. But the true meaning of the dream had escaped him. The god was forewarning Cyrus that he was about to meet his death, and Darius would thereby come to the throne.

Hystaspes replied, "O king, may there never be born a Persian who would plot against you, and if there be, may he straightaway die. You found the Persians slaves and made them free; you found them subject to others and made them rulers over all men. If a dream has told you that my son is stirring up revolution, I give him over to you to do as you will." With this answer he crossed the Araxes to return to Persia and keep watch over his son Darius for Cyrus' sake.

[1.211] Cyrus now advanced a day's march from the Araxes and carried out Croesus' plan. Then he retired with the flower of his army, leaving behind some inferior troops. A detachment of the Massagetae, one-third of their army, fell upon these troops, overcame their feeble resistance, and slew them all. After this victory, seeing a banquet laid out before them, they betook themselves to feasting, and, sated with good food and wine, fell asleep. The Persians attacked, slew many of them, and took prisoner an even greater number, among whom was their general, Spargapises, Tomyris' son.

[1.212] The queen, learning of these events and of her son's capture, sent the following message: "Cyrus, you who cannot get your fill of blood, do not pride yourself on what you have accomplished. The fruit of the vine, wherewith you fill yourselves until you are so maddened that as the wine goes down shameful words float up on its fumes[24]—*that* is the treacherous poison whereby you have got my son into your power, not by strength in battle. Now listen to me for your own good. Restore my son to me and get out of my land without hurt, gloating over your triumph over a third part of the Massagetae. If you refuse, I swear by the sun, our lord, that for all your gluttony I will give you more blood than you can drink."

[1.213] Cyrus paid no heed to this message. As for Tomyris' son, Spargapises, when he was sober again and realized the nature of his misfortune, he begged Cyrus to have his fetters removed, and as soon as he had the use of his hands, he did away with himself.

[1.214] When Cyrus had rejected her message, Tomyris gathered all her forces and met him in the field, and the battle that followed was, I consider, the most violent that has ever been between foreign nations. According to what I have learned, the manner of it was this. At first, the two sides stood at a distance and fired arrows at each other; then, when all their shafts were exhausted, they came into close combat with lances and swords. They fought this way for a long time, with neither side willing to retreat. Finally, the Massagetae got the upper hand. The greater part of the Persian army was destroyed

---

24. The elaborate description shows that, to these nonagricultural peoples, wine was as yet an unfamiliar substance. In many stories, Herodotus contrasts different types of civilization by way of their experience of wine; the Massagetae can thus be compared to the Scythians (1.106) and the Ethiopians (3.22). The pattern is disrupted, however, at 6.84, where Scythians are said to be harder drinkers than the Greeks.

on the spot, and Cyrus himself was killed. He had reigned twenty-nine years. Tomyris sought out his body among the dead, flung his severed head into a wineskin filled with human blood, and, enraged, spoke these words: "Though I have conquered you, and I live and you are dead, yet you have destroyed me by treacherously capturing my son. Now, as I promised you, I shall give you your fill of blood."

Of the many accounts of Cyrus' death, this is the one I believe true.[25]

[1.215–16][26] The Massagetae dress as the Scythians do and have a similar way of life. In battle they fight both mounted and on foot, and some use the spear, bow and arrow, and the *sagaris* or battle-ax. The only metals they use are gold and bronze . . . for they have no iron or silver in their land, but gold and bronze in great quantity. The following are their customs: Each man takes a wife, but the wives are all held in common. The Greeks think it is the Scythians who do this, but in fact it's the Massagetae. Whenever a Massagetan man desires a woman, he simply hangs up his arrow case on the front of her wagon[27] and enjoys her freely. As to life span, they set no other limit but this to old age: When one of them becomes very old, all his kin gather and sacrifice him, along with various animals, and then they roast all the meats and hold a huge feast. This they deem the happiest death, and they take pity on anyone who dies from disease, since this person must be buried in the ground and not eaten. They grow no crops but live off their flocks and also fishing, for fish are plentiful in the Araxes. They are great drinkers of milk. As to deities, they honor one alone, the sun; and to it they sacrifice horses, in the belief that the swiftest of creatures is owed to the swiftest of gods.

25. Accounts of Cyrus' death were indeed various. Other Greek writers depict him dying at home in his palace or on campaign against the Scythians. Cyrus' tomb can still be seen today in Iran.
26. These two chapters were translated by the editor.
27. Presumably as a kind of "do not disturb" sign.

IV

The Growth of Persia:
Cambyses Conquers North Africa
(c. 530–22 B.C.E.)

After taking the story of the Persian empire as far as the death of Cyrus, Herodotus enters into a long description of the land and people of Egypt, comprising about one-eighth the length of the entire Histories. This section, like the other ethnographies contained in the work, is connected to the main story by the organizing pattern of Persian expansion: Herodotus opens Book 2 by telling us that Cyrus' son, Cambyses, inherited his father's throne and made ready to attack Egypt; at that point he "pauses" the story to relate everything he knows about that ancient land. Then he restarts the narrative "clock" with the account of the Persian invasion of Egypt, at the beginning of Book 3. Each of the earth's regions is dealt with in turn by Herodotus as it becomes a target of Persian imperialism.

The Egyptian material divides roughly into three sections: the geography of the country, especially its great river, the Nile; the customs and religious rites of the people; and the history of the land under successive kings going back to Min, the first Egyptian ruler of whom Herodotus has knowledge (c. 3,000 B.C.E.), and ending with King Amasis, a contemporary of Croesus and Cyrus. The brief excerpts below are designed to give a sampling of each of the three sections of this remarkable Egyptian account.

[2.2]¹ Before the reign of Psammetichus,² the Egyptians used to think that of all the peoples of the world they were the most ancient. But ever since Psammetichus came to the throne and made up his mind to inquire into this matter, the Egyptians have believed that the Phrygians are the more ancient, and that they themselves take second place. Psammetichus, finding that all his inquiries into this question proved fruitless, devised the following plans. He took two newborn babes at random from their parents and gave them to a shepherd to

---

1. All Book 2 excerpts were translated by the editor.
2. Psammetichus or Psamtik reigned from about 664 to 610. According to Herodotus' later acount of his reign, he was the first pharaoh to hire Greek mercenaries to augment his army and even gave a grant of land for these newcomers to settle in.

bring up among his flocks, with strict orders that no one was to utter a word in their presence. They were to live on their own in a lonely cottage; at times goats were to be brought in to them to provide them with milk, and their other needs were to be supplied.

In giving these instructions, Psammetichus had this in mind, to find out what word they would first utter when they had outgrown their meaningless babbling. In this he was successful. For two years the shepherd continued to carry out his orders; then once, as he opened the door and entered the cottage, both children ran up to him with outstretched hands, uttering the word "becos." The first time this happened, the shepherd kept silent; but when this word continued to greet him whenever he visited the children to minister to them, he informed his master and at his bidding brought the children to him. When Psammetichus himself heard this word spoken, he sought to discover what language this word belonged to, and found that this was the Phrygians' word for "bread." So the Egyptians gave way and agreed that the Phrygians were a more ancient people than they. That this is what really happened I was assured by the priests of Hephaestus at Memphis.[3] But the Greeks, in a number of other absurd versions, say that Psammetichus arranged for the children to be reared by women whose tongues he cut out.

One of the unique features of Herodotus' Egyptian account is the insight it displays into scientific questions, especially those concerned with geography, geology, and climate. These questions were hotly debated by the Ionian thinkers of the previous generations, and Herodotus often brings new and remarkably astute observations into the attempt to find solutions. Note, for example, his keen eye for physical evidence in the discussion below of how the land of Egypt was formed.

[2.4–5] The priests at Memphis told me that, in the time of Egypt's first king, Min,[4] the whole country was swampland except the district around Thebes, and that none of the land north of Lake Mo-

---

3. These priests were Herodotus' principal informants during his stay in Egypt. The city of Memphis had been home to the Greek settlement in Egypt ever since the time of Amasis, so many Egyptians spoke Greek there and some, even the priests charged with upkeep of sacred shrines, profited from the Greek tourist trade. The god that Herodotus calls Hephaestus is in fact the Egyptian deity Ptah.

4. About 2,500 years before Herodotus' time.

eris, to a distance of seven days' journey up the Nile, was then above water. And they seem to me quite correct. For it's clear to anyone who sees firsthand and who has understanding, even if he has not been told in advance, that Egypt—I mean the land to which the Greeks now voyage—is newly made land and the gift of the river; and I know this is true also of the region south of Lake Moeris for an additional three days' sail, even though the priests said nothing to me about this tract. For the quality of Egypt is such that, if you sail as far as a day's journey off the coast and drop a plumb line into the sea, you will bring up silt from the bottom and find the depth to be only eleven fathoms. This evidence shows how far out the soil is carried by the river's flow.

[2.10–11] It seems to me that Egypt is indeed newly made land, as the priests claim. I believe that the whole region in between the mountain ranges south of Memphis was once a gulf of sea. . . . There is another such gulf in Arabian territory, projecting out of the Red Sea, which is so long that a ship under oars would need forty days to traverse it, though its width is only a half-day's sail at its widest point; and in it each day the tide ebbs and flows.[5] I believe that Egypt was once a gulf like this one, extending from the northern sea to the Ethiopian, almost merging with the other one that extends from the southern sea to Syria, with only a small strip of land separating them. If someone diverted the Nile so that it flowed into this eastern gulf, who's to say it would not fill it up with silt in the course of 20,000 years? I myself suspect that even 10,000 years would suffice. So isn't it likely that, in the vast stretch of time before my birth, a gulf even larger than this one would be filled in, given that such a huge and productive river flows into it?

[2.12] Therefore, I trust the priests in what they tell me about Egypt, and what is more I am confident for my own part that they are right, for I have seen that Egypt sticks out into the sea, compared with the land around it; I have seen seashells discovered in the mountains; I have seen salty extrusions that corrode even the pyramids; and I've noted that the mountains south of Memphis are the only ones in Egypt containing sand, and that Egypt, unlike the countries of Arabia and Libya that border it, has a blackish and clod-filled soil, as though it were formed from mud and silt carried down by the river. Libyan soil is redder and sandier, as I have observed, while that of Arabia and Syria is more clayey and almost rocky.

---

5. Herodotus here describes what we call the Red Sea.

The river Nile especially interests Herodotus, being the defining feature of the land of Egypt and a geographic anomaly, in that it floods in the summer rather than (as all Greek rivers do) in the rainy winter. Herodotus goes to great lengths to explain this bizarre summer flooding and also to trace the source of the Nile, a geographical mystery that remained unsolved until the nineteenth century. (He himself had explored the upper Nile but had gotten no farther south than the city of Elephantine, near the edge of Ethiopian territory.) Reasoning from the general principle that the southern half of the globe mirrors the northern half, he theorized that the Nile followed a course that parallels that of the Danube, the great northern river whose mouth lies at approximately the same longitude as the Nile Delta. That hypothesis then governed his observations on the customs of the Egyptian people, as seen below.

[2.35] Just as the Egyptians have an opposing climate and a river whose nature is different from that of other rivers, so they have established customs and ways of life entirely opposite to the rest of humankind. For example: The women go to the market and do business, while the men stay at home and weave cloth. . . . Men carry loads on their heads, women on their shoulders. Men urinate while sitting, women while standing. They go to the bathroom indoors and eat outside in the streets, explaining that they feel they must perform necessary but embarrassing functions in a hidden place but other, less embarrassing things in public. No woman can be a priest there, either of a male or female deity, but all gods are served by men.

[2.36] Priests in other countries let their hair grow long, but in Egypt the priests shave their heads. . . . Other peoples live with their domestic animals outside the home, but the Egyptians live with theirs. Others make wheat and barley the staples of their diet, but Egyptians who do this are greatly ridiculed; they make bread out of rye, which some of them call *zeia*. They knead their dough with their hands but clay with their feet. . . . Whereas the Greeks write their letters and add numbers going from left to right, the Egyptians go from right to left; and in doing so they claim they are in the "right," while the Greeks are just "backward."

About half of Book 2 is devoted to a history of Egypt, surveying the reigns of twenty major kings going back to Min, around 3,000 B.C.E. Herodotus provides thumbnail sketches of each ruler in turn, ending with the most recent and the most colorful, Amasis (who reigned from 570 to 525). At the outset of this mini-biography, Amasis is not yet king but the trusted subordinate of the reigning pharaoh, Apries, whose poor leadership of the army has provoked an insurrection.

[2.162] When King Apries learned of the rebellion against him, he sent Amasis to negotiate with the rebels and stop the uprising. While Amasis was speaking to the rebels and urging them to stop, someone standing behind him put a helmet on his head and, as he did so, declared he was crowning a king. Amasis was not displeased by this move, as soon became evident; for when the rebels did in fact choose him to be king, he prepared to lead them into battle against Apries. Meanwhile Apries, learning of this treachery, sent to Amasis a trusted servant whose name was Patarbemis, with orders to capture Amasis alive and bring him before Apries. But when Patarbemis arrived at the camp and summoned Amasis, Amasis rose in his saddle (for he was at that moment mounted on horseback) and, letting out a fart, said "Take *this* back to Apries!"

[2.169] Battle finally broke out near the city of Memphis, with Apries leading a body of foreign mercenaries and Amasis leading native Egyptians. The foreigners fought well but were not nearly as numerous as the natives and so were defeated. Apries is said to have entertained the notion that not even a god could overthrow him, so secure was his rule; yet for all that, he was defeated in battle and taken as a prisoner to Sais.

[2.172] And so with Apries deposed, Amasis came to the throne, a man from the region of Sais, from a town known as Siouph. At first the Egyptians looked down on their new king and held him in contempt, since he had formerly been a common man from an undistinguished background. But Amasis used his cleverness to win them over rather than reacting out of arrogance. He possessed many fine things, among which was a golden vessel in which he and his guests used to wash their feet. He broke this vessel apart and used it to make a statue of a god, and erected this statue in a convenient spot in the city, where the Egyptians, as they passed before the statue, stopped to pay it great reverence. Learning how things had gone, Amasis called the Egyptians together and revealed that the statue had been made from a footbath, into which the Egyptians used to vomit, urinate, and wash the filth off their feet; and now, he said, they revered it as a god! "I myself," he told them, "am just like that footbath; though I was once humble, I am now your king; honor and respect me as you do the statue." In this way he seduced the Egyptians into accepting his mastery.

[2.173] Here was the way he conducted his business: In the morning, up to the time when the marketplace fills up, he pursued zealously whatever affairs were pressing; but after this time he drank, laughed with his drinking buddies, and became a useless jokester. His friends grew annoyed with this behavior and admonished him: "Sire, you conduct yourself badly, always indulging in what is base; you should act in accordance with the solemn throne on which you sit, and stay by your tasks throughout the day. Then the Egyptians would know they are ruled by a great man, and you would be better spoken of by your subjects. What you do now is not the least bit royal." Amasis replied as follows: "Men who wield bows and arrows string their bows when they need them and unstring them when they don't. If the bows remained strung all the time, they would break and could no longer be used when needed. Such also is the way of human conduct. If we remain always dutiful and never relax with revelry, we would, before we know it, go insane or have a breakdown. Since I understand this principle, I give equal time to each pursuit." Thus he answered his friends.

[2.174] It is said that Amasis, while he was still a commoner, was a big drinker and prankster and in no way a person of substance. Indeed, when he had finished drinking and enjoying himself he would go around stealing things. If people accused him of taking their property, he denied it, and they would haul him off to some oracle or other; sometimes the oracle convicted him, other times it exonerated him. After he became king, he did the following: He ignored the oracles that had let him off the hook and made no provision for their upkeep, and never made sacrifices there, seeing that they were false and worthless; but he took special care of the ones that had convicted him, since these were true oracles and spoke on behalf of the gods.

Having surveyed Egyptian history up to the time of Amasis—the narrative present—Herodotus returns to the main story of the development of the Persian empire. Cambyses, son of Cyrus, assumes the throne, conquers Egypt with ease and, while based there, begins plotting further invasions of surrounding African territories.

[3.17–19][6] Cambyses planned three different campaigns: one against the Carthaginians, one against the Ammonians, and a third against the Long-lived Ethiopians, who inhabit the part of Libya nearest the southern sea.[7] Against the Carthaginians he sent his navy, and against the Ammonians, a select part of his army; but to the Ethiopians he

6. Chapters 17–33 were translated by the editor.
7. By the term "southern sea" Herodotus probably meant the waters off southernmost Africa, though neither he nor his audience had more than the vaguest idea where this was or how far away from Egypt. Both the name of the tribe, "Long-lived Ethiopians," and their location are intended to convey

first sent spies, to see whether there really was such a thing as the so-called Table of the Sun and to spy on the country generally. He gave these spies gifts to present to the Ethiopian king as a pretext for their visit. (The Table of the Sun, reportedly, is something like this: In front of the Ethiopian city there is a meadow, and it is filled with cooked meats from every type of animal; state officials go there every night to set out these meats, and in the daytime, anyone who wishes can come and partake of them. But the Ethiopians say that these meats spring forth from the earth itself.)[8] Having decided to use spies, then, Cambyses immediately sent for some of the Fish-eaters who live in Elephantine,[9] since these men understand the Ethiopian language.... When they arrived, he sent them on their mission, giving orders what to say and loading them up with gifts: a purple cloak, a necklace and bracelets of gold, a container of myrrh, and a jar of Phoenician wine.

[3.20] The Ethiopians to whom Cambyses sent these men are said to be the tallest and most beautiful of all peoples. Their customs are unlike those of other peoples, especially as concerns the kingship: They select as king whomever they deem to be the tallest and to have strength commensurate with his size.

[3.21] So, the Fish-eaters arrived and presented the king with their gifts, saying: "Cambyses, king of the Persians, has sent us to negotiate with you and to give you these gifts, items that he himself most delights in, in the hopes of becoming your ally and visiting you in person." The Ethiopian king realized that they were spies, however, and spoke as follows: "It's not true that the Persian king has sent you here because he hopes to become my guest; nor do you fellows speak the truth (for it's obvious you're spying on my realm); nor is your king a righteous man; for if he were, he would not feel tempted to conquer land outside his own territory, nor would he enslave men who have done him no wrong. Here, give him this bow and say to him, 'The

---

a sense of extreme remoteness and unfamiliarity, like Herodotus' later phrase "at the ends of the earth." It is worth noting that the Ethiopians known to Greek legend prior to Herodotus were a race of semidivine beings who held elaborate feasts and entertained the Olympian gods as their guests. Herodotus' portrait is not quite so fantastic but contains many of the same elements.
8. An interesting example of rationalization: Though treading perilously close to the borders of fairy tale, Herodotus keeps from stepping over by offering a plausible account of how the meats are replenished.
9. Elephantine or "Ivory City" was a real locale, at the southernmost boundary of Egypt. Nothing is known of the Fish-eaters prior to Herodotus' account; later, they appear in Greek lore as a fairy-tale race of happy primitives.

king of the Ethiopians advises the king of the Persians thus: If the Persians can draw bows as big as these with as much ease as we do, then let them come in full force against the Long-lived Ethiopians; if not, let them give thanks to the gods, who have never inspired in the children of the Ethiopians any desire to gain lands beyond their own.'" Then he picked up a bow, unstrung it, and handed it to them.[10]

[3.22] Then, picking up the purple clothing, he asked what it was and how it had been made. The Fish-eaters gave him a true account of how purple cloth is dyed, to which he replied: "Disguised clothing for disguised men." Next he asked about the gold necklace and bracelets; when the Fish-eaters explained that they were jewelry, he laughed, thinking they meant shackles. "We have shackles in our land far stronger than this," he said. Then he asked about the myrrh, and when they described its manufacture and its use as a perfume, he said the same thing he had said about the clothing. Finally he came to the wine; after learning how it was made and drinking some, he declared himself delighted. Then he asked what the Persian king ate and how long the oldest Persians lived. They described the making of bread out of grain and said that eighty years was the greatest complement of years allotted to their race. To this the Ethiopian replied that he was not surprised they lived such a short time while feeding on dung;[11] moreover, he said, they would not live even as long as eighty years if not for their drink (pointing to the wine); in this alone, he said, the Ethiopians were outdone by the Persians.[12]

[3.23] Now the Fish-eaters asked in their turn about the Ethiopian way of life, and the king told them that many Ethiopians lived to 120 years, and some even longer than that, eating meat and drinking milk. When the spies expressed amazement at their longevity, the king led them to a spring, whose water made their skin glisten just as if it were olive oil and gave off a smell of violets. The spies later

10. Later we learn, in a passage not presented here, that only Cambyses' brother, Smerdis, proved strong enough to draw this bow, and even he could draw it only a little way. Jealous of Smerdis' superior strength, Cambyses sent his brother back to Persia and later ordered his murder.

11. Being the product of a nonagricultural society, the king is disgusted by the idea of eating foods that grow out of the fertilized earth.

12. An interesting variation on the theme encountered earlier in Cyrus' attack on the Massagetae (1.207 ff.): Though innocent of wine, like all nonagricultural peoples, the Ethiopians do not seem vulnerable to its effects. By contrast, Cambyses, though he belongs to a wine-drinking race, is said to have become deranged by alcoholism (see 3.34 below).

reported that this water was so light that nothing would float on it; even wood, or things lighter than wood, would sink to the bottom. (If this water is really such as they described, then it must be through their constant use of it that they have become long-lived.) Next after the spring, he showed them the prison, where all the prisoners were bound with shackles of gold. (Bronze is the rarest and most precious substance among these Ethiopians.)[13] After their visit to the prison, he also showed them the so-called Table of the Sun.

[3.24] Finally the king showed them the Ethiopian tombs, which are said to be made of crystal and used in the following manner: After embalming the corpse (either in the Egyptian manner or some other way), they whiten it with gypsum and paint on it as close a likeness of the living person as they can. Next they surround the body with a pillar of crystal, hollowed out to form a chamber (this crystal is mined easily and in great quantities in their land). In the middle of the pillar stands the corpse, where it can be clearly seen from outside; no unpleasant smells or anything else unseemly can be sensed; the image of the corpse is not distorted in any way by the crystal. For the space of a year, the nearest and dearest of the dead person keep the pillar in their home, bringing it sacrifices and offering it the finest foods; after that they carry it outside and set it up in a circuit around the city.

[3.25] Having seen all this, then, the Fish-eaters departed and, returning to Egypt, made their report to Cambyses. Immediately Cambyses, enraged, marched against the Ethiopians, without first ordering provision of food or reckoning with the fact that he was setting out for the ends of the earth; when he heard what the Fish-eaters had to say, he became maddened and no longer in his right mind, and he marched. He ordered the Greeks who were with him[14] to remain there in Egypt and took with him his entire infantry corps. When he came to Thebes in the course of his march, he split off five myriads[15] from the army and sent them to attack the Ammonians,[16] enslave

13. Unlike gold, bronze is an alloy and must be smelted; presumably the Ethiopians get their bronze through trade and lack the knowledge to produce it, just as they are ignorant of the other manufacturing and agricultural processes described to them by the Fish-eaters.
14. As subjects of the Persian empire, the Greeks of Asia Minor were compelled to take part in Cambyses' military expeditions, even against other Greek cities. In this case the Greeks serving in Egypt constituted part of his navy.
15. A myriad is a company of 10,000 men.
16. The Ammonians were a real people, inhabiting the oasis of Siwa in the deserts west of Egypt. There was found the famous oracle of the Egyptian

them, and to set fire to the local oracle of Zeus; while he himself took
the remaining forces and proceeded against the Ethiopians.

When Cambyses had not yet completed even a fifth of the
march, his food supplies began to fail. Next the pack animals gave
out—for they were devoured by the soldiers. If under these circumstances Cambyses had come to his senses and turned the army around,
he would have been a wise man despite his original error; but in fact
he paid no heed to his difficulties and pressed ahead. As long as the
soldiers could, they foraged grass and plants from the ground, but
soon they came to the desert sand, and there some of them did a terrible thing: Drawing lots, they chose one man out of ten and the rest
ate him. When Cambyses learned of this, shaken by the spectacle of
his men devouring each other, he at last gave up his Ethiopian campaign and turned around, and got back to Thebes after having lost
most of his army. From there he went north to Memphis and discharged the Greek fleet.

[3.26] Thus fared the campaign against the Ethiopians. As for
those who were detached to attack the Ammonians: These troops set
out from Thebes, with guides in the lead, and are known to have arrived at the city of Oasis, a seven days' journey across the desert (Oasis is settled by Samians, reportedly of the Aeschrionian tribe).[17] This
place has a name that translates to "Islands of the Blessed." The army
is said to have arrived at this place, but neither the Ammonians nor
their neighbors nor any other sources know what happened thereafter. The men never reached the Ammonians and never returned
home. This much, however, is told by the Ammonians: When the
men were midway between Oasis and themselves on their journey
through the desert, they stopped to prepare a meal and a violent south
wind arose and buried them under heaps of sand; in this way they disappeared forever. So the Ammonians say regarding the expedition
against them.

Herodotus shows how Cambyses, already behaving irrationally in his pro-
ceedings against the Ethiopians, completely lost sanity after his return to oc-
cupied Egypt. According to Herodotus, he antagonized Egyptian religious

---

god Amun (identified with Zeus by the Greeks), from whom their tribal name
is derived.

17. The term "oasis" has obviously been misinterpreted by Herodotus as a
proper name. Nothing else is known of the Samians said to live here—Greek
islanders dwelling in the Sahara Desert?

feeling by trying to kill a holy calf called the Apis after mistaking a festival in honor of the calf for a celebration of his African defeats. Next, he turned on his own closest kin, sending his trusted aide Prexaspes to murder his brother, and killing his own sister himself, after first incestuously marrying her. As this portrait of cruelty and paranoia reaches nightmarish proportions, Herodotus pauses to speculate on the cause of Cambyses' madness, which the Egyptians attributed to divine revenge for the wounding of the Apis calf.

[3.33] Such were the crimes that Cambyses, in his madness, committed against his closest kin, whether it was because of the Apis or for some other reason; for many are the ills that humankind is subject to. Indeed Cambyses is said to have suffered since his birth from the disease some call "sacred," a great affliction.[18] And it seems reasonable that a man whose body was thus diseased would also be sick in his mind.

[3.34] Other Persians, too, suffered as a result of his derangement: Prexaspes was a man most honored by him, one who used to bring him his dispatches and whose son was the king's cupbearer—a post of considerable distinction. It is said that one day Cambyses addressed him thus: "Prexaspes, what sort of man do the Persians consider me to be, and how do they speak of me?" "My lord," said Prexaspes, "in all other respects they lavish praises on you, but they say that you are overmuch fond of wine." Cambyses flew into a rage. "So now the Persians think I am crazy and out of my mind," he said. "What they previously said, then, was not the truth." For on some previous occasion, when the Persians were sitting in council with him along with Croesus, he had asked them how they thought he compared with his father Cyrus. They answered that he was a better man than his father, for he had extended Cyrus' empire by acquiring dominion over Egypt and the sea. Croesus, however, was not satisfied with this judgment, and said, "Son of Cyrus, in my opinion you are not the equal of your father. For as yet you do not have a son such as he left us." Cambyses was delighted and praised Croesus' judgment.[19]

[3.35] It was with these events in mind that Cambyses, in hot temper, said to Prexaspes, "Learn now whether the Persians are speaking the truth or whether what they say is an indication of their own madness. If I shoot your son, standing there at the door, right

18. The "sacred disease" is generally thought to be epilepsy.
19. Croesus of Lydia, having been appointed by Cyrus to look after his son (1.208 above), is depicted by Herodotus as Cambyses' senior counselor in occupied Egypt. But this, like the earlier passage in which the Greek sage Solon visited Croesus, may well be a thematically convenient fiction.

through the heart, I shall prove that the Persians are talking nonsense. If I miss, then it can be said that the Persians are right and I am not of sound mind." So speaking, he drew his bow and shot the boy. Then he ordered the fallen body to be cut open and the wound examined. When it was found that the arrow was lodged in the heart, he laughed and gleefully said to the boy's father: "Prexaspes, it must now be clear that I am not mad and that it is the Persians who are out of their minds. Tell me, have you ever seen anyone shoot so straight?" Prexaspes, realizing that the man was deranged, feared for his own safety and replied, "My lord, I do not believe that God himself can shoot so straight."[20]

[3.36] On another occasion, Cambyses arrested twelve high-ranking Persians for no good reason and had them buried alive upside down.[21] When he did this, Croesus the Lydian ventured to give the following advice: "O king, do not always give way to your youthful impetuosity; hold yourself in check and keep control over yourself. It is a good thing to look ahead and a wise thing to have regard to the future. For no good reason you arrest and kill men who are your own subjects; yes, and you kill children too. If you continue to act thus, beware lest the Persians revolt against you. Your father Cyrus bade me many a time to give you my counsel and my suggestions for your own good."

It was with all good will that Croesus delivered this advice, but Cambyses replied, "So you dare give me advice, you who were such a fine ruler over your own country, you who gave such good advice to my father! You urged him to cross the Araxes and attack the Massagetae, when they were willing to cross over to our territory.[22] You destroyed yourself by your misgovernment of your own country and destroyed Cyrus, who listened to you. But you will not get away with it. I have long been looking for an excuse to pay you out."

With these words, he seized his bow to shoot him, but Croesus leapt up and rushed from the room. Failing to shoot him, Cambyses ordered his servants to seize him and kill him. But his servants, know-

20. Remarkably, Prexaspes never sought revenge for the murder of his son, according to Herodotus, but continued to serve Cambyses faithfully until the monarch's last days. Later, when the Magi priests usurped the Persian throne by installing a pretender, Prexaspes reportedly denounced the conspiracy from the top of a high tower and then leapt to his death.
21. The Greek phrase might also mean "buried them up to their necks." In either case it's not clear exactly what sort of torture Herodotus here describes.
22. See 1.207 ff.

ing their master's ways, concealed Croesus with this intention, that if Cambyses should change his mind and ask for Croesus, they would bring him forth and be rewarded for saving his life; but if the king should not change his mind or miss Croesus, they could then do away with him. And indeed, not long afterward Cambyses did miss Croesus; and when the servants saw this, they announced that he was still alive. Cambyses said he was glad to hear it, but those who had saved Croesus would not escape; he would kill them. And so he did.[23]

[3.37] These are examples of the utter madness that Cambyses exhibited in his conduct toward the Persians and his allies. And during his stay at Memphis he broke open ancient tombs and examined the bodies and even went so far as to enter the temple of Hephaestus and jeer at his statue. (This statue of Hephaestus is very like the Pataici of the Phoenicians, which they take around with them on the prows of their warships. For those who have never seen one, I can tell you that it is like a pygmy.) He also entered the temple of the Cabiri, which only the priest is permitted to do. He scoffed at the images and even burned them. (These images resemble those of Hephaestus and are said to be his sons.)

[3.38] This indicates to me that Cambyses was completely out of his mind; otherwise he would not have poured ridicule on holy things and sacred traditions. For if one were to ask men of any nation to choose the traditions that they think best in the world, after examining each of them, they would choose the traditions of their own country; such is the reverence in which all hold their own traditions.[24] So it is only a madman who would make a laughingstock of such things.

One can conclude on the basis of many different indications that this is the universal sentiment of humankind toward their own customs, and the following anecdote is but one example. When Darius became king of Persia, he summoned the Greeks who were at his court and asked them what it would take to persuade them to eat the dead bodies of their fathers. They replied that nothing could persuade them to do such a thing. Thereupon Darius summoned some Indians of the tribe called Callatiae, who do actually eat their parents'

---

23. This is the last we hear in the *Histories* of Croesus, Herodotus' most fully developed character. The story of his life remains curiously open-ended, given that the great lesson he is said to have learned from Solon is to "look to the end of all things."

24. Herodotus here ignores the many instances he himself gives of a people adopting foreign customs when they regard them as better than their own.

corpses,[25] and in the presence of the Greeks (who understood through
interpreters what was being said), he asked the Indians what it would
take to persuade them to *burn* their fathers' dead bodies. With a cry
of horror they urged him not to speak of such a thing. Such, then, is
the force of tradition, and I think that Pindar was right in saying "custom is the king of all."

[3.39] While Cambyses was making his expedition against
Egypt, the Lacedaemonians sent a force to Samos against Polycrates,
son of Aeaces, who ruled Samos as the result of a coup.[26] Originally
he had divided the realm into three, sharing rule with his brothers
Pantagnotus and Syloson, but thereafter he slew the former, banished
the younger brother, Syloson, and ruled the whole of Samos. He then
formed a close friendship with Amasis, king of Egypt, confirmed with
an exchange of gifts. It was not long before his extraordinary good
fortune became the talk of Ionia and the rest of Greece. Wherever he
chose to campaign, he met with marked success. He had a fleet of a
hundred penteconters and a thousand archers. He raided and plundered without discrimination, for he used to say that a friend would
be more grateful for the restoration of what had been taken from him
than if it had not been taken in the first place. He captured quite a
number of islands and many towns on the mainland as well. Among
other successes, he defeated at sea and captured the Lesbians who
were coming with full force to the help of the Milesians. They were
put in chains and made to dig the ditch that surrounds Samos' walls.[27]

[3.40] Amasis the Egyptian[28] became aware of Polycrates' remarkable good fortune, but it made him uneasy, and as Polycrates'

25. Like the Massagetae described above (1.216). The neutral tone of Herodotean ethnographies, even when subjects like incest or cannibalism are being
described, shows that in general he observed the principle of cultural rela-
tivism he articulates here. Nevertheless, there are a few passages in which he
abandons the stance of a neutral observer and passes judgment, either posi-
tive or negative, on non-Greek ways.
26. Polycrates is one of the great Greek *tyrannoi* or unconstitutional rulers
whose careers Herodotus follows in the *Histories*. During his reign (c.
535–22), the island of Samos established a naval empire in the Aegean that,
had it continued along the lines he laid down, could have become the domi-
nant power in the Greek world—what Athens would later achieve.
27. Samos, largely as a result of Polycrates' leadership, was famous for its vast
and ingenious engineering projects.
28. This highly successful monarch has been encountered twice now, once
as an ally of Croesus (1.77) and again as the colorful 'party boy' who over-
throws Apries to gain the Egyptian throne (2.162 ff.).

successes still mounted, he wrote the following letter and sent it to Samos. "Amasis to Polycrates. It is a pleasure to hear of the prosperity of a close friend and ally; but knowing as I do the jealousy of the gods, your striking successes do not bring me joy. What I would like for myself and for those I care for is to meet with good fortune in some things and ill fortune in others, and to pass through life with alternating good and ill fortune rather than with continuous good fortune. For I have never heard of any man who, after enjoying continuous good fortune, did not in the end meet with utter disaster. Take my advice and deal with the problem of your extraordinary successes as follows. Consider what it is you value most, something whose loss would cause you the greatest grief, and throw it away, so that it will never be seen again. If thereafter you do not find good fortune alternating with misfortune, then continue to follow my suggestion until you do."

[3.41] On reading the letter, Polycrates accepted as sound the advice it contained and began to consider which of his treasures it would grieve him the most to lose. He decided on a signet ring he wore, an emerald set in gold, the work of a Samian named Theodorus, son of Telecles. Being resolved to throw it away, he acted as follows. He manned a penteconter, went aboard, and ordered it to put to sea. When he had gone a good way from land, taking the ring from his finger, in full view of all on board, he hurled it into the sea. Thereupon he rowed back to land, returned to his home, and lamented his misfortune.

[3.42] Five or six days later, this is what befell him. A fisherman who had caught a perfectly fine, large fish thought it would make a suitable present for Polycrates. He went to the palace gates, sought an audience with Polycrates, and when this was granted, he presented him with the fish, saying: "O king, when I caught this fish I did not think it proper to take it to market, though I am but a poor laboring man. It seemed to me worthy of you and your greatness, so I have brought it as a present for you."

Pleased with the fisherman's words, Polycrates replied as follows: "You have done very well, and I thank you twice, both for your words and for the gift. Take supper with us." The fisherman, proud of this invitation, went home. Meanwhile the servants cut up the fish and found Polycrates' ring in the belly. On seeing this, they took it and hastened with great jubilation to Polycrates, gave him the ring, and related how it had been found.

[3.43] Seeing in this a divine hand, he wrote a letter to Amasis in Egypt, recounting all he had done and what had befallen him. On reading the letter from Polycrates, Amasis realized how impossible it

is for one man to save another from what is destined for him, and that
Polycrates, a man who was so constantly favored by fortune that he
even found what he had thrown away, would meet a miserable end.
He sent a herald to Samos to announce the dissolution of their alliance. His purpose in so doing was to avoid the distress he was bound
to feel for one who was a friend and ally when a terrible calamity
should finally overtake Polycrates.[29]

*While Cambyses was losing his sanity in Egypt, a pair of Magi priests seized
the Persian throne, exploiting the coincidence that one of them resembled
and had the same name as Cambyses' royal brother, Smerdis. In Herodotus'
account, a messenger from the Magi found Cambyses, with his army, at Ecbatana in Syria and delivered a proclamation that royal power now resided
not in Cambyses but in Smerdis—implying the royal Smerdis, Cambyses'
brother. But Cambyses had in fact had his brother secretly killed some time
before this, and he now correctly deduced that Smerdis the Magus had taken
the throne under a false identity. Distraught, Cambyses leapt onto his horse
to ride to Susa, the Persian capital, and expose the impostor; but in his haste
he wounded his thigh on his own sword, in the same spot, significantly,
where he had once struck the sacred Apis calf. Realizing that he was fated
to die from this wound and that he had in fact not only lost the throne but
destroyed the only legitimate heir, Cambyses, as depicted by Herodotus, uttered these last words to the assembled Persian nobles:*

[3.65][30] "Persians, I am forced to reveal to you now what I have most
of all kept hidden. While I was in Egypt, I had a dream that I wish I
had never had. I dreamed that a messenger arrived from the palace
and announced to me that Smerdis was sitting on the royal throne and
that his head was touching the sky. In fear lest my brother rob me of
my crown, I acted more in haste than in wisdom: For though men cannot avert what is to be, I rashly sent Prexaspes to Susa to kill Smerdis.
With this foul deed done, I lived at peace, never imagining that, with
Smerdis out of the way, any other challenger could arise. Alas! I failed
to see anything of what was coming; I killed my own brother when
there was no point in doing so, and now I am losing my crown anyway. It was Smerdis the Magus whose revolt the god warned me of in
the dream! Yet the deed is done; you must recognize that Smerdis, son
of Cyrus, is no longer living. The Magi rule your realm, both the one
I left in charge of my house and his brother, Smerdis. The man who

---

29. The "calamity" is described in the sequel to this story, 3.128 ff.
30. This selection has been translated by the editor.

could best have avenged this outrage against my rule, my brother, is dead—foully murdered by those who were closest to him. But with him gone, Persians, it is you who must stand in for him and carry out my dying wishes.

"I command you, with the gods of my royal house as my witness: All of you here, but especially those of the Achaemenid line,[31] do not allow sovereign power to revert back to the Medes. If they use trickery to get it, take it back from them by trickery; if they seize it by force, protect it with even greater force. If you do this, I pray that the earth bear fruit for you, and your wives and flocks bear young, and that you stay forever free. But if you fail to preserve our power or do not even try to do so, I lay this curse on you: May you get the opposite of all this and also suffer a death as bad as mine, each of you."

[3.66] As he spoke, Cambyses began to weep for all his misdeeds, and the Persians, when they saw him crying, began as one to tear the clothes they had on and to wail and groan piteously. After that, his leg wound having become infected and rotten, the end came for Cambyses, son of Cyrus, who had ruled seven years and five months altogether and who died completely childless.[32]

Soon after this, the Magi, exposed as pretenders to the throne, were killed by a band of seven Persian nobles, among them Darius, son of Hystaspes. This left a power vacuum in the palace, with no direct descendant of Cyrus still surviving. In this crisis the seven conspirators who had killed the Magi held a conversation that modern scholars have dubbed the Debate on Government or Constitutional Debate. Despite Herodotus' protestations, it is almost certainly fictitious, an early experiment in what would later become political philosophy.

[3.80] The Persians who had overthrown the Magi took counsel among themselves, reviewing the whole situation before them. Certain speeches were made that some Greeks find incredible, but were

---

31. The Achaemenid tribe was the highest in rank among the Persian nobility.
32. A somewhat different account of Cambyses' death, and the events surrounding the Magi conspiracy, is given in a stone inscription found in 1836 in a place called Behistun. The inscription was set up by Darius as part of a propaganda campaign to legitimize his rule, so the narrative it presents is highly suspect. It describes the revolt of a Magus named Gaumata and claims that Cambyses died by his own hand. Nevertheless, the essential outlines of Herodotus' story are here confirmed, as are the names of six out of the seven nobles who overthrew the Magus.

nevertheless made. Otanes, speaking as follows, recommended that all Persians should share in the government. "I do not think it right that any one of us should become the sole ruler, for that is neither a happy nor a good thing. You have seen to what lengths the intoxication of power carried Cambyses, and then you had to endure the same thing from the Magus. How can monarchy be a well-adjusted system when the monarch can do whatever he wants unchecked? Even the best of men, placed in such a commanding position, would change from his previous way of thinking. His elevation breeds arrogance in the man, while jealousy is instinctive in all men. With these two qualities he possesses every form of vice. Many of his acts of savagery are due to a surfeit of arrogance, others to jealousy. Absolute power ought to render a man free from jealousy, possessing as he does all that he could wish for, but the opposite proves to be the case in respect of his conduct toward his subjects. He is jealous of the best of the citizens for surviving and continuing to live, and he rejoices in the worst; thus, he is always ready to welcome slanderers. Of all people he is the most awkward to deal with. If you show him reasonable reverence, he is angry that you do not utterly abase yourself; if you do the latter, he resents your servility. But I am just coming to the worst of his excesses— he disregards our traditional customs, violates women, and puts men to death without trial.

"Now the advantages of majority rule are, first, it possesses the fairest of all names, *isonomia*, or equality before the law; secondly, it is not guilty of any of the excesses of monarchy. Magistrates are appointed by lot; they are accountable to the people, and all their deliberations are in public. I therefore recommend that we abolish monarchy and give power to the people. For in the many lies the totality of the state."

[3.81] Such was the opinion put forward by Otanes, but Megabyzus was in favor of establishing an oligarchy and spoke as follows: "What Otanes has said in criticism of monarchy I agree with entirely, but in speaking in favor of democracy he has missed the mark. There is nothing more stupid and more violent than an ignorant mob. It would be quite intolerable for men, in seeking to escape the unbridled violence of a despot, to fall victim to that of an undisciplined rabble. The despot, in all that he does, at least acts with understanding, but the mob does not even have the ability to understand. How can it, when it has not been taught nor does it know what is its own good? It rushes blindly into decisions, sweeping all before it like a river in flood. No, let those who bear ill will to the Persians embrace democracy, but let us choose a number of the best men and entrust the government to them. We shall be among them, and from the best men the best policies are likely to emerge."

[3.82] Such was the opinion of Megabyzus. Darius was the third to speak, and he spoke as follows: "I agree with what Megabyzus has said about democracy, but not with his advocacy of oligarchy. Of the three suggested forms of government—democracy, oligarchy, and monarchy—if we examine the best example of each kind, I maintain that monarchy takes first prize by a long shot. There can be nothing better than the one best man. Gifted with such character, his care for the people would be beyond criticism, and being sole ruler he would find it easiest to keep secret the measures he plans against his enemies. In an oligarchy, many who distinguish themselves in public service are wont to develop bitter private feuds. Each desirous to achieve pre-eminence and have his counsels accepted before others, they fall to bitter quarreling, which leads to party strife, which leads to bloodshed, and bloodshed ends in monarchy, thus proving how much this is the best form of government. As for democracy, this form of government cannot avoid corruption, and when this develops in the public service, those who are corrupt do not engage in feuds but in close associations, the malefactors making common cause with one another. And so it goes on, until somebody comes forward as the people's champion and puts a stop to all this. As a result, he is much admired by the people, and from being admired he finds himself established as a monarch—which again shows that monarchy is the best form of government.

"The essence of the matter is this: Where did we get our freedom from, and who gave it to us? Was it from the people, an oligarchy, or a monarch? In my opinion, we gained our freedom through one man.[33] Furthermore, we ought not discard our ancestral traditions, which have served us well. To do this would not be the better course."

With these three opinions set before them, the remaining four of the seven men voted in favor of monarchy.

A contest is now held to determine which of the seven will rule; Darius wins the contest by means of a cunning ploy and assumes the throne.

****

Herodotus now provides a remarkable survey of the entire Persian empire under Darius, divided into twenty provinces or "satrapies," each paying a

33. Meaning Cyrus, who liberated the Persians from the Medes as described in Book 1.

*fixed amount of yearly tribute into the Persian treasury. The account is re-
markably detailed and must have come directly from some written document, which Herodotus somehow or other obtained and had translated into
Greek. At the end, he gives the grand total of annual Persian revenue as
14,560 talents of silver—a fantastic sum, ten times as much as Athens, which
grew to be the wealthiest Greek city, received at the height of its imperial
power.*

*The largest single contribution to Persia's wealth comes from its Indian
subjects, who pay tribute out of the vast quantites of gold found in their
country. The idea of India's gold deposits then leads Herodotus into the following observation.*

[3.106][34] The farthest reaches of the inhabited world have been
blessed with the finest things, just as Greece has been blessed with the
best mixture of hot and cold weather. For example, India is the east-
ernmost of inhabited lands, as I have described, and in it are creatures
of all kinds, both land animals and birds, whose size far exceeds those
in other lands (except for their horses; for the Indian horses are
smaller than those called Nesaean, raised by the Medes). And India
has gold in great quantities . . . and its trees produce a kind of fruit
that, in beauty and quality, surpasses sheep's wool; they get their
clothing from these trees.[35]

[3.107] Then again in the south, Arabia is the farthest land in the
inhabited world, and alone of all countries it has frankincense, myrrh,
cassia, cinnamon, and a gum called ledanon. However, all these, except the myrrh, are very hard for the Arabians to harvest. For instance,
they must burn storax (the same stuff that the Phoenicians import into
Greece) in order to get at the frankincense; for the trees where frankincense grows are surrounded by flying snakes, small creatures with
mottled skin that swarm in great numbers around each tree. They
can't be driven off except by smoking them with the burning storax.

[3.108] The Arabians also say this: Their whole land would be
filled with these flying snakes, except that something happens to reduce their numbers—the same thing that, as I have learned, happens
to vipers. It seems that the divine mind, which plans wisely (as by all
indications it does), has arranged that creatures that are timid and
make easy prey are also very prolific in the bearing of young, so that
they are not preyed upon to the point of extinction; while fierce and

---

34. Chapters 106–16 were translated by the editor.
35. Herodotus refers here to cotton, a substance almost totally unknown to
Greeks of his era.

menacing creatures bear few young. So, on the one hand, we have the hare, a creature hunted by every other animal as well as men and birds, which is so prolific that, of all the animal kingdom, it alone can conceive while already pregnant; in its womb you can find the furry fetuses beside the ones still hairless, or the embryos already developing beside the ones just starting.[36] On the other hand, we have the lioness, strongest and fiercest of beasts, which bears only once in its lifetime, and then only one cub; for when it gives birth, it ejects its womb along with its offspring.[37] The cause of this is the following: When the unborn cub begins to move around in its mother's womb, its sharp claws—sharpest of any creature—begin to scratch, and the more the cub grows, the more he scratches. By the time of delivery there is no womb left intact at all.

[3.109] Similarly, vipers and the flying snakes in Arabia, were they able to reproduce as freely as nature allows, would soon make human life unlivable. But in fact, during mating, when the male is fertilizing the female, just as he releases his seed, she grabs him by the neck with her teeth and doesn't let go until she bites clean through. Thus the male snake dies; but later his death is avenged on the female, in the following way: The young in her womb pay her back for their father's death by eating a hole through their mother—gnawing through her belly until they gnaw their way out.

Other kinds of snakes, which are not harmful to humans, reproduce simply by laying eggs, and they have huge broods. Vipers, by the way, can be found everywhere, while the flying snakes are concentrated in Arabia and nowhere else. That's why they seem so numerous.

[3.114] In the southwest, the farthest country in the inhabited world is Ethiopia; this land has much gold, elephants everywhere, all sorts of wild trees, ebony wood, and the tallest, loveliest, and most long-lived races of men.

[3.115] Such are the farthest lands of Asia and Africa. As for those of Europe, toward the extreme west, I cannot say anything with certainty. For I don't accept that there is a river called Eridanus by foreigners, which flows into a northern sea and which, as legend has it, carries amber in its stream; nor do I know whether the Tin Islands, which supply us with tin, exist. As for the Eridanus, the very name testifies against it, for it comes from Greek and not a foreign tongue;

36. Entirely untrue, though Herodotus expresses the idea with remarkable force and conviction.
37. Also untrue. Simple mathematical logic refutes this idea, since with such a low birthrate the race of lions would soon be extinct.

some poet made it up. Also I have never been able to find anyone, though I have tried, who has seen that this part of Europe is bordered by sea. In any case, tin and amber *do* come to us from the earth's edge.[38]

[3.116] The northernmost part of Europe seems to have a huge amount of gold. How it is extracted I can't say with certainty either. There's a story that Arimaspians, one-eyed men, steal it away from griffins; but I can't accept the idea that men can be one-eyed, yet normal humans in every other way.[39]

So then, the farthest parts of the earth, which enclose the rest in a circle and hem it around, seem to have the things we deem most beautiful and hardest to find.

After these pronouncements on the global distribution of resources, Herodotus returns to the story of the growth of Persian power. At this point he turns the clock back slightly in order to recount the conclusion of the tale of Polycrates, the ruler of Samos who had tried but failed to discard his ring (3.39 ff.).

[3.120] At about the time of Cambyses' illness, the following events occurred. A Persian named Oroetes had been appointed by Cyrus as governor of Sardis. This man conceived a most unholy project. Although he had never received injury by word or deed from Polycrates of Samos and had never even met him, he planned to seize him and kill him. The reason generally accepted for his determination is as follows. Oroetes and another Persian named Mitrobates, governor of the province of Dascyleium, were sitting at the gates of the royal palace when they fell into quarreling, Mitrobates claiming to be the better man. "What kind of man do you call yourself?" said he. "Although the island of Samos lies close to your province, you have not added it to the king's dominions. Yet it is so easy to subdue that one of the natives with fifteen soldiers gained mastery over the island and now rules it." The story goes that Oroetes was nettled by his reproach, but instead of seeking revenge on the speaker for this insult,

38. Herodotus insists on having it both ways: He disclaims knowledge of *specific* places in the far west, or even refutes their existence; but he still uses the tin and amber said to come from these places to support the *general* principle that precious goods belong to the farthest countries.
39. An interesting objection; Herodotus has no such problem in the case of griffins, mythical creatures usually imagined as a composite of bird, snake, and lion.

he sought the utter destruction of Polycrates as being the cause of his disgrace.

[3.121] There is a less well-authenticated account, that Oroetes sent a herald to Samos to make some request (what that was is not clear), and Polycrates happened to be sitting in the men's apartments in company with Anacreon of Teos. Now, it is not clear whether this was deliberate or a chance occurrence, but when the herald advanced and spoke, Polycrates, who happened to be turning away from him facing the wall, did not bother to turn around and made no reply. Both these stories are told to account for the death of Polycrates, and you may take your choice.

[3.122] Oroetes, residing at Magnesia on the river Maeander, now sent Myrsus, son of Gyges, a Lydian, with a message to Samos. Oroetes knew of Polycrates' ambitions, for Polycrates was the first Greek we know of to plan to become master of the seas—if we except Minos of Cnossus and prior to him any others who may have been rulers of the seas. But as far as authentic history goes, Polycrates was the first,[40] and he had great hopes of becoming ruler over Ionia and the islands. Knowing of his intentions, Oroetes sent him the following message: "I know that you have great enterprises in mind and that your resources do not match your designs. If you act as I suggest, you will achieve greatness for yourself and safety for me, for I have it on good authority that Cambyses is plotting my death. Get me away from here and share my wealth with me; with such resources you will rule the whole of Greece. If you doubt my wealth, send your most trustworthy emissary, and I will reveal to him what I possess."

[3.123] Polycrates, who had a great desire for money, received this proposal with joy and accepted it. He first sent his secretary, a townsman named Maeandrius, son of Maeandrius, to investigate on his behalf. (Not long afterward, this Maeandrius sent as an offering to the temple of Hera all the magnificent furniture of Polycrates' men's quarters.) Learning of his approach, Oroetes acted as follows. He filled eight chests with stones, almost all the way to the brim, and then put gold on top of the stones; then he fastened the chests securely and kept them in readiness. Maeandrius arrived, beheld the gold, and reported back to Polycrates.

---

40. Herodotus here makes a crucial distinction between Polycrates, who belongs to the recent past and so to investigable history, and Minos, who belongs to mythology and fable. Compare his dismissal, in 1.1–5, of the Persian stories about Io, Europa, and Medea in favor of his personal knowledge of the historical figure of Croesus.

[3.124] In spite of the earnest protests of his soothsayers and his friends, Polycrates now prepared to depart. His daughter too tried to dissuade him because of a vision she had seen in a dream. She saw her father suspended in the air, washed by Zeus, and anointed by the Sun God. Because of this vision, she did all she could to prevent her father from leaving the country to visit Oroetes. She even pursued him to the ship with words of ill omen. He replied with this threat, that if he returned safe he would put off her marriage for many a year. She then prayed that his threat would be fulfilled; she would rather remain a virgin for a longer space of time, she said, than be bereft of her father.

[3.125] But Polycrates, disregarding all good counsel, sailed to meet Oroetes, taking with him among other companions Democedes of Croton, son of Calliphon, the most distinguished physician of his time.[41] On reaching Magnesia, Polycrates met a dreadful end, quite unbefitting his own distinguished life and ambitions—for with the exception of the rulers of Syracuse, no other Greek ruler[42] can be compared with Polycrates for splendor. Having killed him in a manner that does not bear repeating, Oroetes hung the body on a cross. Of his followers, he released the Samians, bidding them thank him for their freedom; the foreigners and slaves he held as prisoners of war.

The crucifixion of Polycrates brought to fulfillment his daughter's vision. He was washed by Zeus when it rained, and he was anointed by the Sun God when moisture dripped from his body. This was how Polycrates' long run of good fortune came to an end.

---

41. Soon to play an important role in world events (3.129 ff.).
42. As stated earlier, the term "ruler" here translates the Greek *tyrannos*, the term for someone who holds absolute power without constitutional authority. Syracuse is a city in Sicily, an island widely colonized by Greeks at this time.

V

The Growth of Persia:
Darius Enters Europe
(521–499 B.C.E.)

Shortly after the death of Polycrates, Oroetes too met a bad end, killed by
his own guards at the request of Darius. But the prisoners seized from Samos
remained in Persian hands, and this circumstance led, in Herodotus' view
at least, to the first inklings of a Persian attack on the Greek mainland, by
way of the odd sequence of events recounted below.

  Darius at this point could truly be called the most powerful man in the
world. His empire comprised virtually all the known world, except for
Greece, Scythia, and remotest Ethiopia. His administrative system had
brought unprecedented unity and efficiency to this vast empire, and a re-
markably fast communications system (see 8.98) enabled him to transmit
royal orders across its length and breadth. Every year, new mountains of trib-
ute were deposited in his storehouses and palaces, more money than his
government could possibly use. Persia had become the mightiest and most
expansive power the world had ever seen. Now the question remained as
to whether, and in which direction, its expansion would continue.

[3.129–30] Soon after Oroetes' wealth was confiscated and conveyed
to Susa, it happened that Darius, out hunting, twisted his foot in
dismounting from his horse. This turned out to be a severe injury, a
dislocation of the ankle. It had long been his custom to keep at his
court Egyptian doctors of the highest esteem, and these he now sent
for. But they wrenched the foot with such force as to make the condition worse. For seven days and seven nights Darius was sleepless
with pain, but on the eighth day, as he lay very ill, someone brought
him news of the skill of Democedes of Croton, which he had heard of
while still at Sardis. Darius ordered the man to be brought to him as
quickly as possible. Finding him somewhere among Oroetes' slaves in
a state of neglect, they brought him to the palace, still dragging his
chains and clad in rags. As he stood before the king, being asked by
Darius whether he understood the art of medicine, he denied it, for
he feared that if he revealed who he was, he would lose any chance of
returning to Greece. But Darius saw that he was lying and ordered

the attendants to send for whips and instruments of torture. Thereupon Democedes owned up to the truth but still declared that he was no expert in medicine, having only a slight understanding of the art from having consorted with a doctor. But thereafter Darius entrusted himself entirely to Democedes, who, using Greek remedies and replacing the severe treatment with milder means, enabled his patient to get some sleep and soon restored him to health.

Darius, who had given up hope of ever using his foot again, made him a gift of two pairs of golden fetters, whereupon Democedes inquired whether Darius was deliberately doubling his affliction as a reward for healing him. Pleased with this reply, Darius sent him off to visit his wives,[1] and when the eunuch who was conducting him told them that this was the man who had saved the king's life, they each drew a cupful of gold coins from a chest and gave them to Democedes. So abundant was the gift that a servant named Sciton, following behind and picking up the coins that fell to the ground, amassed quite a fortune.

[3.132] After he had cured Darius, Democedes lived in a spacious house in Susa, dined at the king's table, and enjoyed all blessings but one: He could not go back to Greece. When the Egyptian doctors who had first treated the king were about to be impaled because they had been surpassed by a Greek doctor, he rescued them by intervening with the king on their behalf. And he also saved a soothsayer from Elis, a follower of Polycrates, who was then languishing among the slaves. Democedes became a big hit with the king.

[3.133–34] Soon after this, it came about that Atossa, daughter of Cyrus and wife to Darius, suffered from a tumor in the breast, which then burst and spread. While it was yet a minor affliction, shame induced her to conceal it and tell no one; but when it became very painful, she sent for Democedes and showed it to him. He said he could cure her, but he exacted an oath from her that in return she would grant him any favor he asked, saying that he would ask nothing that would make her blush. Thereupon he treated her and cured her, and she, following instructions given by Democedes, had the following conversation with the king while the two lay in bed. "O king," she said, "with such power at your disposal you lie idle, making no further conquests to enlarge the Persian empire. Surely one who is in his prime, master of mighty resources, should engage in some enterprise so as to show the Persians that they are ruled by a man. There are two reasons why this is advisable: First, the Persians should know

---

1. That is, to the royal harem.

that their ruler *is* a man, and second, they will use up their strength in war and have no leisure to plot against you. Now is the time for notable deeds, while you are young. For as the body increases in strength, so does the mind; but as the body goes, so does the mind, losing its keenness for action."

Thus did Atossa speak, as instructed by Democedes, and Darius replied as follows. "Wife, what you have said is exactly what I intend. I have resolved to build a bridge between Asia and Europe and take the field against the Scythians. This will come to pass quite soon."[2] "Look now, do not make your first venture an attack on the Scythians," said Atossa; "they will be there for you whenever you wish. You would please me by campaigning against Greece; from what I have heard of the girls of Sparta, Argos, Attica, and Corinth, I long to have them as handmaids. You have a man of all the world best fitted to give you the information about Greece and to be your guide—I mean the man who healed your foot." "Wife," replied Darius, "since you think we should make Greece our first objective, it would be better for me to begin by sending over there some Persian spies, accompanied by the man you mention, to bring back a report of all that they have seen and heard. Then when I am fully informed, I shall set about the campaign."

[3.135] His words were immediately followed by action. As soon as day dawned, he sent for fifteen Persians of eminence and instructed them to sail along the Greek coast in company with Democedes but never to allow Democedes to escape them, making sure that they brought him back. Then, summoning Democedes himself, he besought him to guide the Persian party over the whole of Greece and then to return. He bade him take with him all his furniture as a gift for his father and brothers, promising to replace this with goods worth many times as much, and in addition he provided a merchant vessel full of all kinds of valuables to accompany him. Now, in my opinion, Darius had no ulterior motive in making this offer; but Democedes, fearing that Darius was making trial of him, was in no hurry to accept all that was given him. His own goods, he said, he would leave where they were so as to have the use of them on his return, but he accepted the merchant vessel that Darius offered as a gift to his brothers.

[3.136] The party made their way to the city of Sidon in Phoenicia, where they immediately manned two triremes[3] together with a

2. The attack on the Scythians, by way of a bridge across the Bosporus, does indeed follow in Book 4.
3. Triremes are military vessels driven by 150 oarsmen.

large merchant vessel filled with precious goods of every kind. When all was prepared, they sailed to Greece, surveyed the coast and wrote down all its most notable features, and then went on to Tarentum in Italy. Here Aristophilides, king of Tarentum, out of kindness to Democedes, removed the rudders from the Persian ships and furthermore arrested the Persians as spies. While they were imprisoned, Democedes got away to Croton. And when he had reached his own country, Aristophilides released the Persians and restored the gear he had removed from the ships.

[3.137] The Persians sailed in pursuit of Democedes and, having reached Croton and found him in the marketplace, they seized him. Some of the men of Croton, fearful of Persian might, were ready to give him up, while others clung onto him and with their cudgels attacked the Persians, who cried, "Men of Croton, beware what you do. The man you are trying to rescue is a runaway slave of Darius. Do you imagine that King Darius will put up with this treatment? And if you rob us of this man, will this deed be to your advantage? Will not this be the first city we attack, the first city we shall seek to enslave?"[4]

These words, however, failed to persuade the men of Croton, and having lost both Democedes and the merchant vessel that had accompanied them, the Persians sailed back to Asia, making no further attempt to survey Greece, since they were deprived of their guide. Before they left, Democedes instructed them to inform Darius that he, Democedes, was taking to wife the daughter of Milo the wrestler,[5] whose name was in high honor with the king. In my opinion, it was in order to show Darius that he was a man of note in his own country as well as abroad that Democedes eagerly pursued this marriage and spent much money to achieve it.

[3.138] The Persians left Croton and were shipwrecked off Iapygia,[6] where a Tarantine named Gillus later found them enslaved, rescued them, and brought them back to Darius. . . . These were the first Persians to travel from Asia into the Greek world, and they did so as spies, as I have related.

With Polycrates dead, a power vacuum developed on the important Greek island of Samos. The Persians attempted to install a puppet ruler, Polycrates'

4. With chilling prescience, the Persian messengers imply that a widespread attack on Greece is already in the cards—and assume that the Crotoniates know this as well.
5. Milo was the most famous and talented athlete of his times.
6. The heel of the Italian "boot."

brother, Syloson. But the plan went awry when the Persian contingent escorting Syloson was attacked by members of a fanatical resistance movement. Taken by surprise, the Persian army overreacted and slaughtered the native population indiscriminately. Syloson took power on an empty island, and Samos became, as Herodotus says with a kind of perverse pride, "the first city either of Greeks or barbarians captured by Darius."

Thereafter the story leaves Samos behind and returns to events in Asia.

[3.150] After the Persian fleet had sailed for Samos, the Babylonians revolted. They had long been planning this, for during the reign of the Magus, the uprising of the seven, and the subsequent confusion, all this time they were making preparations—which somehow went undetected—to resist a siege. When the time came for rebellion, they acted as follows. With the exception of their mothers, each man chose only one other woman to bake his bread and, bringing together all the rest of the women, they strangled them so as to economize on the consumption of food.

[3.151] When this news reached Darius, he marched against them with all his forces and laid siege to the city. But the Babylonians, climbing onto their battlements, jeered at him, insulting Darius and his army. One of them shouted out this jibe: "Why are you sitting there, Persians? Why don't you go away? When mules give birth, that's when you will capture our city." The man who spoke thus, of course, never thought that a mule could give birth.

[3.152] When a year and seven months had passed by, Darius and his army were disheartened at their failure to capture Babylon in spite of all the devices and various stratagems to which they had resorted, including that which Cyrus had used with success.[7] The Babylonians displayed quite extraordinary vigilance in keeping watch, and Darius was making no progress.

[3.153] Then, in the twentieth month of the siege, Zopyrus, son of Megabyzus, who was one of the seven that had destroyed the Magus, met with a strange portent: One of his pack mules gave birth. When this news reached Zopyrus—who refused to believe it until he had seen the foal with his own eyes—he forbade all those who had seen it to speak of it, and took counsel. Remembering those words of the Babylonian at the beginning of the siege, that only when a mule gave birth would the city be taken, he made up his mind that the time had come for the capture of Babylon. That the man had uttered these

7. 1.191 above.

words, and that he himself had seen a mule foal, must surely be a divine sign, he thought.

[3.154] Convinced now that Babylon's fate was sealed, he went to Darius and inquired whether the capture of Babylon was of vital importance to him. Being assured that this was really so, he began to consider how he might be the one to take the city, and how the deed might be his alone; for among the Persians noble deeds are held in high honor as the path to greatness. He decided that, to bring the city into subjection, there was no other way but this, to mutilate himself and go over to the enemy as an apparent deserter. Thereupon, making light of his sufferings, he subjected himself to a frightful mutilation. He cut off his nose and ears, shaved off his hair in a disfiguring fashion, and had himself flogged, and appeared thus before Darius.

[3.155] Aghast at seeing a man of such eminence so mutilated, Darius leapt from his throne with a cry of horror and demanded to know who had inflicted this dreadful punishment and for what reason. "There is no one else but you," replied Zopyrus, "who has the power to bring me to this state. I, and no other, have done this to myself because I could not endure to see the Babylonians mocking the Persians."

"O, most rash of men," cried Darius, "in saying that our besieged enemies have caused you to disfigure yourself, you are giving a fair name to a most shameful deed. Foolish man, do you think you can hasten to defeat our enemies by mutilating yourself? You must have taken leave of your senses to destroy yourself thus."

"Had I told you what I intended," replied the other, "you would not have permitted it; but now it is on my own responsibility that I have done this. And now, if you will do your part, Babylon will be in your hands. Just as I am, I shall desert to the other side, telling them that this is what you have done to me. When I have persuaded them, I expect that I shall be able to take control of their army. For your part, on the tenth day after I have entered the town, station a thousand men, whose loss would be of no great concern to you, at the gates of Semiramis. Seven days later, station another two thousand at the Nineveh gates, and after twenty days, another four thousand at the Chaldaean gates. None of these detachments should be armed with anything but daggers. After twenty days, order the army to make a general assault on the defenses from all sides, but station the Persian troops at the Belian and Cissian gates. It is my belief that the Babylonians, seeing how I have benefited them, will give me greater responsibilities, among them the keys to the gates. Thereafter it will be for me and our Persians to do what is necessary."

[3.156] With these instructions, he fled toward the gates of Babylon, looking behind him as if he were indeed a deserter. When the soldiers on watch on the tower saw him, they ran down and, opening the gate just a little, demanded his name and business. He told them that he was Zopyrus and a deserter to the other side. Thereupon the sentries took him before the people's assembly. Standing before them, he bewailed his fate, declaring that Darius had inflicted on him those injuries (which were in fact self-inflicted) because he had advised him to give up the siege, there being no way to capture the city. "And now, men of Babylon," he said, "I come to you as a great boon, but to Darius and his army a great bane. Having mutilated me in this way, he is not going to get off scot-free. I know every detail of his plans."

[3.157] The Babylonians, seeing a man of such distinction among the Persians with his nose and ears cut off and his body all bloodied with lashes, being now completely convinced that he was speaking the truth and had come to their assistance, were quite ready to give him what he asked, and what he asked was command of some troops. He obtained his request and proceeded to execute the plan he had arranged with Darius. On the tenth day after his arrival, he led out his troops, surrounded the first detachment of a thousand men that he had instructed Darius to station, and slew them all. Seeing that his deeds corresponded with his words, the Babylonians were delighted and ready to put themselves at his service in every way. After an interval of the agreed number of days, he led out another party of Babylonian troops and slew Darius' detachment of two thousand. As a result of this second exploit, Zopyrus rose high in esteem, his name on the lips of every Babylonian. Again after the agreed interval, he led out his troops as arranged and slew the detachment of four thousand. With the accomplishment of this deed, Zopyrus rose to the pinnacle of fame with the Babylonians, who made him commander in chief and guardian of the walls.

[3.158] When Darius, as arranged, made a general assault on the city from every side, Zopyrus revealed the full extent of his craftiness. While the Babylonians mounted the walls to repel the attack, he opened the Belian and Cissian gates and admitted the Persians. Of the Babylonians, those who saw what had happened fled to the temple of Bel, while the others remained, each man at his post, until they too realized that they had been betrayed.

[3.159] Thus was Babylon captured for a second time.[8] Darius, after destroying the city's defenses and pulling down all its gates

8. The first time was by Cyrus in Book 1.

(which Cyrus had omitted to do on its first capture), impaled three thousand of its leading citizens[9] and allowed the rest to continue to dwell in their city. To provide the Babylonians with wives and save the race from extinction (as has been related, the Babylonians had strangled their wives to save food), Darius made the following provision. He arranged for the neighboring peoples to send women to Babylon, each its own quota, to the number of fifty thousand. It is from these that the Babylonians of today are descended.

[3.160] In Darius' eyes, no one surpassed Zopyrus in noble deeds, either before or after him, except only for Cyrus, with whom no Persian ever dared to compare himself. It is related that Darius would often display the greatness of his esteem, declaring that he would rather have Zopyrus free of his disfigurement than acquire twenty more Babylons. Every year he sent Zopyrus the gifts that Persians most prize, and among other gifts he granted him Babylon, free of tax, for his lifetime.

Having secured his hold over Asia, Darius apparently moved to attack the Scythians, a nomadic European people living north of the Black Sea (c. 515 B.C.E., but the date is inferred only from the chronology of the Histories; *there is no independent evidence to substantiate any of Herodotus' account). Herodotus now follows the same pattern he used in Book 2, when Cambyses decided to invade Egypt: He "pauses" the narrative to conduct a long, detailed exploration of the lands and peoples that are now in the Persians' crosshairs and even those farther afield, in the cold hinterlands of the far northeast (where Siberia is today). Here he gives ethnographies of a wide variety of Scythian tribes, describing a tough, rugged, warrior race similar in many ways to the Massagetae of Book 1. The passage below singles out their most distinctive feature, which will also figure prominently in their struggle against Persia.*

[4.46][10] The Black Sea region, which Darius now planned to invade, has the most ignorant peoples in the world, except for the Scythians. I can't give an example of a single tribe in this region notable for its wisdom, and I know of no individual worthy of mention, except the Scythian tribe and its former prince Anacharsis.[11] The Scythians,

---

9. The cruel punishments inflicted on Babylon after its revolt are attested by Darius in his rock inscription at Behistun, though there are two different insurrections mentioned there, one dated to 522 and the other to 521. Herodotus, whether deliberately or not, seems to have merged the two.

10. This selection was translated by the editor.

11. A story concerning Anacharsis is told elsewhere by Herodotus (4.76), though it is not excerpted in this volume. Anacharsis was a rare non-Greek

however, do have a claim on wisdom, indeed the cleverest single contrivance of any I know of in all humankind (though in other respects I don't find the Scythians admirable). This one great thing allows them to prevent any invader from getting away unscathed, to avoid being found by an enemy if they wish to hide, and to make it impossible for any pursuer to catch them: They do without cities and fortified walls but carry their homes with them, they fight by shooting arrows from horseback, they live off their flocks rather than agriculture, and they dwell aboard horse-drawn carts. So how, I ask you, would an enemy engage them in battle or even make contact with them?

Not understanding the strategic problem presented by the Scythians' mobility, Darius prepares his expedition, pressing the whole empire into his service.

[4.83] While Darius was preparing his expedition against the Scythians, sending messengers to all parts so as to raise troops here, arrange for ships there, and organize a bridge over the Bosporus, his brother Artabanus[12] urged him strongly not to march against the Scythians, stressing what a difficult people they were. This good counsel having no effect, Artabanus desisted from his efforts, and Darius, his preparations completed, marched out of Susa with his army.

[4.84] A Persian named Oeobazus, having three sons in the army, begged Darius' permission for one of them to remain behind. Darius replied, as if to a friend who had made a modest request, that he would leave them all behind. Oeobazus was overjoyed, thinking that his sons were excused from military service, but Darius ordered those who were concerned with such tasks to put to death all of Oeobazus' sons. Thus these men were indeed left behind—slaughtered.

Darius moved his army into Europe by way of a bridge across the straits of Bosporus, made out of warships lashed together with rope. Darius then crossed the Danube River as well, using a similar bridge, and entered Scythian territory, leaving a contingent of Ionian Greeks to guard this Danube bridge and protect his line of retreat. What followed, as described by Herodotus, can barely be called a war, because there was very little ac-

who came to be included among the legendary Seven Sages of the archaic age, along with men like Solon and Thales.
12. The first appearance of Artabanus, who will be an important character in Book 7.

tual fighting. Rather, the Scythians made use of their great strategic advantage, mobility, to elude the Persians and draw them ever deeper into the hinterland, destroying food and water supplies as they went (a strategy still known today as a "Scythian defense"). Sensing that their strategy was succeeding, the Scythians then took the steps described below to cut off the Persians' retreat and so destroy them.

[4.133][13] The contingent of Scythians that had been stationed to guard the shores of the Maeotian Lake[14] now came to negotiate with the Ionian Greeks at the Danube. Approaching the bridge, they spoke as follows: "Ionians, we bring you freedom from slavery, if you will listen to us. We know that Darius has ordered you to wait sixty days here at the bridge and then, if he has not yet appeared, to go back to your own homeland. Do as he says, and you will be blameless in his eyes as well as in ours. Stand guard here for just sixty days and then go home." The Ionians agreed to do as they said.

[4.134] Meanwhile, the rest of the Scythian army drew up their infantry and archers opposite Darius' forces, seemingly intent on offering battle. But as they stood in battle formation, a hare ran through the lines between the two armies, and each Scythian soldier started chasing it as it ran past him. Darius, seeing the Scythians falling into disorder and raising a great din, asked what the cause of the uproar was. When he learned that they were merely chasing a hare, he turned to those he normally spoke with and said: "These men don't think much of us. . . . I now believe that it's time to find a wise plan for a safe retreat out of this country."

His counselor Gobryas replied: "Sire, I had already heard from report how impossible these men can be, and now I've learned it myself, seeing how they make sport of us. But here's an idea. Tonight we shall light the campfires as we usually do and then sneak away, leaving behind the weaker soldiers who aren't up to it (we'll keep the plan secret from them) and the donkeys. We must get to the bridge across the Danube before either the Scythians break it up or the Ionians conceive the idea that they are now able to destroy us."

[4.135] That was Gobryas' advice, and that night Darius put it into effect. He left behind in the camp the men who were sick or fatigued and those of least worth, and also the donkeys, tied with tethers. The point of leaving the donkeys was so that they would con-

---

13. This and the next three chapters were translated by the editor.
14. See map p. xxii.

tinue braying;[15] the men were left because of their weakness but were told that they were being deployed to guard the camp while Darius led the stronger troops in an attack on the Scythians. Darius made this pretense to the men he was abandoning and then, after lighting his campfires, he made his way with all speed toward the Danube.

[4.136] At daybreak, the abandoned Persians realized that they had been betrayed by Darius, and they stretched out their arms to the Scythians in entreaty and told them what had happened. The Scythians wheeled around as soon as they heard . . . and started pursuing the Persians toward the Danube.

The majority of the Persian army was on foot and not sure of the route—since there were no finished roads—whereas the Scythians were mounted and knew all the shortcuts; so the Scythians actually got to the bridge well ahead of the Persians. Seeing that the Persians had not yet arrived, they spoke to the Ionians in their ships as follows. "Men of Ionia, the sixty days have passed by, and still you remain here, contrary to what is right. Hitherto fear has kept you at your post, but now you can break up the bridge and depart, rejoicing in your freedom and giving thanks to the gods and the Scythians. As for your former master, we will deal with him in such a way that nevermore will he go campaigning."

[4.137] The Ionians took counsel. Miltiades the Athenian, who was in command and was the ruler of the Chersonese on the Hellespont, was in favor of accepting the advice of the Scythians and setting Ionia free. But he was opposed by Histiaeus of Miletus, who reminded them that they each owed their present position as ruler of their respective cities to Darius and that with the downfall of Darius neither he nor any others would be able to maintain their rule. Every one of their cities would prefer democratic government to the rule of tyrants. So he spoke, and whereas all had previously favored the view of Miltiades, they now turned completely around and voted in favor of the view expressed by Histiaeus.

[4.139] Having reached this decision, they then resolved to proceed as follows: to remove a part of the bridge on the Scythian side to the length of a bow shot, with a view to be appearing to take action while in fact preventing the Scythians from using the bridge to force

---

15. Earlier, as Herodotus reports, the braying of the unfamiliar donkeys had badly upset the horses of the Scythian cavalry. Compare the ruse of Cyrus in Book 1, who used camels against the Lydians (1.80).

a crossing of the Danube.[16] And while demolishing this portion of the bridge, they would assure the Scythians that they would do anything to please them. So this is how they intended to carry out Histiaeus' proposal, and then Histiaeus spoke for them all. "Men of Scythia, glad are the tidings you bring us, and you have come just at the right time. Clearly we two nations can do each other mutual benefit here. As you see, we are already destroying the bridge and will eagerly finish the job, wanting our freedom. While we are so engaged, it is time for you to seek out these men and, when you find them, to inflict on them a fitting punishment on behalf of us both."

[4.140] Once again the Scythians put their faith in the Ionians and turned back in search of the Persian army but failed to make any contact with it. The Scythians themselves were the cause of this: For they had deprived the Persians of their water supplies and the pasturage for their horses; if they hadn't done so, they could have easily found the Persians, but as it was, the thing they had planned best caused them to fail of their goal. For the Scythians now sought the Persians where the country still had drinking water and pasturage, thinking the Persians must escape by that route. But the Persians stuck to their original route even though it was now denuded. And so it was with difficulty that the Persians reached the crossing, arriving in the dark.

[4.141] Finding the bridge apparently broken, they first fell into a panic, thinking that the Ionians had deserted them. But in Darius' retinue there was an Egyptian who happened to have a remarkably loud voice. This man Darius ordered to stand on the bank and shout for Histiaeus. Hearing him at the very first shout, Histiaeus brought all the ships to ferry the army across and to restore the bridge.

[4.142] Thus did the Persians make their escape, the Scythians having once more failed to make contact. "If the Ionians are to be regarded as free men," say the Scythians, "they are to be judged the basest and most cowardly of all men; but if they are looked upon as slaves, they are the most subservient to their masters and least likely to run away." Such are the taunts that the Scythians fling at the Ionians.

Though he failed to subdue the Scythians, Darius nevertheless established a beachhead in Europe, the land south and west of the Danube known as Thrace. He left behind an army here, under the command of Megabazus, with orders to conquer all of this wild and primitive land for the Persians.

16. That is, to prevent them from crossing in advance of the Persians and denying them the bridgehead.

Later Megabazus tried to extend Persian rule even farther westward, to Macedonia, but apparently without success (see 5.17–21 below). In any case, the Persians' relentless expansion into Europe clearly posed a major threat to the cities of mainland Greece, which now stood directly in Darius' westward path.

The Persian operations under Megabazus give Herodotus an opening to provide an ethnography of certain Thracian tribes, as well as of a nameless group of lake dwellers who also came under attack. These, it should be noted, are the last ethnographies contained in the Histories; *at the midpoint of his work, Herodotus has completed his survey of all the known peoples of the earth.*

[5.2][17] Megabazus marched his army through the whole of Thrace, bringing every city and every tribe into subjection to the king; for Darius had ordered him to conquer Thrace.

[5.3] The Thracian race is, after the Indians, the largest in the world. If the Thracians were led by a single chief or could share a common purpose, they would be invincible and the most powerful of any nation, in my opinion. But this is impossible for them and there is no way to achieve it, so they remain correspondingly weak. Their tribes have different names according to the regions where they live, but they all share common customs, except the Getae, the Trausi, and those dwelling north of the Crestonaeans.

[5.4] The customs of the Getae, who believe they are immortal, I have already described. The Trausi have the same customs as the rest of the Thracians with this exception, their attitude to birth and death. When a baby is born, the relatives sit all around it and bewail it on account of all the evils it must suffer now that it has come into the world, going through the entire list of human sorrows. But when someone dies, they bury him to the accompaniment of merriment and rejoicing, stressing how happy he is now and recounting all the troubles he had now escaped.

[5.5] The Thracians who live beyond the Crestonaeans have the following custom. Each man has several wives, and when a man dies, his wives enter into a keen debate, in which his friends join with enthusiasm, as to which of them was most beloved by the deceased. She who has the honor of being so judged is first of all praised by both men and women and then slaughtered over the grave by her closest relatives and buried beside her husband. The other wives are deeply distressed for not being chosen, for this is regarded as the greatest possible disgrace.

17. This chapter and the one following were translated by the editor.

[5.17–18] Having subdued the Paeonians,[18] Megabazus sent to Macedonia an embassy consisting of seven Persians of his army who ranked next to himself. These men were sent to Amyntas, king of Macedonia, to demand earth and water as a mark of submission to Darius.[19] . . . When the seven envoys arrived and, obtaining audience with Amyntas, demanded earth and water, their request was granted, and Amyntas, extending all hospitality, invited them to a magnificent banquet that he had prepared. After dinner, as the wine was circulating, the Persians said: "Our good Macedonian friend, it is the custom with us Persians, when we arrange an important banquet, to have our concubines and our wedded wives sit beside us. Now since you have welcomed us so cordially and are entertaining us so magnificently and are giving earth and water to King Darius, please fall in with our custom." "Men of Persia," replied Amyntas, "this is not our custom; we keep men and women separate. But since you, our masters, make this request, even this shall be granted."

Thus speaking, Amyntas sent for the women, who, on entering, seated themselves in a row opposite the Persians. Thereupon the Persians, seeing that the women were beautiful, remonstrated with Amyntas, saying that it would have been better for the women not to come at all than to come and sit, not beside them, but opposite them, tantalizing them painfully. Amyntas reluctantly bade the women to sit beside the guests, who, being well and truly drunk, began to fondle their breasts, and one of them even tried to steal a kiss.

[5.19] His great dread of the Persians enabled Amyntas to contain his displeasure and remain unmoved. But his son Alexander,[20] beholding this, being young and without experience of the ills of this world, was no longer able to restrain himself, and in his resentment he said to Amyntas: "Father, in concession to your age, go and rest, and stay not for the drinking. I will remain here and see that our guests are suitably entertained." Suspecting that Alexander intended to do something rash, Amyntas said: "My son, I understand from your words that you are all but consumed with anger and that you want me out of the way so as to do something ill-advised. I beg you not to do

18. The Paeonians were another non-Greek people of eastern Europe, whom Darius had ordered to be deported en masse into Asia.
19. The giving of earth and water was the standard ritual by which a country formalized its submission to the Persian empire.
20. Not the famous Alexander but his remote ancestor, Alexander I. He will play an important role later, after assuming the Macedonian throne, as an intermediary between Persia and Athens (8.140).

anything rash to these men so as to bring ruin upon us, but to endure seeing what is done. As for me, I will listen to you and leave this scene."

[5.20] With this request Amyntas departed, and Alexander addressed the Persians as follows: "My friends, these women are entirely at your disposal, whether you want to go to bed with any or all of them. You have only to say what you want. But now, since it is nearly time for bed and I see that you have had enough to drink, allow these women, if you please, to leave in order to bathe themselves, after which they will return to you." So he spoke, and with the Persians assenting, he sent the women away to their quarters while he himself put women's dress onto an equal number of beardless youths, gave each one a dagger, brought them into the banquet hall, and said to the Persians: "Men of Persia, you have enjoyed, I think, a very good dinner. Everything we possessed and everything we could procure is yours. And now, to crown it all, we freely make you a present of our mothers and sisters, so that you may be sure that we hold you in the high esteem that you deserve, and can report back to the king who sent you that a Greek, ruler of Macedonia, entertained you well with bed and board." Alexander then seated beside each Persian a Macedonian man in the guise of a woman, and, when the Persians tried to fondle them, these men killed them.

[5.21] Thus did they perish, they and their retinue, for along with them there went their carriages, their servants, and all their lavish equipment—everything disappeared with them. Not long afterward, the Persians organized a thorough search for these men, but Alexander cleverly thwarted their efforts by bribing Bubares, the Persian leader of the search party, giving him a large sum of money and his sister Gygaea. Thus the affair was concealed and hushed up.

VI

The Greek Revolt from Persia

(499–94 B.C.E.)

After following the Persian advance into Europe as far as Macedonia, Herodotus turns his attention to Asia Minor, which was fast becoming a friction point between the Persians and the subject Greek cities of Ionia, in particular Miletus.

Miletus had for a long time been ruled by Histiaeus, the man who had preserved the Danube bridge (4.133 ff.) so as to retain his role as puppet dictator. But some years after the Danube episode, he fell under suspicion of acting against Persian interests and was summoned to the side of Darius in the Persian capital, Susa. In his absence, Histiaeus entrusted the rule of Miletus to his son-in-law Aristagoras, a shady character who immediately began conniving at ways to increase his power in the region. To ingratiate himself with Artaphernes, Darius' half-brother and the newly appointed governor of Sardis, Aristagoras promised to conquer the island of Naxos for the Persians, and Artaphernes gave him money and troops to mount a surprise attack. But the campaign suffered a fatal setback when Aristagoras quarreled with the Persian general accompanying him, Megabates, who then spitefully informed the Naxians that an attack was imminent. The expedition thus resulted in a long siege that used up the Persians' money but accomplished nothing. Aristagoras also had spent much of his own money on the project. His mounting troubles and his alienation from his Persian overlords now put him in a very difficult position.

[5.35] Aristagoras was unable to keep his promise to Artaphernes to deliver Naxos into his hands; he couldn't pay off the debts incurred in the campaign and furthermore he feared that, with the failure of the expedition and the accusations brought by Megabates, he would be deprived of command over Miletus. These fears drove him to contemplate rebellion, and he was further encouraged by the arrival of a man sent by Histiaeus from Susa, with a message pricked on his scalp urging Aristagoras to revolt. Histiaeus had long wanted to urge this course on Aristagoras, but since all the roads were guarded he could think of no other safe way but this to transmit the message. Taking the most trustworthy of his slaves, Histiaeus had shaved his head, pricked the message on his scalp, waited for the hair to grow again, and then immediately sent him to Miletus with no other instructions than that Aristagoras should shave his head and examine his scalp. The message found there was, as I have said, an instruction to revolt. Histiaeus took this course because he grieved so much at being detained at Susa, and he had high hopes that, if there were a rebellion, he would be sent to the coast to deal with it, whereas if Miletus remained at peace he reckoned he would never see it again. It was with this in mind that he dispatched the messenger, and this happened to coincide with other circumstances persuading Aristagoras in the same direction.

As a first step, Aristagoras arrested the pro-Persian Greek leaders who had sailed with him against Naxos and who as yet had no inkling that he had changed his political sympathies. In a deeply cynical passage, Herodotus describes how Aristagoras used these arrests and a newly adopted democratic philosophy to manipulate popular opinion in his favor.

[5.37–38][1] Aristagoras was now openly in revolt and started planning every possible way to harm Darius. First of all, he disbanded his tyranny over Miletus—or so he said—and installed a democratic regime so that the Milesians would be more willing to join with him in rebellion. He did the same throughout Ionia, chasing out tyrants from some places and, in the case of the rulers he had seized from the Naxos expedition, handing them over to their own cities so as to make himself popular with the citizens there. The inhabitants of Mytilene got their tyrant, Coes, sent back to them and promptly stoned him to death. But the Cymaeans and most other states let their former tyrants off unpunished.

Thus came about an end of autocratic rule throughout the cities, and Aristagoras, having thrown out the tyrants, told the people to elect generals to lead each city's war efforts. Then he himself departed in a trireme on a diplomatic mission to Sparta, for he needed to secure a powerful ally against Persia.

[5.49][2] Aristagoras arrived in Sparta when King Cleomenes held sway, and so he went to speak with Cleomenes. He brought with him (so the Spartans say) a bronze tablet with a map of the earth carved on it, showing all the seas and rivers. When admitted to a parley with Cleomenes, Aristagoras spoke thus: "Cleomenes, don't be surprised

1. This section was translated by the editor.
2. Chapter 49 was translated by the editor.

by my eagerness for this meeting; the circumstances are these. We have long felt the pain and the shame of the enslavement of the sons of Ionia; but this is your shame too, in that you Spartans are leaders of Greece. Now I ask you by the gods to rescue the Ionians, men of your own breed, from slavery. You can accomplish this easily enough. The barbarians are poor soldiers, whereas you, in your pursuit of excellence, have made yourselves supremely prepared for war. Their method of fighting uses bows and short spears, and they go to battle wearing leather pants and cloth helmets called *kurbasias*. So their defeat is assured. And what is more, the continent these men inhabit has more riches in it than the other two together, starting with their gold, and also silver, bronze, precious cloth, pack animals, and slaves. I will show you all the countries one by one, going west to east. Next to the Ionians, here are the Lydians, who have a rich land and much silver besides." As he spoke, he pointed out the places on the map he had brought, which was engraved on a bronze plaque. "East of the Lydians lie the Phrygians, who have the most flocks and the richest harvests of any people I know. Next to the Phrygians are the Cappadocians (we Greeks call them Syrians), and next to them the Cilicians, dwelling on the coast (see, this island here is Cyprus); they pay the king an annual tribute of five hundred talents. Next to the Cilicians are the Armenians, who also have rich flocks, and next to them the Matieni over here; and next to them is the land of Cissia, in which lies Susa, a city on the river Choaspes, where the king makes his home and where he keeps his storerooms full of money. Capture this city and, rest assured, your riches will rival those of Zeus himself!

"Why should you make war as you do now, fighting over small boundaries in a small and worthless region, challenging Messenians and Argives and Arcadians who are closely matched with you in strength and who have no gold or silver—things for which one could really be eager to risk one's life—when rule over Asia is there for the taking? Why would you do anything else at all?"

Thus spoke Aristagoras, and Cleomenes responded, "Visitor from Miletus, I will give you an answer in three days."[3]

[5.50] When the day appointed for an answer came around and they met again, Cleomenes asked Aristagoras how many days' jour-

---

3. The speech of Aristagoras and Cleomenes' reply are among Herodotus' most deft pieces of characterization, illustrating the contrast between the high-strung, greedy optimism of the Ionian adventurer and the stolid conservatism of the Spartan "man of few words."

ney from the Ionian coast was the residence of the Persian king. Aristagoras, who had so far shown great cunning in misleading the king, now made a mistake. If he wanted to persuade the Spartans to send a force to Asia, he should have concealed the truth; but in fact he said it was a journey of three months. As Aristagoras was continuing to describe the road to Susa, Cleomenes hastily interrupted him. "Visitor from Miletus," he said, "you must leave Sparta before sunset. Quite out of the question is the proposal you make, which would take the Spartans a three months' journey away from the sea."

[5.51] With these words, Cleomenes went back home, but Aristagoras followed him to his house, clasping an olive branch and begging him as a suppliant to listen to him and send away the child— for Cleomenes happened to have at his side his daughter, Gorgo, an only child of eight or nine years. "Say what you want," said Cleomenes, "and never mind the child." Thereupon Aristagoras began with an offer of ten talents for Cleomenes if he would grant his request. When Cleomenes refused, Aristagoras continued to increase his offer until it reached fifty talents, whereupon the little girl cried out: "Father, the stranger will corrupt you if you don't get up and leave." Well pleased with his daughter's advice, Cleomenes went into another room, and Aristagoras left Sparta once and for all, with no further opportunity to discuss the road to Susa.

Aristagoras, having failed to gain Spartan support for the Ionian rebellion, went on to Athens, where he hoped to have better success. This visit prompts Herodotus to survey the political situation at Athens, which had been changing rapidly over the previous decade. After a reign of more than fifty years, the Pisistratid family had been ousted from power in 510 B.C.E., thanks in large part to an invasion mounted by the Spartans under Cleomenes; the reigning tyrant, Hippias, had been given safe conduct out of the city. In the political struggle that followed, Cleisthenes, leader of the popular party and a member of the liberal Alcmaeonid family, began to get the upper hand over the more conservative Isagoras, prompting a second Spartan invasion aimed at preventing a tilt toward democracy. But this time the Athenian people united against the Spartans, blockaded them in the acropolis at the center of the city, and forced them to negotiate a humiliating retreat. Cleisthenes' faction was victorious, and immediately a sweeping set of democratic reforms was enacted.

The new regime sought a cordial relationship with Persia and sent envoys to the court of Darius. There the ambassadors were asked to give earth and water, the tokens of submission to Persia, and, perhaps believing that their revolution would not survive without Persian support, they agreed to do so.

*However, after they returned home, their fellow Athenians were appalled at
what they had done and repudiated the pact. This was the first contact we
know of between Athens and Persia and certainly the friendliest.*

*Meanwhile, on the home front, Athens achieved a series of striking mili-
tary successes against its neighbors and traditional rivals, prompting the following comments from Herodotus:*

[5.78]⁴ Athens grew strong, and in this strength we see that, not in
one respect only but in all ways, democracy is a force to be reckoned
with; for while the Athenians lived under rulers, they failed to equal
their neighbors on the battlefield, but when freed of rulers they became very much the leaders. While they were the subjects of a ruler,
they refused to give their all, since it seemed that they were fighting
under the compulsion of a master; but once freed, each man was eager to do his job, knowing that his efforts were on his own behalf.

*However, though the young democracy thrived, the threat of tyranny had
not been dispelled. Hippias, the Pisistratid ruler exiled in 510 B.C.E., was still
alive and well and hoping to get back into power at Athens. For a time it
looked as though the Spartans might support him by mounting yet another
invasion, but after conferring with their allies, who opposed the plan, they
abandoned it. Hippias then elected to seek help from an even greater superpower, the Persian empire. The nearest Persian capital to Greece was
Sardis, then governed by Darius' half-brother Artaphernes; so it was there
that Hippias landed.*

[5.96] When Hippias reached Asia, he made every effort to set Artaphernes against the Athenians and resorted to every device to bring
Athens into subjection to himself and to Darius. Learning what Hippias was trying to do, the Athenians sent envoys to Sardis urging the
Persians to give no heed to these Athenian exiles. But Artaphernes
replied that, if they cared for their own safety, they must take Hippias
back. When this reply was conveyed to the Athenians, they refused to
accept it, being resolved instead to be at open enmity with the Persians.
[5.97] It was at this crucial moment, when the Athenians had
made this decision and had alienated the Persians, that Aristagoras of
Miletus, expelled from Sparta by Cleomenes, arrived in Athens, a city
that was the next most powerful after Sparta. Appearing before the
people's assembly, he made a speech in which he repeated what he had

4. This chapter was translated by the editor.

said at Sparta with respect to the abundance of good things to be found in Asia; he described the Persian method of warfare, saying that they were not accustomed to use either shield or spear and could easily be overcome. In addition, he reminded them that Miletus was a colony founded by Athens, and that it was only right that the Athenians, now so powerful, should come to her assistance. So urgent was he in his entreaties that there was no limit to his promises, until he won them over. Indeed, it seems that it is easier to deceive a large crowd than a single man, since he had failed to hoodwink the Spartan Cleomenes, just one man, but had succeeded with thirty thousand Athenians.[5] Being thus persuaded, the Athenians voted to send twenty ships to the assistance of the Ionians, appointing as their commander Melanthius, a man of high repute. It was these ships that were the beginning of much trouble both for Greeks and barbarians.

[5.99] The Athenians arrived with their fleet of twenty ships accompanied by five triremes of Eretrians, who joined the expedition not for the sake of the Athenians but to repay a debt to the Milesians. Some time previously, the Milesians had fought with the Eretrians in their war against the Chalcidians, who in turn had been helped by the Samians. When these ships arrived and were joined by the rest of the allies, Aristagoras proceeded to attack Sardis. He did not himself take part in the expedition but remained at Miletus, putting in command his brother, Charopus, and another citizen, Hermophantus.

[5.100–01] The expedition sailed for Ephesus, where the ships were left at Coressus in Ephesian territory. The troops, in strong force, marched inland with Ephesian guides. They followed the course of the river Cayster, crossed the ridge of Tmolus, and came down upon Sardis, which they took without opposition. They captured everything except the citadel, which was held by Artaphernes himself with a considerable force. But they were hindered from plundering the captured city by the fact that most of the houses in Sardis were constructed of reeds and even the houses of brick were reed-thatched. One of these houses was set alight by a soldier, and the conflagration immediately spread from one to another and consumed the entire town. The town being ablaze, the Lydians together with such Persians as were staying there, encircled on all sides as the flames reached the outskirts and unable to escape, poured into the marketplace on

5. This appears to be the number of the entire citizen body, not the number present in the assembly when Aristagoras spoke. All citizens had the right to attend the assembly and cast votes, but fewer than half were probably present on any one occasion.

the banks of the river Pactolus. (This river, bearing gold dust from Tmolus, flows through the marketplace and joins the river Hermus, which then flows into the sea.) Assembling in crowds by this river in the marketplace, the Lydians and Persians mounted a defense; the Ionians, seeing these offering resistance and others in considerable numbers coming to join them, retired to Tmolus in alarm and, as night fell, made off to their ships. In the burning of Sardis, the temple of the native goddess Cybebe was destroyed, and this provided the Persians at some later time with an excuse for burning Greek temples.

[5.102] Thereupon all the Persians stationed west of the Halys, hearing of what had happened, gathered together and came to the help of the Lydians. Finding that the Ionians had already quit Sardis, they followed on their tracks and caught up with them at Ephesus. The Ionians drew up in battle-order against them but suffered a severe defeat in the ensuing engagement. Among the many casualties was Eualcides, the commander of the Eretrians, a man who had won crowns in the Olympic games and had been much praised by Simonides of Ceos.[6] The survivors of the battle dispersed among neighboring cities.

[5.103] Thereafter the Athenians entirely abandoned the Ionians. Although Aristagoras appealed earnestly to them through envoys, they refused any further help. The Ionians, deprived of Athenian assistance, nonetheless continued to prosecute the war against the king, for they had gone too far in their defiance of Darius.

[5.105] News was brought to Darius that Sardis had been taken and burned by the Athenians and Ionians and that the originator of this rebellion was Aristagoras the Milesian. It is said that on hearing this he gave little attention to the part played by the Ionians, knowing full well that they would pay dearly for their action, but he inquired who were the Athenians. When he was informed, he asked for his bow, fitted an arrow into it, and shot it up into the sky, crying as he let fly: "Grant, O Zeus, grant that I may punish the Athenians!" After this, he commanded one of his servants to repeat to him three times a day, whenever he sat down to a meal, "Master, remember the Athenians."

[5.106] Then he summoned to his presence Histiaeus the Milesian, whom he had long detained at his court, and said, "I gather, Histiaeus, that your deputy, to whom you entrusted Miletus, has raised a rebellion against me. He has brought men from another continent against me and, persuading the Ionians—who will pay dearly for it—

6. Simonides was one of the most famous poets of the day.

to join forces with him, he has deprived me of Sardis. Come, now, was this well done? How could such a thing have happened without your being privy to it? Beware, lest hereafter you may yourself be implicated in this."

"O king," replied Histiaeus, "what words are these that you have uttered, that I should plan anything, great or small, to your injury? What would be the purpose of such an action, and what is it that I now lack? All that is yours is mine, and I am deemed worthy to take part in your counsels. If indeed my deputy is guilty as you say, be assured that he has done this on his own initiative. For my part, I shall never believe that the Milesians and my deputy are engaged in a rebellion against you. But if indeed they are so doing and the report is true, you can see, o king, how imprudent you were in forcing me to come away from the coast. With me out of sight, the Ionians, it appears, have done what they have long wanted to do. Had I been still there, not a city would have stirred. Allow me, therefore, to hasten to Ionia and restore things to their original state, delivering up to you that deputy of mine who has caused all this commotion. And having done this to your satisfaction, I swear by the gods of your royal house not to put off the clothes I shall be wearing when I reach Ionia, until I have made Sardinia, the biggest island of all, a tributary to you."

[5.107] The purpose of all this was to deceive Darius, and Darius was indeed persuaded to let him go, instructing him to return to Susa when he had done what he promised.

Histiaeus returned to Asia Minor to find that he was no longer trusted by either the Persian governor, Artaphernes, or his former fellow Greeks in Miletus. He raised a private army and had some success conducting raids on the islands of the Aegean but eventually was captured by the Persians and sent to Artaphernes, who had him killed and sent his severed head to Darius. Herodotus reports with great poignancy that Darius, who had never lost affection for Histiaeus despite the Milesian's double dealings, ordered that the head be washed and given an honorable burial and was incensed at Artaphernes for the execution. Meanwhile Aristagoras, the other Milesian rebel leader, died an even less noble death, according to Herodotus in the following account.

[5.124–26][7] When the Greek cities had been recaptured, Aristagoras the Milesian proved that he was a man of low character; for after having put all Ionia into an uproar and stirred up big troubles, he looked

---

7. This section was translated by the editor.

at the results and began to plan a getaway. It now seemed impossible to him to prevail over Darius. . . . On the whole, he thought Myrcinus the best place for an escape. So he left Miletus in the care of a respected citizen named Pythagoras and, taking with him anyone who wanted to go, he set sail for Thrace and got possession of Myrcinus. But then he and his followers were killed by the Thracians while besieging a different town, even though the inhabitants had already agreed to leave the place.

The Ionian revolt dragged on for several more years after the deaths of its leaders, since the Greek navy was still capable enough to withstand the Phoenician ships fighting on behalf of the Persians. But in a great naval showdown at Lade, just offshore from Miletus, Ionian morale collapsed and many Greek ships deserted to the enemy side. Resistance was no longer possible, and the Persians sacked and burned the city of Miletus, killing the men and enslaving the women and children (494 B.C.E.). The whole rebellion had lasted five years and had produced no results except the total destruction of the leading city of Ionia.

VII

Persia versus Greece: Darius' Wars

(494–90 B.C.E.)

The reconquest of the Ionian Greeks by Persia left the mainland Greeks deeply unsettled. Since Athens and Eretria had taken a small but significant part in the burning of Sardis, Darius remained determined to have revenge on those two cities at least. Beyond that, the Persians faced the larger question of whether their rule over Ionia could ever be secure as long as the mainland Greeks remained free. Perhaps supposing that it would be safer to conquer all the Greeks than only some, Darius began in the years 494 and 493 to lay plans for the subjugation of the Greek mainland. Many Greek cities were all too willing to surrender without a fight.

[6.48–49] After this, Darius began to make trial of the spirit of the Greeks, to see whether they would offer resistance or submit to him. He therefore sent heralds to various places throughout Greece to demand earth and water for the king. At the same time, he sent other messengers to the coastal towns already under his dominion, requiring them to provide warships and cavalry transports. These vessels were duly provided, and many of the mainland cities of Greece gave the tokens demanded by the king, as did all the islanders whom the heralds visited.

Among the latter who gave earth and water were the Aeginetans. This act of submission immediately aroused the anger of the Athenians, who believed that they intended to join Darius in attacking Athens. Gladly seizing on this as a pretext, the Athenians put the matter before the Spartans, accusing the Aeginetans of having betrayed Greece by their action.

[6.50] In response to this accusation, Cleomenes, son of Anaxandrides and king of Sparta,[1] crossed over to Aegina with the intention

---

1. We have already met this colorful Spartan monarch on two previous occasions, as the leader of the series of Spartan interventions in Athenian politics between 510 and 508 (p. 93), who later refused to help Aristagoras in his revolt from Persia in 499 (5.49 ff.). He reigned roughly from 520 to 490 and,

of arresting those Aeginetans who were most responsible for policy. But when he was attempting to do so, he found himself opposed by many of the Aeginetans and particularly by Crius, son of Polycrites. This man declared that Cleomenes would be made to rue it if he tried to carry off a single man, and that he was acting without the authority of the Spartan government, being bribed by the Athenians; otherwise he would have been accompanied by the other king. (These words had been supplied to him by Demaratus, the other Spartan king, in a letter.)[2] Cleomenes, on quitting Aegina, asked Crius his name and, when he was told it, "Get your horns tipped with brass as soon as you can, Crius,"[3] he said, "for you are going to meet with much trouble."

[6.51–52] Meanwhile, Demaratus, who had remained behind at Sparta, was making accusations against Cleomenes. He was the other of the two Spartan kings but of the inferior house—not that it is inferior in any respect (for they have a common ancestor) other than the esteem due to the house of Eurysthenes as being the elder.

For the Spartans, diverging from all the poets, maintain that it was Aristodemus himself who, as their king, brought them into territory that they now possess, and not the children of Aristodemus.[4] Soon thereafter his wife Argeia gave birth to twins. . . . Aristodemus lived long enough to see his children but then fell sick and died. The Lacedaemonians of that time were resolved, in accordance with their custom, to make the elder of the two children their king but were unable to choose between them, the children being the same in size and exactly alike. Finding themselves in this difficulty, they questioned the mother, but she insisted that she herself could not distinguish between

his reluctance to help the Ionians notwithstanding, pursued a strongly anti-Persian policy throughout. Herodotus here begins a series of tales involving his bitter rivalry with Demaratus, who was his coregent from about 515 to 491. The peculiar Spartan institution of dual kingship often led to such power struggles.

2. That is, Demaratus had conspired with Crius in an effort to embarrass Cleomenes, by instructing the Aeginetan how best to undermine Cleomenes' authority. It's not clear whether Demaratus was motivated by policy differences with Cleomenes, i.e., a more pro-Persian outlook, or simply by personal antagonism.

3. Cleomenes puns on the name Crius, which is Greek for "ram."

4. Here Herodotus makes a digression from his main story, the feud between Cleomenes and Demaratus, to explain the origin of the dual kingship at Sparta. No other Greek state of Herodotus' day had two kings sharing power.

them. No doubt she knew very well but said this in the hope that both might become kings.

The Spartans, in this dilemma, sent to the oracle at Delphi to inquire how they should deal with this situation. The Priestess replied that they must make both children kings but give the greater honor to the elder. This answer did nothing to solve the difficulty confronting the Spartans as to which was the elder, but the following suggestion was made by a Messenian named Panites: The Spartans should keep watch to see which of the babes the mother washed and fed first. If she always kept to the same order, this would tell them what they wanted to know; if she varied, giving preference to the one and then to the other, it would be clear that she knew no more than they, and they must then resort to another plan.

The Spartans accepted the Messenian's suggestion and, by keeping watch over the mother, who had no idea that she was being watched, they found that in feeding and washing the babes she did indeed give preference to one over the other. So they accepted the child that was preferred by the mother as being the elder and brought it up at public expense. This elder boy had the name Eurysthenes, and the younger, Procles. When the children grew to manhood, it is said that, in spite of being brothers, they were always at loggerheads, and their descendants continued to feud.

[6.61] To return then to the the time when Cleomenes was in Aegina, pursuing the common good of Greece: Back in Sparta, Demaratus was bringing accusations against him, prompted not by any regard for the Aeginetans but by jealousy and enmity toward his fellow king. So upon his return from Aegina, Cleomenes began to consider how he might deprive Demaratus of his kingship. And he discovered some ground for this in the following circumstance.

When Ariston was king of Sparta, he was twice married but had no children. Unwilling to recognize that he was himself the cause of failure, he married a third time.[5]

[6.63] His new wife, before the full term of ten months had elapsed, gave birth to this same Demaratus. Ariston was sitting in council with the Ephors[6] when one of his servants came to tell him

5. At this point Herodotus tells a long story, omitted here, concerning this third wife, who was said to have been made beautiful by a supernatural apparition.
6. Under the Spartan constitution, five Ephors were charged with overseeing a wide array of state functions and even had jurisdiction over the kings in certain matters.

that a son was born to him. Recalling the date of his marriage and counting off the months on his fingers, Ariston cried out, with an oath, "The boy can't be mine." This was said in the hearing of the Ephors, but at the time they paid little attention to it. The boy grew up, and later Ariston regretted what he had said, feeling quite certain that the boy was his. (He gave him the name Demaratus for the following reason. Some time before this, the Spartans had offered public prayers, praying that Ariston, whom they esteemed as the most distinguished of all the kings who had ever reigned in Sparta, should be granted a son. Hence the name: Dem-aratus—prayed for by the people.)

[6.64] In the course of time, Ariston died and was succeeded by Demaratus as king. But it was fated, it seemed, that the question of legitimacy would become public and would deprive him of the kingship. In this Cleomenes played the major part, being at enmity with Demaratus on two counts, that Demaratus had withdrawn the army from Eleusis, and then again in the affair of the Aeginetans when Cleomenes had crossed over to deal with those who favored the Medes.[7]

[6.65] Eager for revenge, he approached Leotychides, who belonged to the same house as Demaratus,[8] and made an agreement with him to the effect that Cleomenes would make him king in place of Demaratus, and then Leotychides would support him in his attack on Aegina. Now, Leotychides had become the bitter enemy of Demaratus for the following reason. When Leotychides was betrothed to Percalus, daughter of Chilon, Demaratus robbed him of his marriage by first carrying off the girl himself and marrying her. This was the origin of the enmity between Leotychides and Demaratus, and now Leotychides, instigated by Cleomenes, swore an oath against Demaratus, declaring that he was not the rightful king of the Spartans, not being Ariston's son. He then proceeded to a formal prosecution, recalling the words uttered by Ariston when his servant announced the birth of a child, and he, reckoning up the months, had cried, "It can't be mine." Relying on these words, Leotychides sought to prove that Demaratus was neither the son of Ariston nor the rightful king of Sparta and furnished as witnesses the Ephors who were present at the time and had heard Ariston's words.

7. Herodotus in the later books of the *Histories* often uses the terms "Medes" and "Persians" indiscriminately. In Greek the verb "to medize" meant to go over to the Persian side.
8. He was in fact Demaratus' cousin.

[6.66] The matter being hotly disputed, the Spartans finally decided to send to the oracle at Delphi to ask whether Demaratus was the son of Ariston. Cleomenes, who had contrived to get the question referred to the Priestess, now won over Cobon, a man of considerable influence at Delphi, who prevailed upon the prophetess Perialla to give the answer that Cleomenes desired. So when the sacred envoys put the question to her, the Priestess replied that Demaratus was not the son of Ariston. Some time afterward, all this became known, and Cobon was exiled from Delphi, while the prophetess Perialla was deprived of her office.

[6.67] Such were the means whereby Demaratus was deposed, but it was an insult that led to his flight to the Persians. After being deprived of the kingship, Demaratus was elected to a lesser domestic office in Sparta. When the festival of Gymnopaedia came around and Demaratus took up his position as spectator, Leotychides, now king in his place, by way of insult and mockery sent his servant to ask him how it felt to be a mere magistrate after being a king. Demaratus, stung by the question, replied, "Tell him I have experienced both, and he has not. Nevertheless, this question will bring to Sparta either thousands of ills or thousands of blessings." Then wrapping his head in his cloak, he left the theater and went home, where he prepared to sacrifice an ox to Zeus and, having done so, sent for his mother.

[6.68] When she had appeared, he put into her hands a portion of the entrails[9] and besought her earnestly as follows. "Mother," he said, "I beseech you by all the gods, and especially by Zeus, god of the hearth, to tell me the truth. Who was really my father? Leotychides said, in the course of the dispute, that you were already pregnant by your former husband when you were married to Ariston, and others tell a more scandalous story, that you had an affair with a stable-boy and that I am *his* son. I entreat you by the gods, tell me the truth. Even if you are guilty of what is alleged, you are not alone among women. There is much talk in Sparta that Ariston was impotent; otherwise, he would have had children by his other wives."

[6.69] "My son," replied his mother, "since you urge me so insistently to tell the truth, you shall have the whole truth. On the third night after my marriage to Ariston, a phantom, closely resembling Ariston, came to me; it lay down with me and decked me with the wreaths it had brought. Then it left, and afterward Ariston came in.

9. As a means of making the oath more binding, similar to placing someone's hand on a Bible.

When he saw me wearing the wreaths, he asked who had given them to me, and I replied that *he* had; but he denied it, though I swore a solemn oath and reproached him for his denial. . . . When he heard me swear the oath, Ariston realized that something supernatural had happened. And the wreaths turned out to have come from the shrine adjoining the courtyard door, belonging to the hero they call Astrabacus; and it was this same hero whom the seers named, when we questioned them, as the one by whom I conceived. So, my son, you now know all that you wanted to know. Either your father is Astrabacus and you were begotten by this hero, or it is Ariston; for it was on that night I conceived. With regard to what your enemies allege, that Ariston, when told of your birth, declared in the hearing of many that you could not be his son because ten months had not elapsed, it was simply his ignorance of such matters that led him to such a heedless utterance. Children can be born not only after ten months but also after nine or seven. Indeed I bore you, my son, after seven months. Ariston himself realized soon afterward that he did wrong to speak as he did. Give no heed to any other stories about your birth; you have heard the honest truth from me. May it befall Leotychides and all who speak like him to have wives who bear children fathered by stable-boys."

[6.70] Now that he had learned all he wanted from his mother, Demaratus took with him provisions for a journey and made his way to Elis on the pretext that he was proceeding to Delphi to consult the oracle. The Spartans, however, suspecting that he intended to flee the country, pursued him, but Demaratus crossed from Elis to Zacynthus before they caught up. The Spartans continued their pursuit and got their hands on him and deprived him of his servants; but as the Zacynthians refused to give him up, he escaped and thereafter crossed over to Asia and presented himself before Darius. The king welcomed him generously, giving him lands and cities. Such, then, was the fate that brought Demaratus to Asia, a man who had won distinction among the Spartans both for his deeds and his wisdom in counsel, and who was moreover the only Spartan king to have gained victory in the four-horse chariot race at Olympia.

[6.71–72] After the deposition of Demaratus, Leotychides succeeded to the kingship. . . . But for him too there was no peaceful old age at home in Sparta, for he suffered a punishment whereby Demaratus was fully avenged. Commanding the army in an expedition to Thessaly, when success was within his grasp he accepted a large bribe. He was caught in the act, sitting in his tent on a glove stuffed with money, and was brought to trial and banished, and his house demolished. He took refuge in Tegea and there he died. All these events, however, took place later.[10]

[6.73] Having thus succeeded in his scheme against Demaratus, Cleomenes, accompanied this time by Leotychides, lost no time in proceeding against Aegina, still incensed by his previous rebuff. Confronted by both kings, the Aeginetans thought it best to offer no further resistance. The kings selected out of the Aeginetans ten men preeminent by wealth and birth, among them Crius and Casambus, the ones who wielded the most influence. These they carried to Attica and handed over to the Athenians, their bitterest enemies, as hostages.

[6.74] Some time later, when the evil devices that Cleomenes had employed against Demaratus became generally known, he became fearful of the Spartans and fled to Thessaly. From there he passed to Arcadia, where he began to make trouble, seeking to unite the Arcadians against Sparta. He made them swear to follow him wherever he might lead them and was especially eager to take the leaders of the Arcadians to Nonacris, so as to make them swear by the waters of the Styx.[11]

[6.75] When the Lacedaemonians heard what Cleomenes was contriving, in their alarm they brought him back home on the understanding that he would be restored to his former office. Even before this he had exhibited some strange behavior, and now he was seized with outright madness that assumed this form, that whenever he met a Spartan of the citizen class he rapped him on the face with his scepter. His kindred, seeing that he was quite out of his mind, restrained him in the stocks. Being so bound and finding himself with but a single guard, he asked the man for a knife. At first the man refused, but in the face of Cleomenes' repeated threats as to what he would do to him when freed, he gave him a knife.[12] As soon as the knife was in his hand, Cleomenes began to mutilate himself, beginning with his legs, and, slicing his flesh, he advanced from his legs to his thighs, hips, and loins until he reached his belly, and, cutting this into strips, he died.

10. As much as twenty years later, long after the events described in the *Histories* had ended. On this and several other occasions, Herodotus turns the clock forward to show us how retribution for a wrong works itself out over the course of decades or even generations.
11. An especially binding oath; in Greek myth the gods themselves swear by the Styx.
12. Herodotus further notes here that the guard was a helot or serf, who would therefore be at the mercy of all Cleomenes' punishments.

The Greeks in general say that he incurred this fate because he had bribed the Priestess to pronounce against Demaratus, but the Athenians attribute it to his destroying the sacred precinct of the goddesses Demeter and Persephone when he invaded Eleusis,[13] while the Argives ascribe it to the occasion when he took from their refuge in the temple of the god Argus those Argives who had fled from battle and executed them, and also set fire to the sacred grove itself, giving no heed to its sanctity.[14]

[6.84] But the Spartans, for their part, deny that Cleomenes' madness was a punishment from heaven; they say that it was caused by his habit, acquired from the Scythians, of drinking his wine without adding water. It seems that the nomadic Scythians, eager for revenge on Darius for his invasion of their country, had sent ambassadors to Sparta to propose an alliance. . . . It is said that when the Scythians arrived on this mission, Cleomenes was continually in their company, much more so than was seemly, and from them he learned to drink his wine without water—and this, the Spartans believe, led him to insanity. (From this episode, the Spartans say, comes the phrase they use when they want strong drink: "Scythian style.")

For my own part, I think that Cleomenes' death was a punishment for what he did to Demaratus.[15]

With Cleomenes dead, the Aeginetans mended their dispute with Sparta in an effort to get back their leading citizens who were being held hostage in Athens. But the Athenians refused to give these men back, prompting a series of hostilities between Athens and Aegina.

Meanwhile, the Persians were preparing a major assault on Athens and Eretria, the two states that had helped the Ionians in the sack of Sardis. An initial invasion, launched in 492 under the general Mardonius, Darius' son-

---

13. This was in 506, during Cleomenes' last, abortive attempt to intervene in Athenian politics and prevent Cleisthenes from coming to power. Eleusis is a shrine near Athens; the Athenians naturally prefer to see the sacrilege done on their turf as the cause of Cleomenes' madness.

14. Herodotus goes on to tell the story of this campaign (494 B.C.E.) in some detail, but the main outlines are clear from the passage excerpted here. The city of Argos had long been Sparta's bitterest enemy, and this episode only deepened the antagonism. In the Persian wars that would follow, Argos refused to take part in any defense of Greece organized by Sparta and thus stayed neutral. It was considered a violation of religious law to execute those who have taken refuge at a holy shrine.

15. A rare case in which Herodotus expresses his own preference for one of the variants he records.

in-law, had failed before getting halfway to its targets. The plan had been for the army and navy to proceed toward Greece together, such that the fleet could land supplies for the men as they marched down the coast. But the army, moving westward across Thrace, was badly mauled in a night battle with the Brygi tribe, while the fleet incurred heavy damage from a storm as it rounded the peninsula of Athos. Mardonius returned in disgrace, having conquered only Macedonia and the Greek island of Thasos. But Darius decided to try a new approach, with new generals, two years later.

[6.94] While war continued between Athens and Aegina, Darius, the Persian king, carried on with his own designs, being exhorted every day by his servant to "remember the Athenians," and urged on by the Pisistratids[16] who never ceased to slander the Athenians. At the same time, he was himself pleased to have this pretext for reducing to submission those Greeks who refused him earth and water. In view of the failure of the previous expedition, he relieved his general Mardonius of command and appointed other generals to lead the attack on Eretria and Athens: Datis, a Mede, and Artaphernes, his own nephew and son of Artaphernes.[17] Their orders were to reduce to slavery Athens and Eretria and to bring the slaves before the king.

[6.95] These new commanders, leaving the king's presence, made their way to the Aleian plain in Cilicia, accompanied by a strong and well-equipped force of infantry. Here they were joined by the entire naval force requisitioned from various communities, and also by the horse transports that Darius had commanded his tributaries to prepare the previous year. The horses were embarked on the transports, the troops on their ships, and together with six hundred triremes they set sail for Ionia. From there, instead of keeping a straight course parallel to the coast toward the Hellespont and Thrace, they sailed westward from Samos across the Icarian Sea through the islands. In my opinion, the reason for this was their fear of the passage around Athos, which had been the cause of a fearful disaster the previous year. A further compelling reason was that the island of Naxos remained as yet unconquered.[18]

16. That is, Hippias, the exiled Athenian tyrant, and his kin. Though he had been out of power for almost thirty years, the aged Hippias, now living at Darius' court, had not given up on his hopes of regaining rule at Athens.
17. The elder Artaphernes has been encountered earlier; he was Darius' half-brother and governor of Lydia (p. 90 above).
18. Naxos had been the target of a joint Samian-Persian attack ten years earlier, when Aristagoras had promised Artaphernes to bring the island under Persian rule (p. 90 above).

[6.96] When the Persians reached Naxos from the Icarian Sea (this being their first objective), the Naxians, remembering what had happened on the previous occasion, offered no resistance but took to the hills. The Persians carried off to slavery those whom they caught, burned the temples along with the town, and then sailed away against the other islands.

[6.97] While the Persians were thus engaged, the Delians also quit Delos and took refuge in Tenos.[19] As the Persian fleet first drew near, Datis, sailing ahead, commanded them not to anchor at Delos but at Rhenaea opposite. He himself, on discovering whither the Delians had fled, sent a herald to them with this message: "Holy men, why have you fled, judging me so harshly? I myself have enough understanding—even if the king had not given me specific orders—to avoid doing harm to the birthplace of the two gods, both the land itself and those who dwell there. Return, therefore, to that which is your own and continue to dwell in your island." This was the message he sent to the Delians, after which he proceeded to heap up on the altar three hundred talents-weight of frankincense and burned it as an offering. Then he sailed with his force against Eretria first, taking with him a number of Ionians and Aeolians.

The Delians say that after his departure, Delos was shaken by an earthquake, the first and, to this day, the last shock experienced there. It may well be that this was a sign whereby the god gave warning of troubles to come, for during the successive reigns of the three kings, Darius son of Hystaspes, Xerxes son of Darius, and Artaxerxes son of Xerxes, Greece suffered more woes than in the twenty generations preceding Darius—some inflicted on them by the Persians, some arising from the struggles for supremacy by their own leading states.[20] It

19. Delos, being the legendary birthplace of Apollo and Artemis, was considered a sacred island by the Greeks, especially the Ionians (for whom it was the center of various cult rituals and festivals).
20. Historians have given much attention to this sentence, since it is the one place in the *Histories* where Herodotus seems to make explicit reference to the Peloponnesian War—the great conflict between Athens and Sparta that began, officially, in 431. But the two Greek superpowers had been skirmishing long before this date, and it is possible that Herodotus' words here could refer to a period decades earlier than the war itself. There has also been much debate over the implications of this sentence for the dating of the *Histories*. If Herodotus implies that he had lived to see the *end* of Artaxerxes' reign, in 424, then this passage would push forward by six years the latest date that can otherwise be assigned to the composition of the text. But some scholars see no such implication here.

was therefore not surprising that Delos should be shaken by an earthquake where there had never been an earthquake before. And indeed there existed an oracle containing the words: "Delos, too, I will shake, though never before shaken." The above names can be rendered in Greek as follows: Darius—worker; Xerxes—warrior; Artaxerxes—great warrior. This would be a correct translation of the names of these kings.[21]

Eretria was a small city in western Euboea, whose only hope of resisting the Persian invasion lay in its walls. Faced with imminent attack, the citizens became fractious, with many inclined to surrender to the Persians; a contingent of support troops from Athens, learning of this divisiveness, hastened to abandon the town. At last the Persians arrived and commenced siege operations. Fighting was fierce for six days, after which two Eretrians treacherously opened the gates to the Persians, allowing them to sack and burn the city and enslave all its inhabitants. Darius had settled one of his scores with the Greeks; now Athens remained.

[6.102] With the subjugation of Eretria, after a few days' delay the Persians sailed for Attica,[22] confident that they could deal with the Athenians just as they had dealt with the Eretrians. Marathon being a place in Attica suitable for cavalry and nearest to Eretria, it was to Marathon that they were guided by Hippias, son of Pisistratus.

[6.103] When the news reached the Athenians, they likewise marched out to Marathon under the command of ten generals,[23] of whom the tenth was Miltiades.[24] Miltiades' father, Cimon, had been banished from Athens by the tyrant Pisistratus. While in exile it was his fortune to win the four-horse chariot race at Olympia, thereby acquiring the same honor as his half-brother Miltiades before him. At the next Olympiad he won the same prize with the same mares but he

21. These are spurious translations.
22. Attica is the peninsula in which Athens is situated.
23. The Athenians elected ten *stratēgoi* or "generals" annually to supervise military affairs, though usually only one or two commanded any single military expedition.
24. Herodotus here interrupts the story of the developing battle to give us background on Miltiades, who will soon be its principal hero. The point of describing the murder of Miltiades' father, Cimon, by the sons of Pisistratus becomes obvious when we consider that one of those same sons, Hippias, is now guiding the Persian attack on Athens. For Miltiades, the coming battle is not only a moment of national peril but a personal grudge match as well.

surrendered his victory and caused Pisistratus to be proclaimed the victor, on the understanding that he would be allowed back to his own country. He won another Olympiad with the same mares, but was murdered by the sons of Pisistratus after their father had died. They set men to waylay him by night, and these slew him near the Council House. He was buried outside the city beyond what is called the Valley Road, and opposite the tomb were buried the mares that had won three prizes. . . . At the time of Cimon's death, Stesagoras, the elder of his two sons, was living with Cimon's brother Miltiades in the Chersonese, while the younger, called Miltiades after his uncle, who had founded the Chersonese settlement, was with his father in Athens.

It was this Miltiades who was then elected one of ten generals of the Athenian troops. He had escaped from the Chersonese and twice come within an ace of losing his life—first when the Phoenicians, eager to seize him and carry him off to the Persian king, pursued him as far as Imbros, and then, after he had escaped that peril and reached his own country and thought himself safe, when his political enemies, having lain in wait for him, arraigned him before the court and prosecuted him for his rule of the Chersonese.[25] This attack he likewise escaped and was appointed general by popular vote.[26]

[6.105] But before leaving the city, the Athenians first sent off to Sparta a messenger, one Philippides,[27] an Athenian who was by profession and practice a courier. According to the account he later gave to the Athenians, this man, when he was in the neighborhood of Mount Parthenion above Tegea, encountered the god Pan, who called him by name and bade him ask the Athenians why they neglected him, though he was well disposed to them and had often been helpful to them in the past and would be so again. The Athenians, believing this to be a true account, when their affairs were once more in good order, set up a shrine to Pan beneath the acropolis, and from the time they received this message, they propitiate him with yearly sacrifices and a torch-race.

[6.106] So Philippides, at this time—that is, when he was sent by the generals and when, as he said, the god Pan appeared to him—

---

25. The younger Miltiades had inherited rule over the Chersonese from his uncle of the same name.
26. Reading between the lines of Herodotus' account of this political trial, we can infer that Miltiades, known for his strong anti-Persian sentiments, was prosecuted by the appeasement faction in Athens, who would have preferred to come to terms with Darius, but was supported by the more influential resistance faction.
27. In some manuscripts he is called "Pheidippides."

reached Sparta the day after leaving Athens[28] and delivered this message to the Spartan authorities: "Men of Lacedaemon, the Athenians ask you to come to their assistance and not to permit a city that is the most ancient in Greece to be enslaved by the barbarians. Already Eretria has been reduced to slavery, and Greece is the weaker for the loss of a notable city." Thus spoke Philippides, as instructed, and the Spartans replied that, although they were willing to send help, they found it impossible to do so immediately because of the restrictions of their own laws. It was the ninth day of the month, and they said they could not take the field until the moon was at the full.[29] So they waited for the full moon.

[6.107] Meanwhile Hippias, son of Pisistratus, was guiding the Persians to Marathon. On the previous night he had dreamed a strange dream, that he was lying in his mother's arms. This dream he interpreted to mean that he would be restored to Athens, would recover his power, and would end his days peacefully in his own native country. Such were his first thoughts about the dream. Acting now as a guide to the Persians, he put the prisoners from Eretria ashore on Aegilia, an island belonging to the town of Styra, and then proceeded to lead the fleet to an anchorage off Marathon, where he landed the Persians and drew them up in formation.

As he was thus engaged, it so happened that he sneezed and coughed more vigorously than was his wont, and, since he was advanced in years and most of his teeth were loose, one of them fell out through the violence of his coughing. It fell somewhere in the sand, and in spite of all his efforts, he could not find it. He heaved a great sigh and, turning to some bystanders, he said: "This land is not ours and we shall never be able to hold it. Whatever of it was my portion, my tooth possesses." So Hippias believed that this was the manner in which his dream had come true.

28. After covering seventy miles per day for two days, fast running indeed! In later legends he is also said to have run the twenty-six miles to Athens from Marathon to announce the Greek victory there—the reason why our modern marathon run is set at just over twenty-six miles. After blurting out two words that proclaimed the victory, Philippides reportedly fell down dead.
29. Not the specious excuse it may at first appear. The Spartans were strict observers of religious ritual, and the law forbidding military maneuvers during the period in question was an ancient one. Nonetheless it is possible to conclude, as some modern historians have done, that the Spartans preferred to avoid a direct confrontation with Persia at this point.

****

[6.108] The Athenians were drawn up in an enclosure sacred to Heracles when they were joined by the Plataeans in full force.[30]

[6.109] The Athenian generals were divided in their opinions, some arguing against risking a battle in view of their numerical inferiority, while others were in favor. Among the latter was Miltiades. Seeing that opinion was divided and that the less valiant view was likely to prevail, Miltiades resolved to approach the Polemarch, who held the eleventh and decisive vote. (At this period of time, the man on whom the lot fell to be Polemarch was entitled to an equal vote with the ten generals.) The Polemarch on this occasion was Callimachus of Aphidna, and it was he whom Miltiades approached, speaking as follows: "It is in your hands, Callimachus, either to enslave Athens, or to make her free, and to leave behind you for all time a memory surpassing even that of Harmodius and Aristogeiton.[31] Never in all their history have the Athenians faced a greater peril. If they bow their necks to the Medes, no one can doubt what they will suffer when given over to Hippias; but if our native city fights and wins, it can become the leading city of all Greece. How such things can be, and how it rests with you to determine the course of events, I shall now make clear. We generals, ten in number, are divided in our opinions, some in favor of risking a battle, some against. If we do not fight now, I expect to see bitter dissension break out in Athens, which will shake men's resolution and lead to submission to Persia.[32] But if we join battle before the rot can spread throughout the citizen body, and if the gods do but grant us fair play, we can win in the engagement. So yours is now the decisive voice; all depends on you. If you cast your vote on my side, your country will be free and the foremost city of Greece. But if you support those who are against giving battle, then the opposite of those blessings I have mentioned will be your lot."

[6.110] These words of Miltiades convinced Callimachus, and with the Polemarch's vote added to the others, the decision to fight

30. Plataea was the only Greek city to come to Athens' aid in this crisis, but her contribution of troops was hardly a voluntary one; in the sections omitted here Herodotus describes how Plataea had become a dependent of Athens decades earlier in order to escape harassment by her neighbors.
31. The illustrious "tyrant-slayers" who had assassinated one of the Pisistratids in 514 and thus ushered in the end of autocratic rule.
32. Miltiades envisions Athens being destroyed by internal factionalism, just as Eretria had been. His own experience since returning to Athens had revealed to him the strength of the accommodationist faction.

was made. Thereupon the generals who had been in favor of fighting, as each one got his turn to exercise supreme command for the day, all resigned authority in favor of Miltiades. He accepted their offer but nevertheless waited until his own turn of command came around before he would join battle.[33]

[6.111] Then the Athenian army was drawn up for battle in the following order. The right wing was commanded by the Polemarch, for it was the custom of the Athenians at the time for the Polemarch to have the right wing. Then, in their regular order, the tribes were arrayed in an unbroken line, and finally on the left wing were stationed the Plataeans. And ever since this battle, whenever the Athenians offer sacrifice at their quadrennial festivals, the Athenian herald prays that the Plataeans, along with the Athenians, receive benefits. Now the way that the Athenian troops were arranged at Marathon had this result, that the extending of the Athenian front to equal that of the Medes left their center the weakest part of the line, being few ranks deep, whereas both wings were strengthened.

[6.112] These dispositions being made and the sacrifices being favorable, with the word being given, the Athenians charged the enemy at a run. The distance between the armies was about a mile.[34] The Persians, seeing them coming on at a run, prepared to receive them; they thought that the Athenians had lost their senses and were bent on self-destruction, for they were inferior in number and came on at a rush without cavalry or archers. Such were the thoughts of the barbarians, but the Athenians fell upon them in close order and fought in a way never to be forgotten. They were the first of the Greeks, as far as we know, to charge the enemy at a run and the first to look unafraid at Median dress and the men wearing it. Before this, the very name "Mede" had been a terror to the Greeks.[35]

33. Much confusion arises from this chapter, as from other aspects of Herodotus' account of the battle of Marathon. Why would Miltiades want to wait before attacking, given his words in the previous chapter about the creeping "rot" that threatened Athenian unity? Probably he was hoping that the Spartan army would arrive to help him—a fact that Athenian legend later conveniently "forgot."

34. Needless to say, it is impossible to imagine men wearing heavy armor running at full speed for a mile without exhausting themselves completely. Legend has clearly exaggerated the distance involved. Probably the troops *did* run for a short ways, if only to avoid the hail of arrows falling on them as they advanced.

35. A striking reminder of the novelty of this confrontation; the Greeks had not faced a barbarian threat on the mainland in all of their recorded history.

The struggle at Marathon lasted a considerable time. In the center, which was held by the Persians themselves and the Sacae, the invaders had the upper hand. It was there that they broke the line and pursued the fugitives inland, whereas on the wings the Athenians and the Plataeans were victorious. Where they had prevailed they allowed the enemy to flee and, uniting both wings, they fell upon those who had broken the center and defeated them.³⁶ They pursued the fleeing Persians and cut them down as they fled to the sea. Then, laying hold of the ships, they called for fire.

[6.114–15] It was in this phase of the battle that the Polemarch Callimachus, who had fought valiantly, lost his life, and one of the generals, Stesilaus, was slain, and Cynegirus, as he was laying hold of the vessel's stern, had his hand cut off by an ax and so perished. So likewise did many other notable Athenians. Nevertheless, in this way the Athenians managed to secure seven of the ships. The rest succeeded in getting away, and the Persians, after taking on board the Eretrian prisoners from the island where they had left them, sailed around Sunium and headed for Athens, hoping to reach it before the Athenian army could return.³⁷ In Athens the Alcmaeonids were accused of suggesting this tactic. They had, it was said, an agreement with the Persians and raised a shield to signal to them when they were embarked on their ships.³⁸

[6.116] So the Persians were sailing around Sunium, but the Athenians made all possible speed in returning to the city and succeeded in arriving before the Persians. Just as at Marathon they had taken up a position in an enclosure sacred to Heracles, so they now

36. A plausible explanation of how the Greeks prevailed; the Persians allowed their "crack" troops in the center to become cut off from the wings and isolated, such that the Athenians could close in on them from both sides. What Herodotus fails to explain, however, is why the Persians' cavalry, which could have given them an easy victory, played no role in the battle. Some have speculated that the Greeks attacked at a moment when the horses were still on board the transport ships and could not be deployed.
37. Having failed at Marathon, the Persians now attempt to take the city of Athens itself while the army is still in the field. However, this entailed a journey all the way around the Attic peninsula, since the harbor of Phalerum lay on its western coast.
38. The Alcmaeonids were a wealthy, politically liberal family at Athens that had produced Cleisthenes, among other populist leaders. There is reason to believe that they may indeed have been involved in a collusion with the Persians, though Herodotus takes pains to refute the charge in a passage omitted here.

stationed themselves in another enclosure sacred to Heracles at Cynosarges. The Persian fleet lay off Phalerum, which was at that time the harbor for Athens, and after riding at anchor for a while sailed away for Asia.

[6.117] In the battle of Marathon some 6,400 were killed on the Persian side, and on the Athenian side 192. In this battle a strange event took place. The Athenian Epizelus, fighting gallantly in the thick of the fray, was struck blind, though untouched either by sword or arrow, and his blindness continued to the end of his life. I am told that in speaking of this event he used to say that there stood against him a man of great stature, heavily armed, whose beard cast a shadow over his entire shield, and that this phantom passed him by and slew the man beside him. Such is his story.

[6.120] When the moon reached its full, the Spartans set out for Athens, two thousand strong, so anxious to be in time that they were in Attica on the third day after leaving Sparta. Too late to take part in the battle, they were nevertheless eager to have sight of the Medes and went on to Marathon to view the bodies. Then, bestowing praise on the Athenians for their achievement, they returned home.

A great victory demands a celebration, and Herodotus closes off his account of Marathon with two of his most delightful stories, both concerning the wealthy and politically influential Alcmaeonid family. Having first tried to refute the charge that the Alcmaeonids helped the Persians at Marathon, Herodotus here traces the early history of the family, going back to the founder of its fortune, Alcmaeon.

[6.125] Even in the early days the Alcmaeonids were a family of distinction in Athens, and from the time of Alcmaeon, and of Megacles after him, they acquired particular fame. When the Lydian envoys sent by Croesus from Sardis arrived to consult the oracle at Delphi, Alcmaeon, son of Megacles, exerted himself to give them every possible assistance. Having learned from the envoys sent on this mission that Alcmaeon had rendered him such good service, Croesus invited him to Sardis and promised him as a gift whatever amount of gold he would be able to carry away on his person at one time. Confronted by this unusual offer, Alcmaeon made the following preparations. He clothed himself in a very large tunic with a bulge at the waist, put on the widest boots he could procure, and thus attired, he followed his guides into the treasury. Falling upon a heap of gold dust, he first crammed into his boots right up his legs as much gold as they would hold, then he filled full the bulging front of his tunic, scattered gold dust all over his hair, stuffed some more into his mouth, and was scarcely able to stagger out of the treasury, looking barely human with his mouth stuffed full and his figure all swollen. When Croesus saw him, he was overcome with laughter and gave him all the gold he was carrying and as much again. Thus it was that the house of Alcmaeon acquired great wealth, and Alcmaeon was able to maintain a racing-stable with which he won the four-horse chariot race at Olympia.

[6.126] Then, in the next generation, Cleisthenes, ruler of Sicyon,[39] raised Alcmaeon's family to even greater heights than they had attained before. Cleisthenes had a daughter named Agariste, whom he wished to marry to the best suitor he could find in all Greece. So at the Olympic games where he himself had won the chariot race, he caused a proclamation to be made that any Greek who wished to become Cleisthenes' son-in-law should come to Sicyon within sixty days, or even sooner; within a year's time from the end of the sixty days, Cleisthenes would decide on the man to marry his daughter. Thereupon all the Greeks who had confidence in their own merit and in that of their country came as suitors to Sicyon, where Cleisthenes had prepared for them a racetrack and a wrestling-ground for this very purpose.

[6.127] From Sybaris in Italy (Sybaris was at that time at the height of its prosperity) came Smindyrides, a man famous above all others for the art of luxurious living; and from Siris, also in Italy, came Damasus, son of Amyris, who was called the Wise. Then there was Amphimnestus, from Epidamnus on the Ionian Gulf, and from Aetolia came Males, brother to Titormus who was the strongest man in Greece and who had sought retirement in the remotest parts of Aetolia so as to avoid his fellowmen. From the Peloponnese came Leocedes. . . . Next was Amiantus from Trapezus in Arcadia, and Laphanes, an Azenian of Paeus . . . and lastly Onomastus, a native of Elis. These were the four from the Peloponnese. From Athens came Megacles, the son of that Alcmaeon who had visited Croesus, and Hippocleides, the wealthiest and handsomest of the Athenians. From Eretria, which at this time was a flourishing city, came Lysanias, the only man from Euboea. From Thessaly came Diactorides, one of the Scopodae of Crannon, and Alcon from the Molossians. This was the list of suitors.

[6.128] When they were all assembled on the appointed day, Cleisthenes first made inquiry as to each one's country and parentage,

---

39. Grandfather of the more famous Cleisthenes who founded the democratic regime at Athens.

and then, keeping them with him for a year, he made trial of their many virtues, their temper, their accomplishments, and their disposition, sometimes conversing with them singly, sometimes drawing them all together. Those who were not too old he took with him to the gymnasia, but the greatest test was at the banquet table. It so came about that the suitors who pleased him best were from Athens, and of these he gave preference to Hippocleides, partly on account of his many virtues, partly because he was related far back to the Cypselids of Corinth.

[6.129] When at last the day arrived for the marriage feast and for Cleisthenes to declare his preferred suitor, he sacrificed a hundred oxen and gave a banquet for the suitors and all the Sicyonians. Dinner being over, the suitors competed with one another in music and in public speaking. As the drinking proceeded, Hippocleides, who far outclassed the others, bade the flute-player play him a tune, which the man did, and Hippocleides danced to it. No doubt he danced well to his own satisfaction, but Cleisthenes looked askance at the entire performance. After a brief pause, Hippocleides bade someone bring a table, and, the table being produced, he danced on it, first some Laconian figures, then some Attic figures, and then he stood on his head on the table, tossing his legs about in the air. Cleisthenes, although he was now quite averse to the idea of Hippocleides as a son-in-law because of his shameless display of dancing, had restrained himself throughout the Laconian and Attic figures, wishing to avoid a public outburst. But when he saw Hippocleides beating time with his legs in the air, he could no longer contain himself and cried out: "Son of Tisander, you have danced away your marriage!" "What does Hippocleides care?" came the other's reply, and that was how the proverb originated.[40]

[6.130] Then Cleisthenes called for silence and addressed the assembly. "Gentlemen, suitors of my daughter, I have the highest esteem for you all, and if it were possible, I would show favor to you all by not choosing one and disappointing the others. But since, with only one daughter, it is beyond my power to please all, I bestow on those of you who have failed to win the bride a talent of silver, in appreciation of the honor you have done me in wishing to marry into my house and to compensate you for your long absence from home. My daughter, Agariste, I betroth to Megacles, son of Alcmaeon, according to Athenian law." When Megacles declared his acceptance, Cleisthenes had the marriage formally solemnized.

---

40. Evidently Greeks of Herodotus' day said "What does Hippocleides care?" to express disregard for conventional opinion.

[6.131] Such was the Trial of the Suitors, and in this way the Alc-maeonids became famous throughout Greece. From this marriage was born Cleisthenes—named after his maternal grandfather, Cleisthenes of Sicyon—who organized the Athenians into their tribes and instituted democratic government in Athens. A second son of Megacles was Hippocrates, whose children were another Megacles and another Agariste, named after Agariste, daughter of Cleisthenes. She married Xanthippus, son of Ariphon, and, being with child, she had a dream wherein she thought she was delivered of a lion. In a few days she gave birth to a son, Pericles.[41]

Herodotus now returns to the narrative present to record the fortunes of Miltiades, hero of Marathon, in the period after the battle. Not content to rest on his laurels, Miltiades promised the Athenians he would make them rich if they gave him money and troops with which to attack an objective he refused to name. The target turned out to be Paros, a wealthy Greek island that had participated, under compulsion, in the Persian attack on Eretria and Athens. Miltiades' forces put the main city of the island under siege but failed to make any headway, and then, while conducting some sort of covert operation, Miltiades himself injured his leg jumping from the top of a fence. Incapacitated by his injury and disgraced by the failure to capture Paros, Miltiades returned to Athens to undergo a second political trial mounted by his enemies. His reputation as the hero of Marathon notwithstanding, he was fined a huge sum of money and soon thereafter died as a result of gangrene in his injured leg.

41. The only mention in the *Histories* of the great statesman who dominated affairs at Athens during much of Herodotus' lifetime.

VIII

Persia versus Greece: Xerxes' War

(484–80 B.C.E.)

With Book 7 we enter the most detailed and least fragmented portion of the Histories. Herodotus "fast forwards" in only a few paragraphs through the final years of Darius' reign, roughly 490–86, to arrive at the accession of King Xerxes in the fifth chapter. From that point on, his narrative pace slows dramatically, such that his next three books cover only five years of historical time, as compared with the decades covered in the previous three books and the centuries of the first three. He follows month by month, and finally day by day, the progress of Xerxes' invasion of Greece in 480, concluding with the defeat of the last remaining Persian forces in Europe in 479. Because of its internal unity, its grand scale, and its focus on the figure of King Xerxes, this section is sometimes referred to as "the Xerxiad," on the analogy of Homer's epic poem the Iliad.

The first major scene of Book 7 is a debate in the Persian council chamber over the question of the proposed war on Greece. It contains some of the longest and most ornately composed speeches in the whole of the Histories, put in the mouths of the three great leaders of the day: Xerxes the king, Mardonius the army commander, and Artabanus the elder sage. The scene must be largely invented, since Herodotus could not have had much information about what was said in secret council meetings far removed from him in both time and space. But the value of these speeches for readers of the Histories goes far beyond the artistry of their composition. Herodotus here attempts an analysis of the internal workings of the Persian political system, as well as providing character sketches of the major "players" of the day. His depiction of how a major decision got made at the Persian court reveals the strengths and (mostly) weaknesses of an entire society. The comparison that can be drawn between this council meeting and two similar scenes in the Greek world, the debates of the admirals at Salamis (8.58 ff.), is inescapable and highly illuminating.

[7.5][1] After Darius' death, the throne passed to Xerxes, Darius' son.[2] At first Xerxes was in no way eager to launch an invasion of Greece;

---

1. The section starting here and ending at 7.12 was translated by the editor.
2. In 486; Xerxes was at this point about thirty-two years old. His succession

rather, he began to muster his forces to put down rebellion in Egypt. But by his side stood Mardonius, son of Gobryas, the most influential man at his court[3]—he was Xerxes' cousin, being the son of Darius' sister—who kept advancing this argument: "Master, it doesn't look right not to punish the Athenians for the great wrongs they have done to the Persians. Go ahead and do what you are undertaking to do, teach Egypt a lesson for its insolence; but then march on Athens, so that your countrymen will speak well of you and so that your enemies will think twice before attacking your land." Vengeance was his main theme, but he also included this as an added spur: That Europe was a very beautiful realm, excellent in every way, where all variety of trees were grown; the king, alone among mortals, deserved to possess it.

[7.6] Mardonius spoke thus out of his restlessness for new enterprises and because he himself wished to become governor of Greece. In time, his arguments persuaded Xerxes, and other circumstances too became his allies in the struggle to convince the king.

[7.7–8] When Xerxes had made up his mind to invade Greece, he first went through with his plan to attack the Egyptian rebels. This was in the second year after Darius' death. He quickly subdued them and made Egypt far more servile than it had been during Darius' reign, appointing his brother Achaemenes to serve as governor. (Later, a Libyan named Inaros, the son of the pharaoh Psammetichus, rose up and slew Achaemenes.) Then, after Egypt had been retaken, when he was ready to undertake the expedition against Athens, he called a council meeting of the Persian nobles to find out what they thought of it and to announce his intentions before all.

When they were assembled, Xerxes spoke as follows: "Persians, it is not I who have introduced this law of conquest among us; I follow what I have received from others. I have learned from my elders that our nation has never been at rest since we took over dominion from the Medes, when Cyrus overcame Astyages. God has shown us this path and sees to it that our many pursuits lead always to our improvement. You know well how many nations Cyrus, and Cambyses,

---

was not assured, as Herodotus relates in the chapters omitted here: He was the youngest of Darius' sons but also the only one born of Atossa, daughter of Cyrus the Great. In the inevitable dispute over succession, Xerxes had gotten valuable advice, according to Herodotus, from the Spartan king Demaratus, now exiled and living at Susa—an authority on succession disputes, to be sure.

3. Mardonius, it will be recalled, had led the first, abortive invasion of Greece in 492 under Darius (p. 106 above).

and my father, Darius, have conquered and added to our empire; why bother to name them? As for me, ever since I have inherited this throne, I have pondered how not to fall short of the standard of honor my ancestors have set, and how not to diminish the power of the Persians. And in my ponderings I have found a way we can acquire glory, along with a land every bit as large and noble as our own and indeed even more fruitful; and vengeance and payback come with it as well. Hence I have gathered you here, to explain to you what I have in mind to do.

"I intend to bridge the Hellespont and take my army straight through Europe and into Greece, to punish the Athenians for what they did to the Persians and to my father. You all saw that Darius, too, was eager to march against these men. But he's dead, and he never got his chance at revenge. On his behalf, and on behalf of all Persians, I vow not to stop before I capture and burn the city of Athens—those Athenians who started this with their attack on me and my father. First they marched to Sardis, together with Aristagoras the Milesian, our puppet, and they set fire to sacred groves and shrines; and then, what they did to us when we landed on their soil, in the invasion led by Datis and Artaphernes—well, I don't need to remind you.[4]

"For these reasons I am preparing to attack them, and in addition I reckon up the following benefits to be gained: If we subjugate these men as well as their neighbors, those who inhabit the land founded by Pelops the Phrygian,[5] our realm will extend to the very sky where Zeus dwells. Indeed, the sun will never look down upon a country outside our empire; you and I together, marching through the length and breadth of Europe, will make all lands one land. For I have learned that, once these people I have mentioned are subdued, there will be no tribe nor city anywhere on earth able to mount a fight against us. So let the blameless ones bear the yoke of slavery along with those guilty of wronging us.[6]

"Your task, if you wish to please me, is this: When I tell you that it's time to come, you must all rush to come; and whoever brings the best-prepared army, to him I will give the gifts that we Persians treasure most highly. Such is your job. But lest I appear to you to be mak-

---

4. The reference is to the battle of Marathon some five years before this.
5. "The land founded by Pelops" means the Peloponnese, the large peninsula named "island of Pelops" in Greek, dominated militarily by the city of Sparta.
6. The "blameless ones" are the Spartans, who, unlike the Athenians, declined to take part in the Ionian attack on Sardis.

ing plans without consultation, I now put this question before the council. Let anyone who wants reveal his own opinion." With that he ended his speech.

[7.9] After this, Mardonius spoke. "Master," he said, "You have proved yourself the best of the Persians, both those who have come before and those who will follow after: Besides your other fine and true words, you have declared that you won't allow the Ionians living in Europe[7] to scorn us when we do not merit their scorn. Let me now add this: It is unthinkable that we should hold in servitude the Sacae, the Indians, and the Ethiopians, and the other great and numerous peoples we have conquered, though they have done us no wrong, while not getting revenge on the Greeks who have started this fight unprovoked. What are we afraid of? Why fear their numbers or their cash reserves, when we know that their style of fighting and their re- sources are both slight? For we can judge them by their offspring, our subjects, the Asiatic Greeks called Ionians and Aeolians and Dorians.

"I myself have made trial of these people, on an invasion ordered by your father. I got as far as Macedonia and almost to the gates of Athens without any of them opposing me in battle.[8] What's more, these reckless, clumsy Greeks, as I have discovered, make war in the most ill-contrived way possible: After declaring war on one another, they find a lovely, smooth plot of land and go there to fight, so that even the victors get badly roughed up, while the losers—I needn't tell you, they're totally destroyed. Since they speak the same tongue, why don't they use heralds and envoys to resolve their differences, or any other means save battle? Or if they must go to war, why don't they choose ground that least favors their enemy and fight there? But no, they persist in this useless behavior and thus they never even discussed armed opposition when I drove my army right up to Macedonia.

"Who will oppose your war aims, sire, when you command the whole population of Asia and all her ships besides? I don't imagine the Greeks have so much gumption. But if I'm wrong and the Greeks bestir themselves, foolishly, to offer battle, they will learn how far beyond other men we are in the skills of war. Let us leave nothing untried, for by trying men accomplish everything; nothing comes to them of its own accord."

7. Another periphrasis showing how a Persian might have understood com- plex Greek geography and ethnic divisions. The "Ionians living in Europe" are the Athenians.
8. Mardonius boldly exaggerates his achievements in 492; in fact, he was a long way from Athens when his army was thrashed and forced to retreat.

[7.10] Thus spoke Mardonius, putting the polish on Xerxes' opinion. Then silence descended on the Persian council, no one being willing to speak in opposition. Finally, Artabanus, son of Hystaspes, brother of Darius, uncle of Xerxes, and trusted adviser to the king, spoke as follows: "It's not possible, sire, to choose the best course of action when there is no free exchange of views; one must simply follow whatever is proposed. But when both sides of the argument are expressed, the right one can be chosen, just as we test the purity of gold not by examining one sample alone but by scratching two together to see which is the purer. I am the man who once told your father, my brother, Darius, not to attack the Scythians, a tribe that has no fixed dwellings anywhere on earth; but in his confidence of victory he heeded me not and then went and lost the better part of his army. You, my king, are about to attack a people who are worthier by far than the Scythians, and who indeed are said to be the worthiest of all, both on the land and on the sea. It's my business to tell you just how much you have to fear from them.

"You say, my king, that you will bridge the Hellespont and march your army right through Europe and into Greece. Let's say, though, that you meet with some reverse either on land or on sea, or even on both at once—for these men are said to be tough soldiers, as one could deduce from the way the Athenians alone defeated the large force that went with Datis and Artaphernes to Attica. But suppose you avoid a double defeat; if they bear down on you with their ships and win a naval engagement and then sail to the Hellespont and break apart the bridge there—a terrible thing to contemplate, my king. For my part, though, I need no special insight to guess at what would happen, since the same thing almost happened to us when your father bridged the Thracian Bosporus and then the Danube to invade Scythian land. The Scythians used all their wiles to convince the Ionians, who had been left as guards of the Danube crossing, to break up the bridge; and if Histiaeus, ruler of Miletus, had followed the will of the other rulers rather than opposing them, the Persian empire would have fallen that day.[9] Is it not terrible even to hear—the idea that your royal fortunes once rested entirely on one man's shoulders?

"Don't take us into such great peril when there is no need. Heed my advice and dissolve this assembly, and then, after you've examined the matter in private, you can announce to us again what you think best to do. For the best benefit of good planning is this: If one is thwarted by some setback, nevertheless one has the sense that the

9. See 5.133 ff.

plans were well laid, but bad luck intervened; whereas if one is a bad planner, but fortune turns out favorably, one has the sense of having thrown a lucky roll of the dice, but still having laid bad plans.

"Do you see how the god hurls his lightning at the outsized beasts and stops their proud displays, while the smaller creatures bother him not at all? Do you see how his bolts fall without fail on the biggest houses and trees? Thus does the god diminish all things outsized. In the same way too, a great army can be destroyed by a smaller one, when the god in jealous spite hurls thunder or puts panic into them so that they are destroyed all out of proportion to their strengths. For the god does not allow anyone except himself to think grand thoughts.[10]

"All things done in haste beget mistakes, and for these mistakes one usually pays a very high price. Restraint brings benefits, whether they are apparent now or only in the fullness of time. That is my advice to you, my king. As for *you* though, son of Gobryas:[11] Stop making such reckless speeches about the Greeks; they do not merit your low opinion. It's obvious that you are so eager to slander the Greeks because you wish to rouse the king toward war. You must not go down this road. . . .[12]

"But if we really must fight the Greeks, then let the king stay here within Persia's borders, while you, Mardonius, lead the invasion with a force of any size you like, any men you like. And let us two put our own children up as a stake against the outcome. If things turn out for the king as you predict, then I forfeit the lives of my children and my own on top of theirs. But if things go as I predict, then let your children suffer the same fate and you too—that is, if you make it home. If you don't agree to this pact but lead the army to Greece anyway, then I proclaim this: Someone of those left behind here in Persia will hear that Mardonius has done great harm to our people and has left his corpse to be torn by birds and dogs somewhere in Attica or Lacedaemon—or perhaps only on the road that leads there[13]—and so has learned what sort of men they were whom he urged the king to attack."

---

10. The idea of a jealous god who destroys the proudest or happiest creatures on earth echoes the moral wisdom of Solon from the outset of the *Histories* (1.30 ff.), along with other prominent passages (3.39–43, 3.108–09).

11. Artabanus directs the remainder of his speech at Mardonius.

12. Two sentences have been omitted here, in which Artabanus moralizes on the evils of slander.

13. This remark contains a thinly veiled jibe against Mardonius, who in his 492 expedition had turned back before even reaching his objectives.

[7.11] So spoke Artabanus, and Xerxes, enraged, replied as follows: "You are my father's brother, Artabanus, and so you will not pay the price your foolish words deserve. But I impose this disgrace on you for your baseness and cowardice: You will not come with me on the invasion of Greece but stay here with the women, and I shall do what I have promised without your help.

"I would be no true offspring of Darius, of Hystaspes, of Arsames, of Ariaramnes, of Teispes, of Cyrus, of Cambyses, of Teispes, and of Achaemenes before him, if I did not pay these Athenians back. And what's more, I know well that if we don't take action, they will; they will invade our territory, to judge by what they have already set in motion when they landed on our continent and burned Sardis. There's no turning back for either side in this conflict, only the question of who strikes first and who gets struck. Either all our land will be theirs, or all theirs will be ours;[14] our mutual hatred allows no compromise.

"I'm glad we were the first ones wronged in this fight, so that when we take revenge I can learn what fearsome things they have in store for me—men who were conquered by my forefathers' slave, Pelops the Phrygian, and subdued so completely that their race and their land still bears the name of their conqueror today!"[15]

[7.12] That was the end of discussion. But later that evening, the opinion expressed by Artabanus began to gnaw at Xerxes; and, after lying awake pondering it, the king realized that indeed it would not benefit him to attack Greece. He made a decision to cancel the war and then fell asleep, whereupon he had the following dream, according to Persian sources: A beautiful, tall man seemed to be standing over him as he slept, saying, "Persian, have you reversed course and chosen not to take your army against Greece, even after proclaiming to your countrymen to ready their troops? This change of course is the wrong thing to do, and the one standing beside you cannot condone it. Go back to your plan from the daytime; stay on that road." And then the man appeared to fly away.

[7.13] When day dawned, Xerxes dismissed the dream from his mind, recalled his council of advisers and said: "Men of Persia, I ask

14. In the large scheme of things, Xerxes' analysis was correct, as would be demonstrated by Alexander the Great and his Greco-Macedonian invasion of Asia, 150 years down the road. But Herodotus could not have known such an invasion would someday be possible, and would probably have thought Xerxes' words here overblown.

15. Xerxes' tone turns mocking and sarcastic at the end of his speech.

your forbearance for my change of mind. I have not yet reached full maturity of understanding, and those who are urging me to this enterprise never give me any peace. When I heard the advice given me by Artabanus, my youthful spirit boiled over and I flung at him words unbefitting an older man. But now I find that I agree with him, and I shall accept his advice. I have changed my mind regarding the invasion of Greece, so be at rest." On hearing this, the Persians rejoiced and did obedience to him.

[7.14] But when night came, the same phantom stood over him as he slept, and said: "Son of Darius, you have publicly renounced the expedition and made light of my words as if they had never been spoken. Now know for certain that, unless you at once go forth to war, this is what will happen to you: Just as you have in short time risen to greatness and might, so you will swiftly be brought low."

[7.15] Terrified by this dream, Xerxes sprang from his bed and, sending for Artabanus, spoke to him thus: "Artabanus, at first I acted foolishly when I gave you harsh words in return for your good advice, but then I had second thoughts and realized that I ought to do as you suggested. But now, much as I wish it, I cannot do so. Since I have turned about and changed my mind, I have been haunted by a dream that forbids me to do so, a dream that has just departed after threatening me. Now, if it is a god who sends me this dream, and it is his pleasure that we should march against Greece, the same dream will visit you and give you the same commands. And this is more likely to happen if you put on all my clothes, sit on my throne, and then go to sleep in my bed."

[7.16] Artabanus, who thought it unseemly to sit on the royal throne, was finally forced to consent, and speaking as follows he did what was asked: "In my belief, o king, to be wise or to be ready to listen to good advice is much the same thing. In you are united both qualities, but the counsels of evil men lead you astray, in just the same way as gales of wind assail the sea and force it to change its own nature, which is to be of the greatest service to humankind. As for me, I was not so much hurt by your abuse of me as by observing that, when two courses were open to the Persians—one tending to increase their arrogance, the other restraining it and showing how wrong it is to encourage the soul always to covet more than it already possesses—you chose the course fraught with more peril to yourself and to the Persians. But now you tell me that, since you have turned to the better course and renounced the expedition against the Greeks, you are haunted by a dream sent by some god, forbidding you to abandon it. But these things, my son, are not divine visitations. I, who have seen

so many more years than you, will tell you what these dreams are that
wander into men's minds: They are nearly always floating phantoms
of what one has been thinking about during the day, and during the
past few days we have been very much occupied with the question of
this expedition. But if my explanation is not correct and there is something of the divine in this, you have in brief said all that needs saying
about it—let it appear to me as it did to you, with the same commands.
However, if it is going to appear at all, it is not more likely to appear
to me wearing your clothes than wearing my own, nor sleeping in
your bed than my own. For this thing, whatever it may be, that appears to you in your sleep is surely not so simpleminded as to think
that I am you because it sees me clad in your dress. Still, if it pays no
regard to me and deigns not to appear to me whether wearing my own
clothes or yours, then this will be the inescapable conclusion: If it per-
sists in haunting you, I would myself say that it is god-sent. Now if
you are so determined and cannot be turned from your purpose and
I must sleep in your bed, very well, then; when I have carried out your
instructions let it appear to me, too. Until then I shall adhere to my
former opinion."

[7.17–18] So spoke Artabanus, expecting to prove Xerxes wrong,
and did as he was bidden. He put on Xerxes' clothes, seated himself
on the royal throne, and in due course went to bed. As he slept, the
same phantom that had visited Xerxes stood over him and said: "Are
you the man who is dissuading Xerxes from marching against Greece,
presumably out of your concern for him? For seeking to avert that
which is fated to happen, you shall not escape unpunished, either now
or hereafter. As for Xerxes, he has been clearly shown what will befall
him if he disobeys me." These were the words the phantom seemed
to utter, and it was just about to burn out his eyes with hot irons when
Artabanus woke with a shriek, leapt from his bed, and ran to Xerxes.
Sitting beside him, he narrated his dream and then went on to speak
as follows: "O king, I am one who has seen many mighty empires
struck down by lesser ones, and thus it was that I sought to prevent
you from being quite carried away by your youthful spirit. I reflected
what an ill thing it is to be over-covetous, remembering how fared
Cyrus' expedition against the Massagetae and Cambyses' expedition
against the Ethiopians. In addition, I myself took part in Darius'
march against the Scythians.[16] With these things in mind, I was con-

16. The three expeditions mentioned by Artabanus have all been excerpted,
in whole or in part, in this volume. Significantly, all three were confrontations
between the Persians and less "civilized" peoples, the nomadic Massagetae

vinced that all men would deem you most blessed if you remained at peace. But since there has been this visitation from the gods, and, as it seems, a heaven-sent destruction is to fall upon the Greeks, I change my mind and reverse my judgment. Do therefore make known to the Persians the vision the god has sent us and bid them make the preparations as first instructed by you, and thus act so as to take full advantage of what the god is offering you."

Such were his words. Now they were both encouraged by the dream. As soon as day came, Xerxes laid these happenings before the assembly, and Artabanus, who previously had been the only dissenting voice, now heartily supported the war.

Once he resolved upon the invasion of Greece, Xerxes set about making elaborate preparations. Besides raising troops and preparing transport and supplies throughout the empire, he undertook two vast engineering projects to pave his way into Europe. First he employed thousands of laborers to dig a canal through the Athos peninsula, so that his fleet would not have to become cut off from his army or sail the stormy waters where the expedition of 492 B.C.E. had been wrecked. Then he laid plans for the bridging of the Hellespont (today called the Straits of Dardanelles), to enable his army to march across the gap between the continents. Egyptian and Phoenician craftsmen were set to work weaving huge, thick ropes out of flax and papyrus, to be strung across rows of ships anchored so as to span the strait. Sites for the bridgeheads were found at the towns of Abydus on the Asian side and Sestus on the European side.

[7.33–34] Xerxes then made preparations to move on to Abydus, where bridges had meanwhile been constructed over the Hellespont from Asia to Europe. Between Sestus and Madytus in the Hellespontine Chersonese there is a rocky headland running out to sea opposite Abydus. (On this spot, a little later on, the Athenians, with Xanthippus as their general, seized a Persian named Artayctes, who was tied alive to a stake.[17] This Artayctes had gathered women together in the shrine of the hero Protesilaus and had done perverse things.) It was to this headland that those charged with this work constructed two bridges from Abydus, one made by the Phoenicians with cables of flax, and one by the Egyptians with cables of papyrus. The

---

and Scythians and the hunter-gatherer (?) Ethiopians, in which the Persians' hopes of easy conquest were dashed.

17. The execution of Artayctes is the final episode of the war narrated by Herodotus; see 9.114 ff.

distance from Abydus to the opposite shore is about three-quarters of a mile.

[7.35–36] When the channel had been successfully bridged, there arose a violent storm that shattered and destroyed all that had been done. On learning what happened, Xerxes was mightily angry, and he gave orders that the Hellespont should receive three hundred lashes and that a pair of fetters should be cast into its waters. I have even heard it said that he sent branders with irons to brand the Hellespont. Then he instructed those who scourged the waters to utter these barbarous and wicked words: "You bitter stream! Your master lays this punishment upon you because you have wronged him without cause, having suffered no wrong from him. Yet King Xerxes will cross you, whether you wish it or no. Well do you deserve that no man sacrifices to you, you muddy and briny river!" He not only commanded the sea to be punished, but also ordered that the overseers of work on the bridge have their heads cut off. Those whose business it was carried out this unpleasing task, and other engineers were appointed to bridge the channel.

[7.36][18] Here's how they built the bridge: They brought ships side by side in the strait, using 360 to form a line on the side facing the Black Sea and 314 to form another line on the other side. . . . Anchors of great weight were let down, two for each ship—one on the ships' eastern ends on account of the winds blowing out of the Black Sea, others on the western ends on account of gales from the Aegean, blowing from the south and east. They left a gap between the ships so that light craft could still sail in and out of the Black Sea. Then they stretched cables from the shore, hauling them by means of winches. They did not use flax and papyrus cables separately, as they did on the first bridge, but combined two ropes of flax and four of papyrus across each of the two lines of ships. Both types had a similar thickness and fine quality, but the flaxen rope was more dense; each yard of it weighed over a hundred pounds.[19]

[7.37] The work on the bridges was now completed, and news came from Athos that the canal was quite finished, including the

18. This chapter was translated by the editor.
19. It's hard to imagine that the rope was actually this heavy, unless perhaps Herodotus gives the weight when soaked with water. These cables loom large in symbolic importance as the physical link imposed by the Persians on the space between the continents. The Greek seizure of the cables at the war's end divides the continents once more and thus provides a capstone to the story Herodotus tells; it is the last event he narrates (9.121).

breakwaters at both its ends to prevent the surf from silting up the entrances. Then the army, having wintered at Sardis and being now fully equipped, began its march the following spring from Sardis toward Abydus. As it was departing, the sun left its place in the sky and vanished—though it was clear and cloudless weather—and the day gave place to night. Seeing and marking this, Xerxes became anxious and inquired of the Magi as to the significance of this prodigy. He was told that God was foretelling to the Greeks the eclipse of their cities, for it was the sun that gave forewarning to the Greeks just as the moon did for the Persians. Reassured by this reply, Xerxes continued with the march.

[7.38] The army had begun its march when Pythius the Lydian,[20] taking fright at the phenomenon in the heavens and emboldened by the gifts he had gotten from the king, approached Xerxes and said: "My lord, please grant me a favor that is for you a light matter but would be for me something of great moment." Xerxes, expecting nothing like that which the request turned out to be, declared that he would grant it and bade him speak out freely. On hearing this, Pythius took courage and said: "My lord, I have five sons, all serving in the army with you in the campaign against Greece. Have compassion on my years, o king, and release from military duty my eldest son to take care of me and my property. Take with you the other four, and may you return in safety, having achieved your heart's desire."

[7.39] Xerxes was mightily angry and answered thus: "You wretch, do you dare to make mention of your son when I myself am marching against Greece accompanied by my sons, my brothers, and friends—you, my slave, and in duty bound to follow me with all your household, including your wife? Now mark this well: A man's spirit dwells in his ears; when it hears good things, it fills the body with delight, but when it hears the contrary, it heaves with fury. When you did me good service and offered more such, you cannot boast that you outdid the king in generosity. And now that you have turned to impudence, your punishment will be less than is deserved. Yourself and four of your sons are saved through the hospitality you gave me, but the one on whom you set most store shall pay with his life." He immediately commanded those on whom the duty lay to seek out the

20. In an earlier episode (omitted here), Pythius, said to be the wealthiest man in the world after Xerxes, had offered to feed and billet the entire Persian army at his own expense and to give Xerxes a war subsidy as well. Determined to outdo Pythius' generosity, Xerxes instead gave money of his own to augment the Lydian's fortune.

eldest of Pythius' sons, to cut him in half, and to fix the two halves, one on the right and the other on the left of the road, so that the army could march between them. The order was obeyed.

[7.44–45] When he reached Abydus, Xerxes thought he would like to hold a review of his entire force. On a hillock a throne of white marble had already been prepared for this purpose by the people of Abydus, at the king's command. He took his seat there, and gazing down on the shore below he beheld both his land forces and his fleet; and as he gazed he felt a desire to witness a competition between his ships. This took place and resulted in a victory for the Phoenicians of Sidon,[21] much to the satisfaction of Xerxes, who was pleased both with the race and with his forces. And as he saw the whole of the Hellespont completely covered by his ships and all the shore and the plains around Abydus thronged with his men, he congratulated himself, but thereafter he burst into tears.

[7.46] The king's uncle Artabanus, he who originally had spoken his mind so freely in attempting to dissuade Xerxes from undertaking the Greek expedition, perceiving the king's tears, spoke to him thus: "O my king, how different is that which you are now doing from that which you did before. First you congratulated yourself, now you weep." "Yes," said Xerxes, "for there came over me a feeling of pity as I considered the brevity of a man's life, and that of all this vast host not one will be alive in a hundred years' time."

"Yet," replied the other, "in our span of life there are things more pitiable than that. In our brief existence there is no one, either present here or elsewhere, who is so happy as not to wish, not once but many a time, that he were dead rather than alive. Calamities befall us, sicknesses trouble us, so as to make life, however short, seem long. Thus, our life being so burdensome, death becomes a refuge most desirable for man, and the god, who gives us but a sip of the sweetness of life, is found to be grudging even in this gift."

[7.47][22] To this Xerxes replied, "Artabanus, let's talk no more of human life, which is very much as you describe; let's not get distracted by ills when we have vital matters in hand. Tell me now, if that dream had not appeared to you so unmistakably, would you now keep to your original opinion and dissuade me from marching on Greece? Or would you change your mind? Tell me truly." And Artabanus replied,

---

21. The Phoenicians, a seafaring people whose colonies were widely scattered around the Mediterranean, contributed most of the ships in Xerxes' navy. The Persians themselves had almost no experience of the sea.
22. From this chapter through Chapter 52 were translated by the editor.

"Sire, I pray that the dream may have a happy result, as we both wish it to have. But as for myself, I am still filled with fear even today and barely able to contain myself. I count many dangers but especially this: I see that the two greatest things of all will be your worst enemies."

[7.48] Xerxes responded as follows: "You bizarre fellow! What are these two worst enemies you speak of? Do you mean the size of our land army, fearing that the Greek infantry will be far more numerous? Or that our fleet will fail to equal theirs? Or both these things together? If you see anything lacking in our preparations, speak; there is still time to gather more forces."

[7.49] "Sire," said Artabanus, "no one in his right mind could find fault with this army, nor with the size of the fleet. But if you were to increase their size, the two enemies I spoke of would be even more opposed to you. I'm talking about the land and the sea. For on the sea there is no harbor or anchorage anywhere, I don't imagine, large enough to shelter your vessels if a storm should arise. And you won't need just one harbor, but many, all up and down the coast we're sailing. There are no such harbors—so recognize that mischances are the masters of mortals, not mortals of mischances.[23]

"Now I'll explain the other of the two enemies I mentioned. This land is hostile territory; even if no obstacle stops your march, it will become more hostile the farther you advance, luring you ever onward; for no one can ever get enough of success. Even with no one opposing you, the land itself will stretch out farther and farther as time goes on, until it gives rise to hunger.

"The best way for a man is this: To fear everything while making plans and to suppose he will encounter every reverse, but then to act boldly in the execution of his plans."

[7.50] To this Xerxes responded, "Artabanus, everything you have said seems reasonable to me, but don't fear everything or weigh the downside equally with the upside. If one were to do this each time a new enterprise goes forward, one would never do anything at all. It's better, I think, to run every risk and take the consequences in half of them than to become paralyzed by fear and never have any consequences. . . . Gains go to those willing to act, never to those who reckon up all the factors and grow timid. You see how far the Persian empire has advanced in power. Well, consider that if the kings who came before me had thought as you do, or even if they had only had advisers like you, you would never have seen it come so far. For these

---

23. The wisdom of these warnings was borne out at Artemisium (see p. 141).

kings have brought it there by being willing to roll the dice. Great undertakings go hand in hand with great risks.

"We are doing as our ancestors did. We have set out in the finest season of the year, and we shall subdue all of Europe and then return home, untroubled by hunger or any other sort of difficulty. For one thing, we're bringing much food along with us, and for another, we shall find provisions in every land and among every people we come to. It's farmers we're attacking this time, not nomads."[24]

[7.51] To this Artabanus said, "Sire, though you bid me dismiss my fears, nevertheless take my advice (and forgive the long discussion, but complex matters require it). Cyrus, son of Cambyses, made subjects of the Ionians, all except the Athenians, and forced them to pay tribute. Do not, I advise you, take these men with you in your attack on their fathers; we can easily prevail over our enemies without their help. If they do go with you, they must either become the most immoral of men by enslaving their own mother city, or the most upright, by helping to set her free. They will offer us little help if they become the most immoral, whereas by acting most uprightly they can do great harm to your army.

"There is an ancient expression you should take to your heart: 'Not every end can be seen in the beginning.'"

[7.52] Xerxes replied as follows. "Artabanus, you're more deceived in your fears over our Ionian conscripts than in any of your other judgments. Our opinion of the Ionians stands very high. You yourself saw, as did the others who accompanied Darius on the Scythian campaign, that when the destruction or survival of the entire Persian army rested on these men, they displayed only trustworthiness and uprightness rather than anything unsavory. And besides, why should we fear that they will cause trouble, when their children and wives and property reside on our land?[25] So don't be afraid on this score. Keep your spirits up and protect my household and my crown; for to you alone out of all men I entrust my royal scepter."

So saying he sent Artabanus back to Susa.

---

24. The implicit comparison is with Darius' campaign against the Scythians (Book 4), who *were* nomads and whose scorched-earth strategy caused starvation in the Persian ranks.

25. The grim implication here is that the Greek cities on the coast of Asia Minor were effectively hostages; they could be destroyed if the conscripts they dispatched did not fight zealously for the Persians. Most of the Ionian troops seem to have done so, despite the efforts of Themistocles to urge them to defect or to fight poorly against their countrymen.

The Persian army now commenced its crossing of the Hellespont bridge, a process that, according to Herodotus, took seven days and nights to complete—and that "under the lash." Once on the European side, the troops gathered at Doriscus, where Xerxes conducted a tally by marching them in groups into a circle that holds 10,000 men, producing a total of 1,700,000 (to quote Herodotus' grossly exaggerated figure). A similar review is held of the fleet, which is found to contain 1,207 vessels (a more plausible number). Herodotus here catalogues the various cities and nations comprising the two Persian armed forces, including in each case a description of the indigenous style of dress and weaponry—a breathtaking roll call spanning many pages and encompassing virtually all the lands of Asia.

Herodotus now represents Xerxes, proud of his enormous might, seeking a colloquy with an adviser, as he had done at the Hellespont; this time his interlocutor is Demaratus, former king of Sparta. The dialogue that results represents Herodotus' most concerted attempt to contrast the political and military culture of Greece, in particular Sparta, with that of Persia.

[7.101][26] After he had sailed through the fleet and disembarked from his ship, Xerxes sent for Demaratus, son of Ariston, who had come with him on the march, and asked: "Demaratus, I would like to put this question to you. You're a Greek, and as I understand from you and from the other Greeks I've spoken with, you hail from a noteworthy and powerful city. So tell me now: Will the Greeks have the courage to put up a fight against me? I myself think not; for even if all the Greeks, and those dwelling west of them, were to join forces, they still would not be strong enough to withstand my attack, since they lack cohesion. But I want to hear what you have to say about these people." "Sire," said Demaratus, "do you want me to give a true answer or to please you?" Xerxes bade him answer truthfully, promising that he would lose none of the king's favor thereby.

"Sire," said Demaratus, "since you want the truth, and since any lie would be detected by you in time anyway, I say this: Greece has poverty as her birthright, but she has also won courage by her own merits, namely by her wisdom and the strength of her laws. With courage Greece is able to keep both poverty and despotism from her shores.

"I have high praise for all the Greeks living in Dorian lands,[27] but in what I will say next I am speaking only of the Spartans. First of

26. This section was translated by the editor.
27. The "Dorian lands" are, principally, those of the Peloponnese. The Dorians were the ethnic subgroup of the Greek people to which the Spartans be-

all, they will never come to terms with you and bring enslavement to Greece. Second, they will stand up to you in battle even if all the other Greeks go over to your side. Don't bother to ask how many they are that they are able to do this; if there are but a thousand in the field, these will fight you; if they are fewer, or more, these will fight you just the same."

[7.103] At this Xerxes laughed and said: "Demaratus, what are you talking about—a thousand men fighting an army of this size? Come, tell me, since you claim to be a king of these men: Would you want to fight alone against ten men? . . . In all reasonableness, how could a thousand men, or ten thousand, or fifty thousand, stand up to an army like ours, especially free and equal men who are not under a single ruler? . . . If they had such a ruler, as our troops do, in fear of him they might become better fighters than their own natures allow, and under compulsion of the whip,[28] few might hold out against many. But with the laxity that freedom allows, there's no way they could do this. For my part I don't believe that Greeks would have an easy time fighting Persians even if the numbers of forces were equal.

"We too possess this quality you speak of, though it's rare; but there are among our Persian lancers some who would willingly fight three Greeks at once. But you know nothing of this, and so your words are meaningless."

[7.104] To this Demaratus replied, "I knew from the outset, sire, that my answer would displease you if I spoke the truth. But it was the truth you urged me to speak, so I told you how things are with the Spartans. You know well enough that I have no love for them; they deprived me of office and privilege, of city and home, and drove me into exile. Your father took me in and gave me both a home and a way to make a living. No man of sense is likely to reject a kindness like this; rather he cherishes it more than anything.[29]

"Speaking for myself, I say no, I would not be able to fight ten men, or even two; indeed I would prefer not to fight even one. But if it came to the crunch and there was some great conflict urging me on, I would most want to fight one of those men of yours who claim to be

---

longed, just as the Athenians belonged to the Ionian subgroup. Thus Demaratus' elaborate praise of Dorian values here cannot be applied to the Greeks generally, and certainly not to Athens.
28. Herodotus later depicts the Persian commanders whipping their men into the thick of battle.
29. The point Demaratus is making here is that he can be trusted since he has no reason to magnify Spartan virtues.

a match for three Greeks. The same is true of my fellow Spartans. They are the equal of any men when they fight alone; fighting together, they surpass all other men. For they are free, but not entirely free: They obey a master called Law, and they fear this master much more than your men fear you. They do whatever it commands them to do, and its commands are always the same: Not to retreat from the battlefield even when badly outnumbered; to stay in formation and either conquer or die.

"If this talk seems like nonsense to you, then let me stay silent henceforth; I spoke only under compulsion as it is. In any case, sire, I hope all turns out as you wish."

[7.105] That was Demaratus' response. As for Xerxes, he turned the whole thing into a joke and didn't get angry, but rather sent Demaratus away with kind words.

The glowing portrait of Spartan military virtue given in the above passage is soon followed up by Herodotus' own personal laudation of Athens, based on that city's refusal to abandon the Greek side even under grave pressure from Persia. In this passage Herodotus assumes a knowledge of the final outcome of the war, in particular the fact that the tide of battle was turned by Athenian naval power.

[7.138] The expedition of the Persian king, though nominally directed against Athens, had as its objective the whole of Greece. The Greeks had long been aware of this, but they were not all of one mind. Those who had given earth and water were confident that they would suffer nothing unpleasant from the barbarian. Others who had refused to submit were in a panic, seeing that there were not enough battle-ready ships in Greece to meet the enemy's attack, nor were most of the Greeks willing to fight, being quite ready to accept Persian rule.

[7.139] At this point I feel myself constrained to express an opinion that most people will find objectionable, but which, believing it to be true, I will not withhold. If the Athenians, through fear of the imminent danger, had abandoned their country, or if they had remained there and made submission to Xerxes, there would certainly have been no attempt to resist the king by sea, and without any resistance at sea, by land the course of events would have been something like this: However many lines of defense should have been constructed across the Isthmus by the Spartans, they would have been deserted by their allies, not willingly but under necessity, as city after city would have fallen to the naval power of the invader. So the Spartans would have stood alone, and in their lone stand they would have performed mighty deeds and died nobly. Either that or, seeing the other Greeks going over to the Persians, they would have come to terms with Xerxes. Thus, in either case, Greece would have been subjugated by the Persians, for I cannot see what possible use it would have been to fortify the Isthmus if the king had had mastery over the sea.

So if anyone were to say that the Athenians were saviors of Greece, he would not be far off the truth. For it was the Athenians who held the scales in balance; whichever side they espoused would be sure to prevail. It was they who, choosing to maintain the freedom of Greece, roused the rest of the Greeks who had not submitted, and it was they who (apart from the gods, that is) repulsed the king. Not even the dire warnings of the oracle of Delphi, striking fear into men's hearts, could persuade them to abandon Greece.[30] They stood their ground and awaited the coming of the invader.

In the weeks following their crossing of the Hellespont, the Persian army and fleet moved relentlessly westward toward the Greek world, drinking rivers dry (in Herodotus' fanciful account at least) as they went. Most of the northerly Greek states, which now would bear the brunt of the invasion, capitulated by giving earth and water to the king's envoys. Xerxes did not bother to send envoys to Athens and Sparta, however, remembering that both cities had murdered ambassadors sent by Darius ten years earlier. Probably he sensed as well that there was no point in seeking cooperation from either of these leading Greek cities.

At Athens there was fierce debate over what course of action the city should take. Inquiry was made of the Delphic oracle, which, according to Herodotus, at first urged the Athenians to "flee to the ends of the earth," but then softened its tone somewhat when asked for a more comforting reply. This second oracular response, while still dire, spoke of safety that could be found behind a "wooden wall" and of a disastrous battle that would take place off the nearby island of Salamis. Now the debate at Athens centered on the meaning of this oracle: Some interpreted the "wooden wall" to mean the wooden fence surrounding the acropolis, others the wooden ships of Athens' newly built navy; while the verse proclaiming that "Holy Salamis will destroy mothers' sons" raised the question of whether Greek or Persian "sons" would be destroyed. In the gloomy atmosphere of a city awaiting a

30. Many cities consulted the Delphic oracle as to whether they should submit to Xerxes or fight for their freedom; usually they were advised to submit. The oracular response given to the Athenians, as will be seen in the next section, was terrifying but ambiguous.

*massive assault, most Athenians assumed that they themselves would be the
casualties at Salamis. Into this debate stepped the emerging leader of the
democracy, Themistocles.*

[7.143] There was someone among the Athenians, a man newly risen
to prominence, Themistocles by name, said to be son of Neocles.[31]
This fellow said that the oracles had been entirely misunderstood; if
the Athenians' interpretation were right and they were destined to die
in a sea battle at Salamis, he said, the oracle would surely have referred
to Salamis as "cursed" rather than "holy." If one interpreted correctly,
he told them, then the oracle had been speaking of the enemy and not
the Athenians when it said "Holy Salamis will destroy mothers' sons."
Themistocles therefore advised them to prepare to encounter the enemy by sea, their ships being the wooden wall indicated by the oracle. When he had made this clear, the Athenians embraced this view
in preference to that of the official interpreters who were against
fighting at sea or lifting a hand against the enemy, who instead urged
them to abandon Attica and settle in another country.

[7.144] There had been a previous occasion[32] when the advice
given by Themistocles had proved its worth. The Athenians had acquired a large sum of money for the treasury, the revenue of the mines
at Laurium, and there was a proposal that they should share this out
between all citizens, ten drachmas apiece. But Themistocles persuaded them to renounce this distribution and to use the money to
build two hundred ships for "the war," meaning the war against Aegina.
It was the outbreak of this war that saved Greece, compelling the
Athenians to become a sea power. In actual fact, the ships were not
used for the original purpose but served Greece in the time of crisis.[33]

31. This introduction of Themistocles is peculiar in two ways, first because
the man was not newly prominent but had in fact held various offices for
years, and second because the phrase "said to be son of Neocles" seems to cast
doubt on his parentage. Like the democratic regime that produced him,
Themistocles is characterized by Herodotus as innovative, self-fashioning,
and somewhat irregular.
32. Herodotus here jumps backward in time a few years, to 483 or 482, to
trace the origin of the naval forces on which Themistocles now proposes to
rely. The brief notice he gives to this episode understates its historical importance: Themistocles had early on committed Athens to a navy-based military posture, which was to be the foundation of her power for more than a
century to come.
33. That is, though built for service against Aegina, the ships actually saved

These ships, already built, were ready for use, and more had to be built to add to their number. In the debate they held after receiving the oracle's reply, they resolved, in obedience to the god, to meet the invaders in their ships in full force, along with such Greeks as would join with them.

In the fall of 481, before the Persians had crossed into Europe, the Greek states that had decided to resist the Persians (now including Athens) had sent representatives to a kind of multi-state congress at the Isthmus of Corinth. The first steps in organizing a joint defense of Greece were to send out a reconnaissance party to spy on Xerxes' forces, and to use diplomacy to resolve long-standing quarrels within the Greek world. Athens and Aegina easily patched up their feud, but Argos remained steadfast in its hatred of Sparta, refusing to serve in any joint force led by its old enemy. Efforts to bring in Greek allies from outside the mainland, principally from Sicily and Crete, also failed.

A second congress of the allied Greek states was held in the spring of 480, under more urgent circumstances. A preliminary line of defense in Thessaly had been abandoned for strategic reasons, causing the Thessalians, who now lay exposed to Persian assault, to go over to the enemy. To prevent the Boeotians and the vital city of Thebes from doing the same, the Greeks had to find a new defensive position that would safeguard these places. The decision was made to take a stand at Thermopylae, where steep mountains running down to the sea would force the Persians to march through a narrow pass; meanwhile the Greek fleet could defend the nearby straits off Artemisium, where again the enemy would be forced into a bottleneck. By defending these spots, the Greeks hoped to offset the great numerical advantage of their enemy, since the narrow passageways would admit only a small portion of the Persian forces at any one time. The Greeks considered it essential to stop the Persian army and navy together; either force could do great damage to their territory even without the help of the other.

As the Persians neared Thermopylae and Artemisium, major confrontations both on land and at sea began to take shape. Herodotus pauses before the outbreak of combat to count up, once again, the immensity of Xerxes' forces. Though precise, his figures are impossibly large. Some scholars have suggested that through a misunderstanding of the Persian regimental system, he accidentally multiplied everything by ten.

[7.184] The Persian fleet had got to Sepias in Magnesia and the Persian army as far as Thermopylae, as yet without loss, and their num-

---

Greece from the Persians. It is possible that Themistocles was targeting Persia from the start of the naval buildup but used Aegina as a politically convenient pretext.

bers were still, by my reckoning, as follows. The fleet that sailed from Asia numbered 1,207 ships of various nations, with their original complement of 241,400, allowing 200 men to a ship. Each of these vessels carried on board, apart from their native soldiers, 30 fighting men, who were either Persians, Medes, or Sacae. This amounted to an additional 36,210 men. To this and the previous figure must be added the crews of the penteconters that each carried an average of 80 men. As I have already said, there were 3,000 penteconters, making an addition of 240,000 men. This was the naval force brought from Asia, amounting to 517,610 men.

As to the army, the infantry were 1,700,000 strong, and the cavalry 80,000. To this must be added the Arabian camel corps and the Libyan charioteers, a total of 20,000 men. Adding together the naval and land forces we get a total of 2,317,610. This is the sum of the forces brought from Asia, excluding camp followers and food transport ships with their crews.

[7.185] To this account we have still to add the forces gathered in Europe, regarding which I can only make a rough estimate. The Greeks of Thrace and the offshore islands provided 120 ships, which would total 24,000 men. The infantry furnished by the Thracians, Paeonians, Eordi, Bottiaei, Chalcidians, Brygi, Pierians, Macedonians, Dolopes, Magnetes, Achaeans, and those who dwell on the Thracian coastlands I would put at 300,000. These figures added to the force from Asia make a total of 2,641,610 fighting men.

[7.186–87] Such being the number of the fighting men, I am of the opinion that the camp followers and the crews of the provision vessels and other transports accompanying the expedition amounted to a number not less but more than that of the fighting men. Still, taking them as equal in number, I arrive at the final estimate, which is that Xcrxcs, son of Darius, brought as far as Sepias and Thermopylae a total of 5,283,220 men. . . . Thus it does not at all surprise me that the streams of rivers sometimes dried up as the army drank from them, but I *do* wonder that the food never gave out for so many millions. For by my reckoning, counting only one quart of grain per person per day, they consumed over 10,000 gallons daily—and I don't include portions for the women, eunuchs, pack animals, and dogs.

Among so many millions of men, no one save Xerxes was so worthy of command, on account of his great height and beauty. [34]

---

34. An oddly laudatory remark, given the context. Herodotus constructs a truly complex portrait of Xerxes, colored in different places by both vengeful anger and affection or admiration.

The first contact between the opposing forces (mid-August 480) came in the form of a small naval skirmish: Three Greek ships out on reconnaissance were spotted by the advancing Persian vessels, which gave chase and captured all three; however, the crew of the Athenian vessel had enough time to beach their craft and flee to safety. Already in this first engagement the Athenians demonstrated the superior naval skills that made them so essential to the Greek defense.

Now that they had actually encountered the enemy, the Greek fleet withdrew to Chalcis, about ninety miles south of their original position, "in a panic" as Herodotus says; but their new anchorage also put them in the lee of the island Euboea in case of bad weather. The Persians, by contrast, were sailing down the exposed and harborless coast of Magnesia.

[7.188] The Persian fleet weighed anchor and made for the Magnesian coast between Castanea and Cape Sepias. The leading ships were moored to the land, while the others, there being little room on the beach, came to anchor offshore in lines eight deep. In this way they passed the night, but when dawn broke, the clear skies and stillness gave place to a raging sea, and a violent storm came upon them with a strong easterly gale, which the natives call a "Hellespontine." Those of them who had marked the wind rising and were conveniently moored anticipated the storm by beaching their ships, thus saving themselves and their vessels. But of those that were caught at sea, some were driven onto a place called Ipni at the foot of Pelion, others were driven onto the coast, others were wrecked on Sepias, while others were thrown onto the shore off Melboea and Castanea. It was a monstrous storm, impossible to weather.

[7.189] The story goes that the Athenians had called on Boreas to assist them in consequence of an oracle that had come to them, bidding them seek help from their son-in-law. For according to Greek tradition, Boreas took to wife a woman of Attica, Oreithyia, daughter of Erechtheus.[35] So the Athenians, as the tale is told, taking Boreas to be their son-in-law through this marriage, when they perceived from their station off Chalcis in Euboea that a storm was rising, then—or even before—they offered sacrifice to Boreas and Oreithyia and called on them to come to their assistance by destroying the Persian ships, as they had done off Athos.[36] Whether this was the reason that Boreas fell upon the Persians as they lay at anchor I cannot say, but the Athenians claim that Boreas had helped them before and was responsible

35. Erechtheus, according to mythology, was the first king of Athens.
36. In 492; see p. 90.

for what now happened. On their return, they built him a shrine on the river Ilissus.

[7.190] At the lowest estimate, four hundred ships are said to have been destroyed in this disaster, together with countless men and an enormous amount of treasure. But for Ameinocles, son of Cretines, a landowner near Cape Sepias, the shipwreck turned out to be a great boon. Many were the gold and silver drinking cups that he gathered, after they washed ashore some time later, and among the finds that came into his possession were Persian treasure chests and other valuable articles beyond count. Thus he became a rich man but did not fare well in other ways: For he ended up as the murderer of his children and thus bore a tormenting grief.

With things at sea having taken this turn, Herodotus returns to the land, where the Persian army was preparing to force the pass at Thermopylae.

[7.201] Xerxes had taken up position at Trachis in Malian territory, while the Greeks occupied the pass generally called Thermopylae, though known by the natives as Pylae. This was the situation of the two armies, the one in control of all the region from Trachis northward, the other of all the country extending south.

[7.202] The Greeks who awaited the Persians at this place were as follows. From Sparta, 300 hoplites;[37] from Tegea and Mantinea, 500 from each; from Orchomenus in Arcadia, 120; 1,000 from the rest of the Arcadia; from Corinth, 400; from Phlius, 200; and from Mycenae, 80 hoplites. Such were the contingents from the Peloponnese. From Boeotia there were 700 from Thespiae and 400 from Thebes.

[7.203] In addition to these, the Locrians of Opus answered in full force, and the Phocians sent 1,000. For the Greeks had summoned these through messengers, saying that they were themselves an advance force, that the rest of the allied force was daily expected, and that the sea was under good guard, watched over by the Atheni-

37. A hoplite is an armed infantry soldier, wearing metal armor and helmet and carrying a spear and shield. It may seem odd that the Spartans, who were leaders of the joint defense forces, sent so few hoplites. Herodotus explains below (7.206) that the 300 were an advance force and that more were to be sent soon. It also bears mentioning that the highly trained Spartan soldier was considered the equal of several of the soldier-farmers enlisted by other Greek states, and that for Sparta, with her tiny citizen population, 300 was not a small number.

ans and Aeginetans and other naval contingents. There was no cause for fear; it was not a god that was threatening Greece but a man. There never was, nor ever would be, a mortal who was not liable to misfortune from the day of birth, and the greater the mortal, the greater the misfortune. So their enemy, too, being but a mortal, would be bound to fall from the height of glory. Thus persuaded, the Locrians and the Phocians sent troops to Trachis.

[7.204–05] The troops from the various cities were commanded by their own officers, but the one who was held in the greatest respect and who held command over the entire force was the Spartan Leonidas, son of Anaxandrides, who in turn was son of Leon, son of Eurycratides, son of Anaxandrus, son of Eurycrates, son of Polydorus, son of Alcamenes, son of Telecles, son of Archelaus, son of Hegesilaus, son of Doryssus, son of Leobotas, son of Echestratus, son of Agis, son of Eurysthenes, son of Aristodemus, son of Aristomachus, son of Cleodaeus, son of Hyllus, son of Heracles.[38] He had become king of Sparta quite unexpectedly. With two elder brothers, Cleomenes and Dorieus, he had no expectation of succeeding to the throne. But when Cleomenes died without male issue, Dorieus having already perished in Sicily, he found himself next in succession, being older than Cleombrotus (Anaxandrides' youngest son), and moreover being married to Cleomenes' daughter. It was he who came to Thermopylae, accompanied by three hundred men whom he had chosen and who all had sons living.[39] He also brought with him the Theban troops as I have listed, who were commanded by Leontiades, son of Eurymachus. The reason why he was concerned to take troops from Thebes, and only Thebes, was the strong suspicion that their sympathies were with the Persians; so his request for troops was intended to find out whether they would answer the call or openly refuse to join the Greek alliance. They did in fact send troops, but their intentions were otherwise.[40]

38. This magnificent fanfare of an introduction should be compared with the understated introduction of Themistocles above (7.143). In contrast to the arriviste leading the Athenians, Leonidas carried with him the full legacy of ancient Spartan tradition.
39. The Spartans considered men with living sons to be the best-motivated soldiers.
40. Since ancient times Herodotus has been accused of anti-Theban bias, and the charge seems justified here. It is unlikely Leonidas would have taken along troops of uncertain loyalty. Probably the Thebans at this point fully intended to resist the Persians; only after the Greek defeat at Thermopylae were they forced to medize.

[7.206] The force accompanying Leonidas was sent by the Spartans in order that their appearance in the field might encourage their allies to fight and not defect to the Persians, as they might have done if they saw the Spartans delaying. It was the intention of the Spartans when the Carneian festival was over—it was this that hindered them—to leave a garrison in Sparta and take the field with all speed with their entire force. The rest of the allies intended to act similarly, for it so happened that the Olympic festival fell just at the same period. None of them expected the action at Thermopylae to be decided so soon, and so they merely sent advance parties.

[7.207] The Greek forces at Thermopylae, as the Persians drew near to the pass, were seized with fear and held a council to consider the question of retreat.[41] It was the general view of the Peloponnesians that the army should retire to the Peloponnese and guard the Isthmus. But with the Phocians and Locrians expressing their indignation at this proposal, Leonidas gave his vote for remaining where they were, while sending envoys to the various cities to ask for help, since they were too few in number to make a stand against the army of the Medes.

[7.208] As they so deliberated, Xerxes sent a spy on horseback to see how many they were and what they were doing. While still in Thessaly, news was brought to Xerxes that a small force had assembled here, led by the Spartans under Leonidas of the house of Heracles. The rider approached the camp and made his survey, but he was unable to see the entire force, for there were troops on the farther side of the wall that had been rebuilt and was under guard. He saw only the troops in front of the wall, who happened at this time to be Spartans. Some of those were engaged in gymnastic exercises, others were combing their hair. The Persian observed them with astonishment, marked their number carefully, and with all this information rode quietly back. No one pursued him; no one took any notice of him. So he returned and told Xerxes all he had seen.

[7.209] Xerxes was quite unable to grasp the truth, which was that these men were getting ready, as best they could, to kill and be killed, and their actions seemed to him simply ridiculous. Sending for Demaratus, who happened to be there with the Persian army, he questioned him about all this, for he wanted to know the meaning of the behavior of the Spartans. "Once before," said Demaratus, "at the beginning of our march against Greece, you heard what I had to say

41. Retreat was now an option because the expected reinforcements had not yet arrived.

about these men and you laughed at me when I told you how things were likely to be.[42] It is my most earnest endeavor, o king, to speak the truth before you, so hearken to me once again. These men have come to fight us for the pass, and it is for this they are preparing. It is their custom, when they are about to fight to the death, to beautify their hair. But mark this: If you can conquer these men and the others left behind at Sparta, there is no other people in the world who will venture to oppose you. You are now face to face with the finest kingdom in Greece and with the bravest men." But Xerxes found his words unbelievable, and once again he asked how so small a force could fight against his army. "O king," said Demaratus, "let me be treated as a liar if things do not turn out as I say."

[7.210] Xerxes was still not convinced and allowed four days to pass, all the while expecting the Greeks to run away. On the fifth day, when they made no move and their continued stand seemed to him sheer impudence and folly, he grew angry and sent against them the Medes and the Cissians, with orders to take them alive and bring them before him. The Medes charged the Greeks and fell in great numbers. But others took their place and would not be beaten off, although they suffered terrible losses. Thus was it made clear to all, and especially to the king, that he had much manpower but few real men.

[7.211] All day long the struggle continued. The Medes, after this rough handling, withdrew from the battle, and their place was taken by the band of Persians whom the king called the Immortals, commanded by Hydarnes. These, it was thought, would soon settle the matter; but when they engaged, they met with no more success than the detachment of Medes. All went on as before; they fought in a narrow defile, having shorter spears than the Greeks and deriving no advantage from their numbers. The Lacedaemonians fought most memorably and showed themselves far more skillful in battle. They would turn their backs in unison as if they were in flight, whereupon the enemy would pursue them with much noise and shouting; then the Spartans, just when the Persians were upon them, would wheel around, face the enemy, and inflict heavy losses on them.[43] Some Spartans also fell, but not many. At last the Persians, finding that all their attempts to gain the pass, whether they attacked by divisions or

---

42. 7.101–04.

43. An excellent illustration of the superiority of Spartan warcraft. Only after constant drill and training could a body of soldiers execute such coordinated movements while under attack, and only the Spartan system provided for, and indeed required, such training.

in any other way, were of no effect, withdrew from the pass. During these assaults, Xerxes, who was watching the battle, is said to have leapt from his seat three times in fear for his army.

[7.212] Next day, the fighting was renewed with no better success for the Persians, who had engaged the enemy in the hope that the Greeks, being few in number and disabled by wounds, would not be able to offer further resistance. But the Greeks had been drawn up in divisions according to their cities, and each division took its share of the fighting except for the Phocians, who had been stationed to guard the track over the mountains. So when the Persians found that they fared no better than on the previous day, they withdrew.

[7.213–17] While the king was wondering what to do in this difficult situation, Ephialtes, a man from Malis, was admitted to his presence. In the hope of receiving a rich reward from the king, he told him of the path that led over the mountains to Thermopylae and by so doing he brought destruction on the Greeks, who were holding the pass. (Some time later this man, in fear of the Spartans, fled to Thessaly, and during his exile a price was put on his head at an assembly of the Amphictyons at Pylae. After some time he returned to Anticyra, where he was killed by Athenades of Trachis. It was actually for a different reason that Athenades killed him, as I shall explain later on,[44] but Athenades was nonetheless honored by the Spartans. Thus did Ephialtes perish some time after these events.) . . . Xerxes was overjoyed; he gave his approval to Ephialtes' proposal and immediately sent forth Hydarnes with the troops under his command, who left camp around the time of lighting of lamps. . . . They reached the summit of the mountain by dawn. This part of the mountain was guarded, as I said earlier, by a thousand Phocian men at arms, stationed here to defend their own country and to guard the path, while the pass below was defended as I have described. The Phocians had voluntarily undertaken to Leonidas to guard the track over the mountains.

[7.218] As the whole mountain was covered with oakwoods, the ascent of the Persians was for a time concealed from the Phocians, who finally became aware of it in the following way. There was a complete stillness, and so the Phocians could hear a lot of rustling, as one hears from leaves trodden beneath trampling feet; they jumped up and seized their arms, and in a moment the enemy came in sight. Seeing armed men before them, the Persians were taken by surprise, coming upon an enemy where they had expected no resistance.

---

44. The promised explanation is not found in the preserved text of the *Histories.*

Alarmed lest the Phocians might turn out to be Spartans, Hydarnes inquired of Ephialtes of what nation were these men and, learning the truth, he drew up the Persians for battle. The Phocians, having to endure a heavy shower of arrows, fled to the crest of the mountain and, supposing themselves to be the main object of attack, prepared to perish. But the Persians with Ephialtes and Hydarnes paid no further attention to them and descended the mountain with all possible speed.

[7.219] The Greeks in the pass at Thermopylae received their first warning from the seer Megistias, who saw in the sacrificial victims the doom that would overtake them with the dawn. Deserters, too, came in the night, bringing news of the Persians' encircling movement, and finally at daybreak scouts came running down from the hills with the same news. Then the Greeks held a council, and opinion was divided, some urging that they must not abandon their post, others holding a contrary view. So the force split up; some departed and made their way in scattered bands to their several cities, while others resolved to remain and stand by Leonidas.[45]

[7.220] There is a story that Leonidas himself sent away the troops that departed, being concerned for their lives, but he thought it ignoble that he and his company of Spartans should quit a post they had come to guard. I myself am inclined to think that Leonidas, seeing that the allies were dispirited and reluctant to share the danger, ordered them to retire, while regarding it as dishonorable that he himself should retreat. And by remaining at this post he left behind a glorious name and avoided the obliteration of Sparta's prosperity. For when, right at the beginning of war, the Spartans sent to consult the oracle regarding its outcome, the answer they received from the Priestess was this, that either Sparta would be overthrown by the foreign invaders, or one of their kings would perish. . . . It was with this answer in mind, I think, and wishing to secure all the glory for the Spartans alone, that Leonidas sent away the allies. This is more probable, I think, than that those who departed did so in an undisciplined fashion because of a difference of opinion.

[7.222] So the allies, thus dismissed, obeyed Leonidas and departed, except for the Thespians and the Thebans, who alone remained with the Spartans. But whereas the Thebans remained reluctantly and

---

45. There has been much debate regarding Leonidas' motives in holding to a now-indefensible position. Some have seen in this episode a delaying action designed to permit the other Greek forces to get away unscathed; others a public-relations move to prevent massive defections from the fragile Greek alliance; others, more cynically, an accident in which the Persians had closed the

with ill grace, being retained by Leonidas as hostages, the Thespians stayed entirely of their own accord, refusing to desert Leonidas and his men. They remained and died with them. Their leader was Demophilus.

[7.223–24] At sunrise, Xerxes made his libations and, having waited until the time of the filling of the marketplace, he moved forward. This was in accordance with Ephialtes' instructions, because the descent from the ridge is much more direct and shorter than the circuitous ascent. As the army of Xerxes drew nearer, the Greeks with Leonidas, knowing that they were going forth to die, pressed forward to the wider part of the pass to a greater degree than previously. Until then, they had been holding the wall and making sorties into the narrower section; but now the battle raged beyond the confined space, and the Persians fell in great numbers, for behind them their company commanders whipped on every single man, urging them forward. Many of them tumbled into the sea and perished, and many more were trampled to death by others. No attention was paid to the dying. For their part the Greeks, knowing that their fate was sealed by those who were coming over the mountain, fought with reckless fury, exerting every ounce of their strength against the enemy. By this time, most of them had had their spears broken and were hewing down the Persians with their swords. It was at this crisis that Leonidas fell, after showing exceptional courage, and with him many notable Spartans whose names, together with the names of all three hundred, I have taken care to learn, they being men of great worth. Among the Persian losses were men of note, among them two sons of Darius, Abrocomes and Hyperanthes, both of them born to Darius by Artanes' daughter, Phratagune.

[7.225] There now arose a fierce struggle between Persians and Spartans over the body of Leonidas.[46] Four times the Greeks drove off the enemy and at last by their bravery succeeded in bearing the body away. Thus did the fighting continue until the troops with Ephialtes were close at hand, when the Greeks, informed of their approach, changed the manner of their fighting. They withdrew again to the narrow section of the pass and behind the wall, and took up a position in close formation on a hillock, all except the Thebans. This

---

trap before Leonidas could effect his planned escape. Herodotus, typically, finds a religious explanation for Leonidas' seemingly superhuman courage.
46. The image of the Greeks fighting to reclaim the body of a fallen hero suits the larger-than-life dimensions of the whole Thermopylae narrative, for this is what Homeric heroes commonly do in the *Iliad*.

hillock is at the entrance to the pass, where now stands a stone lion in honor of Leonidas.[47] Here they resisted to the last, with their swords if they had them, if not, with their hands and teeth, until they were overwhelmed by the encircling Persians, of whom some came on from the front after demolishing the wall, while others closed in from behind.

[7.226] Thus valiantly did the Spartans and the Thespians behave; but one man, Dieneces the Spartan, is said to have distinguished himself above all others. They say that before the battle, a man of Trachis told him that when the Persians discharged their arrows, they made such a dense multitude that they hid the sun. Dieneces, not at all dismayed by these words, made light of the numbers of the Medes and replied: "Our Trachinian friend brings us very good news. If the Medes hide the sun, we shall be fighting in the shade instead of the sunshine." He is said to have left behind him many sayings of this kind in popular memory.

[7.228] The dead were buried where they fell,[48] and in their honor, and likewise in honor of those who fell before Leonidas dismissed the allies, an inscription was set up as follows:

Against three million on this very spot
There fought four thousand—but these were Dorian Greeks.

This was in honor of the entire force. For the Spartans alone there was this:

Go tell the Spartans, thou that passeth by,
That here, obedient to their words, we lie.

[7.229] It is said that two of the three hundred, Eurytus and Aristodemus, suffering from a severe disease of the eyes, had been dismissed by Leonidas before the battle and were recuperating at Alpeni. These two men might have agreed together to return safely to Sparta, or if they did not wish to do so, to die with their countrymen. While either course was open to them, they could not agree but were of different minds. Eurytus, learning of the encircling movement of the Persians, called for his armor, buckled it on, and ordered his helot[49] to lead him to the scene of battle. When they arrived, the helot fled, and

47. The name Leonidas carries within it the Greek word for lion.
48. An unusual mark of respect in the Greek world.
49. Each Spartan warrior went to battle accompanied by several helots, essentially slaves who carried his weapons and tended his needs.

Eurytus rushed into the thick of the fray and perished. But Aristodemus, faint of heart, remained behind. Now if Aristodemus alone had been sick and had returned to Sparta, or if both had returned together, I do not think the Spartans would have been angry. But with the same excuse open to both, and one giving his life while the other declined to do so, the Spartans could not but be very angry with Aristodemus.

[7.230] This is one account to explain how Aristodemus returned safely to Sparta; but there is another story, that he in company with another had been sent from the camp with a message, and though he might have returned in time for the battle, he lingered on the road and so survived, whereas his fellow messenger came back in time and perished.

[7.231] When Aristodemus returned to Sparta, he was met with reproach and disgrace. His disgrace took this form, that no Spartan would provide him with a light to kindle his fire or speak to him, and his reproach was to be called "Shaky Aristodemus." However, in the battle of Plataea he would later cleanse himself of all the shame that had been heaped on him.[50]

[7.232] There is a story that one more of the three hundred, named Pantites, survived. He had been sent with a message to Thessaly, and on returning to Sparta he found himself in such dishonor that he hanged himself.

[7.233] The Thebans under Leontiades stayed together for a while with the Greek force and were compelled to make some show of fighting against the Persian army. But when they saw the Persians gaining the upper hand, they took advantage of Leonidas' retreat to the hillock to detach themselves from the main body. With outstretched hands they approached the Persians, saying (as was quite true) that they favored the Persian cause and had been among the first to give the king earth and water; they had come to Thermopylae under compulsion and were guiltless of any injury done to the king. By so saying they saved their lives, for the Thessalians bore witness to the truth of their claim. Nevertheless, they did not get off entirely without misfortune. Some of them were slain by the Persians at their first approach, while the greater number, at Xerxes' command, were branded with the royal mark, beginning with their commander, Leontiades. (Much later, this man's son, Eurymachus, was killed by the Plataeans as he led a contingent of four hundred Thebans attempting to seize Plataea.)[51]

50. 9.71 below.
51. One of several fascinating passages in which Herodotus draws links be-

[7.234] So went the battle mounted by the Greeks at Thermopylae. Xerxes went over the battlefield to view the bodies and, learning that Leonidas was the king and commander of the Spartans, he ordered his head to be cut off and impaled on a stake. This is one piece of evidence among many others that convinces me that King Xerxes was more angry with Leonidas, while the Spartan yet lived, than with any other man. Otherwise he would not have committed this outrage against his body, since the Persians more than any other nation are accustomed to honor men who have distinguished themselves in battle. But the king's orders were carried out.

At nearly the same time as the battle of Thermopylae (mid-August 480), the collective Greek fleet was engaging the Persian navy in the waters off Artemisium. In contrast to the land battle, these first naval confrontations went rather well for the Greeks, and in addition the Persian forces were again weakened by a terrible sea-storm. A contingent of Persian vessels that had been sent around Euboea to outflank the Greeks—just as the detachment under Hydarnes had outflanked them on land—was caught by the storm in open water and destroyed. Herodotus comments, in one of his most pious pronouncements, that "the god was doing his utmost to make the Persian forces equal to the Greek, instead of more numerous."

The successes at Artemisium dwindled in importance, however, once the sailors learned that the defense of Thermopylae had failed. It would do little good now to hold the Persians' ships at bay while their army marched unimpeded into the Greek heartland. So the Greek navy now withdrew at once, slipping away under cover of darkness, to find a safer, more southerly base. Themistocles, commander of the large Athenian contingent, tried a form of psychological warfare during the retreat: He stopped at water sources along the way to leave rock-carved messages, urging the Ionian sailors serving in Xerxes' fleet to desert or at least to fight slackly in the next engagement against their countrymen. He hoped that, even if no desertions resulted, he might at least trouble Xerxes' mind with the fear that they might.

Stripped now of both land and sea defenses, the entire region of Boeotia, with the sole exception of Phocis, went over to the Persian side, including the all-important city of Thebes. Even the sacred oracle at Delphi, with its vast store of riches and precious art objects, lay open to a Persian plundering raid; but Herodotus reports that a series of miraculous portents put the Persians into a panic and drove them from the site. The Delphians even wit-

---

tween the two great wars of his day, the Greco-Persian conflict and the Peloponnesian War between Athens and Sparta, which was just beginning at the time he finished writing the *Histories*. Readers of Thucydides' history of that later war will vividly recollect the Theban attack on Plataea in 431 (2.2 ff.).

*nessed two gigantic soldiers helping to cut down the fleeing invaders—gods
fighting in human form, an apparition straight out of the poetry of Homer.
The city of Athens, meanwhile, knew better than to expect help from mir-
acles and soon learned that they could also expect none from the Spartan-
led Greek army. There were no readily defensible barriers between Boeotia
and Attica, and in any case the Spartans were disinclined to run risks now
that they had lost Leonidas and the three hundred at Thermopylae. They led
the joint Greek army straight to the Isthmus of Corinth, where there was a
fair chance of defending the Peloponnese (Sparta's own backyard) but none
at all of protecting Attica. Athens knew now that it could not avoid a full Persian assault and at this point, according to Herodotus, began evacuating its
people and property to the islands of Salamis and Aegina and the town of
Troezen in the Peloponnese. (A recently discovered inscription called the
Troezen Decree gives evidence that the evacuation had in fact begun well
before this, but no one knows whether it is genuine.) A few thousand stal-
warts remained in the city, perhaps trusting that the "wooden wall" oracle
referred to the acropolis and not the navy after all. When the Persians arrived (early September 480), they quickly smashed this desperate band of
holdouts and put the now-empty acropolis to the torch.*

*Athens itself had fallen into Persian hands, but its people had become "a
city on the sea." The refugees at Salamis were soon joined by the retreating
Greek navy, which itself had roughly 200 Athenian ships and therefore
40,000 Athenians. Themistocles had engineered this retreat to Salamis so
that the navy could be used to defend the refugees and, if possible, fight to
reclaim the city of Athens itself. But command of the allied fleet was not in
his hands; Athens had agreed at the start of the war to allow Sparta to lead
both land and sea forces. And the Spartan admiral, Eurybiades, inclined toward the Peloponnesian defense strategy, which meant abandoning Attica
as well as Salamis and taking the navy to the Isthmus of Corinth. The conflict between Peloponnesian and Athenian war goals broke out into the open
in a series of urgent meetings of the Greek naval commanders at Salamis,
superbly dramatized by Herodotus as part of his inquiry into how the Greek
"nation" had united under one banner.*

[8.49][52] The commanders of the various allied naval contingents met
to make plans, and Eurybiades asked for recommendations as to
where would be the most suitable place for a seafight in all the territory still under Greek control (Attica he excluded as being already lost
to the enemy). The majority opinion was for sailing to the Isthmus
and fighting to save the Peloponnese; the reasoning was that if they
were defeated at Salamis they would be bottled up on an island with
no possibility of rescue, whereas at the Isthmus they could always find

52. From here through chapter 58 were translated by the editor.

safety by fleeing to their own cities. While the Peloponnesian commanders were advocating this course, an Athenian messenger arrived and reported that the barbarians had arrived in Attica and were burning the whole region.

[8.56] When the Greeks heard the report that the Persians had seized the Athenian acropolis, they were thrown into confusion, and some did not wait for a vote on their proposed strategy but dashed for their ships and hoisted sail as if to start out at once. But the others, who stayed at the council meeting, passed the proposal to stage their sea battle at the Isthmus. Then night fell and they broke up the council meeting and returned to their ships.

[8.57] When Themistocles arrived at his ship, a certain Athenian named Mnesiphilus asked him what strategy had been adopted. When he learned that the course was set for the Isthmus and a defense of the Peloponnese, Mnesiphilus said: "But once you sail away from Salamis, you will no longer be fighting for a united homeland; each contingent will peel off and return to its own city, and not even Eurybiades—not anyone!—will stop the fleet from splitting apart. Greece will be wrecked by bad strategy. If in any way you can, go and try to reverse this decision; perhaps you can persuade Eurybiades to change plans and stay right here." This idea greatly pleased Themistocles, and without even making a reply he went off to Eurybiades' ship.

[8.58] When he got there, he told Eurybiades he wanted to discuss something of common concern, and Eurybiades invited him to come on board. There Themistocles sat down and repeated everything he had heard Mnesiphilus say (though pretending the arguments were his own) and added much more besides. Finally he persuaded Eurybiades to disembark and summon all the commanders, once again, to a council.

[8.59] The council met, and before Eurybiades even had time to explain why he had recalled them, Themistocles broke into a long and passionate speech. As he was speaking, he was interrupted by Adeimantus, the Corinthian commander. "Themistocles," he said, "at the games, those who start the race before the signal are whipped." "Yes," said the other, defending himself, "but those who are left behind do not win the crown."

[8.60] Thus he gave the Corinthian a mild answer—for the moment.[53] Turning then to Eurybiades, he used none of his previous ar-

---

53. Later (8.61) the polemics between these two will grow harsher. As a Peloponnesian state, an oligarchy, and a long-standing commercial rival of Athens, Corinth had little love for democratic upstarts like Themistocles.

guments—that if they left Salamis their force was likely to disperse—for he deemed it unseemly to accuse any of the allies to their face. Instead, he adopted another line and said: "It now lies with you to save Greece, if you will hearken to me and engage the enemy here, and disregard the suggestions that we should withdraw to the Isthmus. Compare the two situations: At the Isthmus you will be fighting in the open sea, very much to our disadvantage with our heavier ships and smaller numbers. Then again, even if we are victorious, you will have lost Salamis, Megara, and Aegina. Furthermore, if their fleet advances south, so will their army, and you will be drawing them to the Peloponnese, thus imperiling the whole of Greece.

"Now if you do as I suggest, you will secure the following advantages. In the first place, we shall be fighting in narrow waters with fewer ships against many, with a good chance of coming off best. Fighting in narrow waters favors us, as fighting in the open sea favors them. Secondly, Salamis, where we have lodged our wives and children, will be preserved. And then there is this further consideration—for you a consideration of the greatest importance—that by fighting here you will be defending the Peloponnese just as well as by fighting at the Isthmus; and, if you act thus wisely, you will not be drawing the enemy on to the Peloponnese. If things turn out as I expect and we beat them at sea, they will not attack you at the Isthmus nor will they advance beyond Attica; they will retreat in disorder, and we shall gain by retaining Megara, Aegina, and Salamis, where the oracle foretold victory for us. When men take counsel reasonably, they generally meet with success; but if they reject reason, the god is unlikely to foster human designs."

[8.61] When Themistocles had thus spoken, Adeimantus again insulted him, bidding him be silent since he was a man without a country and calling on Eurybiades not to allow a vote to be taken on a proposal by a man without a city. Themistocles, he said, should indicate which city he represented before adding his voice to their counsel. The point of this gibe was that Athens had been captured and was in enemy hands. Thereupon Themistocles launched into a long and bitter attack on him and the Corinthians, making it quite clear that the Athenians had a city and a country greater than theirs, as long as they had two hundred ships fully manned; for none of the Greeks were capable of resisting these, should the Athenians attack.[54]

[8.62] After this, he turned to Eurybiades, speaking with even greater urgency. "If you remain here," he said, "you will be playing a

---

54. A pregnant observation, in light of the strong-arm tactics Athens would later use to maintain its naval empire.

man's part; if not, you will be the ruin of Greece. In this war everything depends on our ships. Be persuaded by me. If not, we will take our families on board and make for Siris in Italy.[55] It has long been ours, and oracles foretell that we must colonize it some day. When you are deprived of allies such as we are, you will remember my words."

[8.63] At these words of Themistocles, Eurybiades changed his mind, mainly, in my opinion, through fear that the Athenians would desert the fleet if he withdrew to the Isthmus; for without the Athenians the remainder of the fleet would be no match for the enemy. So he came to the decision to remain where they were and fight it out.

[8.74] Meanwhile, the Greeks at the Isthmus toiled away as if they had no confidence in success at sea and realized that everything was at stake. The news of their activities caused great alarm at Salamis; they feared not so much for themselves as for the Peloponnese. At first they talked among themselves secretly, expressing amazement at Eurybiades' folly. Then this undercurrent broke out into the open, and another council was called. They went over the old ground again: Some maintained that they should withdraw to the Peloponnese and fight for that, and not stay to fight for land already lost, whereas the Athenians, Aeginetans, and Megarians urged that they should stay and fight where they were.

[8.75] Then Themistocles, seeing that the Peloponnesians would carry the vote against him, quietly left the meeting and sent a man in a boat to the Persian fleet, instructing him what to say. This man was Sicinnus, one of Themistocles' household slaves and tutor to his children. (Some time later, when the Thespians were admitting others to citizenship, Themistocles made him a Thespian, and a rich man, too.) Arriving in his boat, Sicinnus addressed the Persian generals as follows: "The Athenian commander has sent me to you secretly, unknown to the other Greeks. He wishes well to the king and hopes for a Persian victory. He bids me tell you that the Greeks are in a panic and contemplate flight, and that you have the opportunity to achieve a brilliant success by not allowing them to get away. They have lost all concord and unity and will not oppose you. Indeed, you will see them fighting among themselves, those who are on your side against those who are not." Having delivered this message, he went off.

[8.76] The Persians, believing what he said, proceeded to put ashore a considerable number of troops on the islet of Psyttaleia, which lies between Salamis and the mainland. Then, about midnight,

55. A desperate threat, though probably not a hollow one.

they advanced their western wing toward Salamis in an encircling movement, while those stationed at Ceos and Cynosura advanced to block the whole channel as far as Munychia with their ships. Their purpose was to prevent the escape of the Greeks, to hem them in at Salamis, and to exact revenge for the battles fought off Artemisium. Troops were landed on the islet Psyttaleia because it lay right in the path of the coming action, and when the battle began, most of the men and wrecks were likely to be carried there; so then they could rescue their own men and destroy the enemy. All this was done in silence, so that the Greeks would not know, and the men had no sleep that night as they prepared for action.

[8.78] Meanwhile, among the commanders at Salamis the battle of speeches continued. As yet they did not know that they were surrounded, thinking the enemy occupied the same position as on the previous day. While they were arguing, Aristides, son of Lysimachus, crossed over to them from Aegina. He was an Athenian who had been ostracized by a vote of the citizenry;[56] yet I gather from what I have learned of his character that he was the best and most upright man among the Athenians. Standing outside the conference, he called for Themistocles, who was by no means his friend but his bitter enemy. But putting all that aside in the face of the impending danger, he called him out to talk to him. He had already heard that the Peloponnesians were anxious to withdraw the fleet to the Isthmus. As soon as Themistocles came out, Aristides spoke as follows: "You and I have been rivals before, but now more than ever we should compete to see which of us can do most good to our country. First let me say that however much the Peloponnesians may talk about withdrawal from here, it will make no difference. With my own eyes I have seen what I now report; even if the Corinthians and Eurybiades himself want to get away, they will not be able to do so. For we are completely cut off and surrounded by the enemy."

[8.80] "Excellent advice and good news," replied Themistocles. "That which I wanted to happen, you tell me you have seen with your own eyes. Know that I am responsible for what the Medes have done. Since the Greeks were not willing to fight here, it was necessary to *make* them fight. But as you have brought the good news, go tell them yourself; if I tell them, they will think I have invented it and will not

---

56. The Athenian constitution allowed the citizen body to "ostracize," or exile for ten years, anyone it wished. The provision was designed to prevent stalemates between two rivals for power, and in fact Aristides had been ostracized in a standoff against Themistocles (483).

believe that the Persians have acted so. Go in and report the facts yourself. If they believe you, well and good; if not, it will make no difference, for they won't go anywhere if we are surrounded on all sides, as you say."

[8.81] So Aristides went in and made his report, saying that he had come from Aegina and had with difficulty slipped through the blockading fleet, and that the entire Greek force was encircled by Xerxes' ships. He urged them to prepare to defend themselves. Having said so much, he withdrew. And now there began another contest of speeches, for most of the commanders refused to believe his report.

[8.82] But while they still doubted, a Tenian trireme commanded by Panaetius deserted from the Persians and arrived with a full account of the truth. For this service the name of the Tenians was later inscribed on a tripod at Delphi among those who helped to defeat the invader. With the accession of this ship that deserted to the Greeks at Salamis, and with the Lemnian ship that had previously joined them at Artemisium, the Greek fleet was brought to the full number of 380 vessels. Previously they had fallen short of this figure by two.

[8.83] Now the Greeks, convinced by what the Tenians had told them, prepared for battle. At dawn the men at arms were assembled, and Themistocles delivered the finest speech of the hour, contrasting the better and the worse in man's nature and condition and urging them to choose the nobler course. Then, finishing off his speech, he gave the order to embark, and they went on board their ships.

[8.84] The Greek fleet now got underway and was immediately attacked by the Persians. Most of the Greek ships backed astern and were close to running aground when Ameinias of Pallene, an Athenian, drove forward and rammed an enemy ship. The two ships became entangled and could not disengage, whereupon the others came to Ameinias' assistance and engaged the enemy. This is how the Athenians describe the beginning of the battle, but the Aeginetans claim that the first to go into action was the ship that had been sent to Aegina to bring the Aeacids.[57] There is also a story that there appeared a phantom in the form of a woman, and in a voice that could be heard from one end of the fleet to the other cheering them on, after first rebuking them with these words: "Incredible! How long are you going to keep on backing water?"[58]

---

57. The Aeacids were mythical heroes. A few days earlier a ship had been sent to Aegina to fetch their cult statues, in the hope that these would aid the fleet with divine power.

58. The playwright Aeschylus, who fought at Salamis and later described the

[8.85] The Athenian contingent, which formed the western wing toward Eleusis, was facing the Phoenicians; the Lacedaemonians, who formed the eastern wing toward the Piraeus, faced the Ionians. Of these last, a few, but not the majority, heeded Themistocles' appeals[59] and held back from the fighting. I could here mention the names of many captains serving in the enemy's fleet who captured Greek vessels, but I shall confine myself to two, Theomestor and Phylacus, both Samians. I mention only these two because Theomestor, in reward for this service, was made ruler of Samos by the Persians, while Phylacus was enrolled among the King's Benefactors and presented with a large estate. The King's Benefactors are called Orosangae in the Persian tongue.

[8.86] But by far the greater number of Persian ships at Salamis were severely disabled, some at the hands of the Athenians, others at the hands of the Aeginetans. For whereas the Greek ships fought in good order and in line, the Persians were not in good array and had no plan in what they did, so that the final issue was bound to be as it was. Nevertheless they fought well that day, far better than in the actions at Euboea. Every man exerted himself to the full in fear of Xerxes, each imagining that the king's eye was on him.

[8.87–88] I cannot give exact details as to the part played in this battle by the various foreign and Greek contingents on the Persian side, but I know that Artemisia[60] distinguished herself in a way that raised her even further in the king's esteem. When there was utter confusion on the Persian side, at this juncture Artemisia's ship was being persued by an Athenian vessel. Having nowhere to flee because directly in her path were other friendly vessels and her own ship was nearest to the enemy, she resorted to a measure that turned out to be to her advantage. Pressed by her Athenian pursuer, she rammed a ship of her own side, a ship of Calynda, which happened to have aboard Damasythimus, the Calyndian king. I cannot say whether she had any quarrel with this man dating from the time when they were at

---

battle in his play *The Persians*, similarly reported a divine voice urging the Greeks on (though with different words) just as the fighting commenced.
59. That is, the rock-carved messages he had left near springs around Artemisium (see p. 151 above).
60. A non-Greek woman who had become ruler of the Greek city of Halicarnassus on the Turkish coast (Herodotus' hometown). In an earlier passage, not included in this volume, she had urged Xerxes not to fight the sea battle at Salamis but to simply wait for the Greek fleet to fall apart.

the Hellespont, nor can I say whether she did this of set purpose or whether the Calyndian ship just happened to be in the way. But by ramming and sinking it, she derived a double advantage for herself. In the first place, the captain of the Athenian vessel, seeing her ramming an enemy ship, thought that either Artemisia's ship was a Greek or that it had deserted from the Persians and was fighting on their side; and so he turned away to attack others. Thus it came about that Artemisia escaped with her life. Secondly, by causing injury to her own side she raised herself higher than ever in the esteem of King Xerxes. It is said that as the king watched the battle, he observed this incident of the ramming, and one of his attendants remarked: "Do you see, master, how well Artemisia fights and how she has sunk an enemy ship?" The king asked if this was really Artemisia's doing and they assured him it was so, for they knew her ensign. (Of course, they supposed that it was an enemy ship that had been sunk. She was indeed fortunate, especially in there being no survivors from the Calyndian ship to accuse her.) The story is that Xerxes said in reply: "My men have become women, my women, men."

[8.89] There fell in this struggle Ariabignes, a commander in the fleet, son of Darius and brother of Xerxes, and with him many other men of note among the Persians, Medes, and their allies. Of the Greeks there perished not many, for, knowing how to swim, those who lost their ships but were not actually slain in combat swam over to Salamis, whereas most of the enemy, unable to swim, were drowned. It was when the enemy's leading ships turned to flee that the greatest destruction took place. For those behind them, being eager to display their valor to the king, pressed forward to the front and became entangled with the ships of their retreating comrades.

[8.90] In the confusion that followed, some of the Phoenicians whose ships had been destroyed came to Xerxes and alleged that the Ionians were responsible for the loss of their ships, accusing them as traitors. But as a result, the Ionian captains escaped death while their Phoenician accusers died instead. For it so happened that while they were still speaking to Xerxes, a Samothracian ship rammed an Athenian ship, and while this was sinking, an Aeginetan vessel attacked and sank the Samothracian ship. But the Samothracians, being skilled javelin throwers, cleared the decks of the vessel that had disabled them, leapt aboard, and captured it. This proved to be the salvation of the Ionians, for when Xerxes saw this remarkable exploit, being already very vexed and ready to blame anyone, he turned on the

Phoenicians and ordered their heads to be cut off, so that they could nevermore blame braver men for their own cowardice.

[8.93] In this sea battle the greatest glory on the Greek side went to the Aeginetans, and after them to the Athenians; and of individuals, to Polycritus the Aeginetan and to the Athenians Eumenes of Anagyrus and Ameinias of Pallene. It was the latter who had given chase to Artemisia, and had he known that Artemisia was on board he would never have desisted from the chase until either he had captured her or else been captured himself. For the Athenians, indignant that a woman should make war on them, had given the captains special orders regarding the queen, and a reward of 10,000 drachmas was proclaimed for whoever would take her alive. However, as I have said, she succeeded in escaping. Her ship and the others that got away now lay at Phalerum.[61]

[8.94] The Athenians say that right at the beginning of the action, the Corinthian commander Adeimantus was seized with panic and, hoisting sail, ran away, whereupon the rest of the Corinthian contingent, seeing their commander in flight, followed his example. But when they were off that part of the coast of Salamis where stands the temple of Athene Sciras, they encountered a small boat, sent by some divine force—since it was never discovered that anyone had sent it to them. Until its appearance, the Corinthians knew nothing of how the battle was going, but from what ensued they concluded that the will of god was there manifested. When the bark came close to them, those on board cried out: "Adeimantus, by turning away in flight you are betraying the Greeks, while they are gaining as great a victory over their enemies as ever they prayed for." When Adeimantus refused to believe these words, they went on to say that he might take them along as hostages and put them to death if he did not find the Greeks having the upper hand. So he and the rest of his ships turned around and rejoined the fleet, but when they arrived the fighting was already over. Such is the story told by the Athenians, but the Corinthians deny this. On the contrary, they claim that they were among the foremost in the fight, and the rest of Greece bears witness in their favor.[62]

[8.97] When Xerxes realized what a disaster he had suffered, he feared that the Greeks, either on their own initiative or prompted by

61. Phalerum was at this time the harbor of Athens.
62. The dispute Herodotus records here reflects the political alignments of his own day. Athens and Corinth had become bitter enemies by the 430s, so the Athenians had ample motive to bad-mouth the Corinthians for not assisting "their" great effort at Salamis.

the Ionians, might sail to the Hellespont to destroy the bridges. He would then be cut off in Europe and in danger of his life. So he made up his mind to take flight, but lest this should become apparent to the Greeks and to his own people, he set to work to construct a mole across the channel to Salamis, lashing together some Phoenician merchant ships to serve as a floating bridge and a wall. At the same, time he made preparations as if to renew the sea battle. Seeing him thus engaged, all were convinced to remain and pursue the war as vigorously as possible. But he did not deceive Mardonius, who well knew Xerxes' mind.

[8.98][63] Xerxes also sent off messengers to Persia to bring them news of his misfortune. (There is nothing in this world faster than these Persian messengers. The Persians run them by the following system: However many days a journey will take, they station that number of men and horses along the way, assigning one horse and rider to each stage of the trip. The riders stop neither for snow, nor rain, nor heat, nor nightfall as they make all haste to complete their stages.[64] The first rider hands off his orders to the second, and the second to the third, and so the messages pass from one to the next just like the Greeks pass torches to each other in the Festival of Hephaestus. This horse-relay system the Persians call the *angareion*.)

[8.99] Now Xerxes' first message to Susa, with news of the capture of Athens, had evoked such joy among the Persians who had remained behind that they strewed all the roads with myrtle boughs and burned incense and gave themselves up to celebration and merrymaking. The second message caused so much distress that they all rent their garments, weeping and wailing without cease, and laying the blame on Mardonius. Their grief was due not so much to the loss of the ships as to their fear for Xerxes' safety. And in this state they continued without a break until Xerxes' safe return.

[8.107] Xerxes summoned Mardonius and ordered him to select those of the land forces that he wished and to see to it that his deeds should be as good as his words. That day nothing more was done, but at nightfall, at the king's orders, the fleet quit Phalerum, each vessel making the best speed it could toward the Hellespont to guard the bridges for the king's return journey. Off Zoster, they saw some rocky headlands projected into the sea and mistook these for ships and took

63. This chapter was translated by the editor.
64. If one substitutes "gloom of night" for "nightfall," this sentence becomes more familiar. Since being inscribed above the U.S. Postal Service building on Eighth Avenue in New York City, it has become an unofficial motto.

flight;[65] then, realizing their error, they joined company again and continued their voyage.

[8.108] The next day, the Greeks, seeing the Persians' land forces still occupying the same position, expected that their fleet would also be at Phalerum, and made preparations to encounter the enemy in another sea battle. When they saw that the fleet had departed, they resolved to pursue them, and they did get as far as the Andros without sighting the Persian fleet. They stopped at Andros and held a council. Themistocles proposed that they should carry on through the islands direct to the Hellespont to destroy the bridges. But Eurybiades put forward an opposing view, declaring that if they destroyed the bridges they would be doing Greece a grave disservice. If Xerxes were cut off and forced to remain in Europe, he was not likely to remain inactive, since this would not improve his chances of success and would deprive him of a return home, while his army was being destroyed by lack of provisions; if he took the offensive and acted with vigor, the whole of Europe might fall to him, city by city and people by people, either by subjugation or by prior agreement, while the annual harvest would allow his troops to live off the land. But, he said, as things stood now, the Persian king, defeated at Salamis, did not intend to remain in Europe, and so he should be allowed to escape back to his own country. Thereafter the war should be transferred to the king's own country, Eurybiades said.

[8.109] Finding that he could not persuade the majority of the allies to advance to the Hellespont, Themistocles changed his ground, and addressing himself to the Athenians—who of all the allies were most vexed at the enemy's escape and were eager to sail on to the Hellespont even by themselves if the others would not accompany them—he spoke as follows: "I have myself seen many instances, and heard of many more from others, where men who have been beaten and driven to desperation have recovered their fighting spirit and made amends for earlier disaster. Now we have had the good fortune to save ourselves and Greece by repelling such a vast horde of men. Let us not pursue those who are in flight. It is not we who have wrought this deed, it is our gods and our divine guardians who begrudged that one man should rule over both Asia and Europe, an unholy and presumptuous man who treats alike things sacred and profane, who burns and casts down the statues of the gods, who scourged the sea and cast fetters into it. For the present, all is well with us; so

---

65. An interesting detail, revealing the fearful state of mind of sailors who have endured a bloody defeat.

let us remain in Greece and see to ourselves and our families. Now that the enemy has been completely driven off, let each man repair his own house and sow his land diligently. And in the spring we can sail to the Hellespont and Ionia." All this he said with the intention of establishing a claim on the Persian king, so as to have a place of refuge if ever he got into trouble with the Athenians—which did in fact come about.[66]

[8.110] Thus did Themistocles speak with ulterior purpose, and the Athenians were persuaded. Since his previous reputation for wisdom and good counsel had been thoroughly vindicated by recent events, they were quite willing to hearken to what he said. Themistocles lost no time in sending a boat carrying Sicinnus his house slave, together with other men who could be trusted to keep silent even under torture, to take a message to the king. When they reached Attica, Sicinnus left the others in the boat, obtained an audience with Xerxes, and spoke thus: "I have been sent by Themistocles, son of Neocles, the Athenian commander, the most outstanding and wisest of the allies, to convey this message. Themistocles the Athenian, desiring to serve you, has held back the Greeks from pursuing your fleet and destroying the bridges at the Hellespont. Now return at your leisure." Having delivered this message, they sailed away.

[8.111] The Greeks, having decided neither to continue their pursuit of the enemy nor to sail to the Hellespont to destroy the crossing, laid siege to Andros, intending to capture it.[67] For the Andrians were the first of the islanders to refuse money demanded by Themistocles. Themistocles had put before them the proposition that the money had to be paid because the Athenians came supported by two

66. The story of Themistocles' medism is told not by Herodotus but Thucydides (1.135–38). Ostracized from Athens and under suspicion of treachery, Themistocles appealed to the Persian king (Artaxerxes at that time) for refuge to escape prosecution by his political enemies. In a letter quoted by Thucydides, Themistocles did in fact claim to have saved Xerxes' life by preventing the breakup of the Hellespont bridge. His machinations succeeded, and he ended his life as a distinguished governor of a Persian province.
67. Themistocles' actions here parallel those of an earlier Athenian war hero, Miltiades: Both men tried to capitalize on a great military success by turning to the extortion of money from Greek islanders. In both cases, the pretext was given that reparations were owed by states that had helped the Persians, but mercantile motives were obviously at work too. The tactics employed by Themistocles here prefigure those of the mature Athenian empire, and his exchange of words with the Andrians contains the germ of Thucydides' Melian Dialogue.

mighty gods, Persuasion and Necessity. To this the Andrians replied that Athens might well be a great and glorious city, being blessed with such useful gods; but the Andrians were wretchedly poor, stinted for land and plagued by two unprofitable gods who never quit their island but always dwelled with them, Poverty and Hardship. Saddled with these gods, the Andrians said, they would not pay the money; for Athenian power could never be mightier than Andrian inability to pay. Having spoken these words and refused to pay the money, they were put under siege.

[8.112] Meanwhile, Themistocles, ever eager for gain, sent threatening demands for money to the other islands, using the same messengers as he had sent to the Persian king. If they did not meet his demand, he said, he would bring the Greek fleet upon them and besiege them until they surrendered. By such threats he collected large sums of money from the Carystians and the Parians, who, learning that Andros was besieged because of its support of Persia, and that Themistocles was the most highly esteemed of the commanders, complied with the demands through fear. I cannot say if any of the other islanders gave money, but I rather think there were some. The Carystians, despite their compliance, were not spared, but the Parians, by appearing before Themistocles with money, escaped a visit from his force. Thus it was that Themistocles, while at Andros, extorted money from the islanders unbeknownst to the other commanders.

IX

Persia versus Greece:
Mardonius' War and After

(480–79 B.C.E.)

The first phase of the war had been essentially a stalemate: The Persians had won a major land battle and thereafter had marched unopposed through central Greece and into Athens, while the Greeks had won a major sea battle, thereby driving the Persian navy and the king back to Asia and establishing total control of the sea. The Greek victory at Salamis certainly loomed larger, in that it was the more recent and more decisive engagement. At the same time, Mardonius' land army, as everyone knew, posed a grave threat to Hellenic freedom.

As the winter of 480 set in, forcing a hiatus in military maneuvers, both sides regrouped and prepared for renewed fighting the following spring. Mardonius and his land forces retired to Thebes, the only large Greek city friendly enough to the Persians to provide food and resources, and the Athenians returned to their own broken homes and ravaged fields. Understanding how badly the Athenians had suffered and sensing their discontent with Spartan leadership, Mardonius now launched a crafty diplomatic initiative in an attempt to split the already fractious Greek alliance. As an envoy to the Athenians he used King Alexander of Macedonia, who was both a long-standing ally of Athens and, in part because of a marital connection with the Persians, a collaborator in Xerxes' cause.

[8.140][1] When Alexander arrived at Athens on his mission from Mardonius, he spoke as follows: "Athenians, here is Mardonius' message: 'The king has instructed me, Mardonius, to say this to you Athenians: "I, Xerxes, do pardon the Athenians for all the wrongs they have done me. And I order you, Mardonius, to give them back their land and to let them take whatever other territory they like and govern it as their own masters. And I order you to rebuild all the temples of theirs that I have burned—provided they are willing to come over to my side." Now that I've gotten my orders I must carry them out, unless your behavior makes this impossible. Here's my message to you: What folly drives you to oppose the king in war? You can't possibly

---

1. This chapter and the two that follow were translated by the editor.

prevail, nor can you hold your own forever. You have seen the size of Xerxes' forces and have felt their strength; you know also how much power I have with me now. Our resources are such that even if you defeat my army—and you would be madmen to think that you will—another force many times as great will replace it. So stop trying to match the king's power; you're only losing your own land and endangering your lives. Lay down your arms. You have an excellent opportunity now to make peace, since the king has taken that line. Come to terms with us without fraud or deceit, and be free men once more.'

"That was Mardonius' message, Athenians, and I, Alexander, urge you to heed it. I needn't remind you of my goodwill toward your city, for you've seen it demonstrated many times. You will never, in my opinion, be able to sustain this war forever; if I thought you could, I wouldn't have brought you the message as I did. The king has superhuman power and his arm stretches everywhere. If you don't meet his terms—and they are generous terms, to be sure—then I fear for you, who of all the allied states lie most in harm's way and have suffered constant hardship, and whose land stands right between the two opposing forces.

"Hearken to the king; he has done you great honor by pardoning your offenses and, to you alone of all the Greeks, stretching out the hand of friendship." Thus spoke Alexander.

[8.141] Now, the Spartans had learned about Alexander's mission to Athens and the offer he bore of reconciliation with the king. And they also recollected a set of oracles saying that one day they and the other Dorians would be thrust out of the Peloponnese by a combined Persian and Athenian army.[2] So they became very fearful that the Athenians would make terms with Persia and sent ambassadors to Athens right away. The timing fell out such that these ambassadors were present at the same time as Alexander.

[8.142] So as soon as Alexander had finished, the Spartan ambassadors got their turn. They said, "The Spartans have sent us to ask you not to swerve from your course regarding Greece nor to go along with the barbarian offer. It wouldn't be right or fitting either to yourselves or to the rest of the Greeks—least of all yourselves, since you were the ones who incited this war, not us;[3] the struggle has been over your territory from the start and now has spread to Greece generally.

2. A rare case in which Herodotus cites an oracle that remained entirely unfulfilled.
3. Referring to 499, when Athens had taken part in the Ionian revolt while Sparta had not. There is an alternate version of this sentence in some Herod-

It would be unthinkable if you Athenians, who have always acted as liberators, were to be the cause of the enslavement of the Greeks.

"We will help you bear the burdens under which you now toil. You have lost two years' worth of crops and have been turned out of your homes for a long time now, so we Spartans and our allies will redress these hardships. Turn your women and all other civilians over to us and we will support them for the duration of the war.

"Do not let Alexander, with his prettying-up of Mardonius' speech, make you change your resolve. He has done what was natural for him to do; as a despot himself, he works hand in glove with a fellow despot. But this is not the path for you, if you can think straight about the matter. For there's no trusting barbarian lies." So said the ambassadors.

[8.143] The Athenians made reply to Alexander as follows. "We know as well as you that the power of the Mede is many times greater than ours; there is no need for you to cast that in our teeth. Nevertheless, we are so attached to freedom that we will fight for it as best we can. As for making terms with the invaders, seek not to persuade us; we will never be persuaded. Take back this message back to Mardonius: The Athenians declare that as long as the sun keeps the same course as it now follows, we will never make terms with Xerxes. We will continue to oppose him, putting our trust in the gods and heroes whom he has insulted, burning their temples and images. As for you, never appear before us again with such proposals, urging us to unholy actions while seeming to do us service. It is not our wish that you, the *proxenos*[4] and friend of our people, should suffer any unseemly treatment at our hands."

[8.144] That was their speech to Alexander. Then to the Spartan envoys the Athenians said: "It was quite natural, no doubt, that the Spartans should be afraid lest we come to terms with the Persians. Yet your fear arises from a base conception of the spirit of the Athenian people. Not all the gold in the world, nor the fairest and richest of lands, could persuade us to embrace the Persian cause and bring slavery to Greece. Even if we could bring ourselves to contemplate such a thing, there are many compelling reasons to prevent us. The first and most important of these is the burning and utter destruction

---

otus manuscripts, according to which the Spartans would be saying: "You incited this war without consulting with us."

4. A *proxenos* was an officer chosen to represent the interests of a foreign state within his own borders. Alexander's status as Athenian *proxenos* meant that he was considered a trusted friend of the Athenians.

of the images and temples of our gods; we must take the utmost vengeance on the perpetrator of these crimes, not strike a deal with him! Then again, there is the nationhood of Greece, our ties of blood and the language that we have in common, the temples of the gods and the rituals that we share, our whole way of life.[5] For the Athenians to betray all this would not be right. Know now, if for some reason you did not know it before, that we will never make terms with Xerxes as long as one Athenian remains alive.

"We are moved by your forethought on our behalf, for your willingness to support our families in our time of need. But while acknowledging your generosity, we shall carry on without causing you any trouble. But now, with things as they are, get your army into the field as quickly as possible. If we suppose right, it will not be long before the enemy invades our territory; he will be there as soon as he gets the message that we will do nothing of what he asks of us. So now, before he can appear in Attica, is the time for you to send a force to Boeotia."[6] After hearing this answer the Spartan envoys returned to their own country.

A few months later, the Persians marched out of Thebes and sacked Athens a second time, forcing the Athenians once again into exile on Salamis and Aegina. Having shown his capacity to harm them, Mardonius again tried to woo the Athenians with an offer of reconciliation.

[9.4] From Athens, Mardonius sent over to Salamis a certain Murychides, a Hellespontine Greek, making the same proposals as had previously been conveyed to the Athenians by Alexander of Macedon. Though knowing full well their far from friendly feelings toward him, he made this second approach in the hope that, with Attica occupied by his troops and in his power, they would abate their obstinacy. It was for this reason that he sent Murychides to Salamis to deliver his

5. These are dramatic statements of a collective national identity, something previously unknown in the Greek world. Most Hellenes identified first with their city, next with their region, and, after that, with their ethnic subgroup (Dorians, Ionians, etc.); in all three categories the Athenians had no reason to make common cause with the Spartans.
6. The Athenians anticipate a second march on their city in the spring of 479 B.C.E. and entreat the Spartans to do what they had failed to do in 480, i.e., march out of the Peloponnese to defend Attica.

message to the council.[7] One of the councilors, Lycidas by name, expressed the opinion that their best course would be to take the proposals as set out by Murychides and submit them to the assembly of the people. It may be that he had been bribed by Mardonius, or perhaps he was just expressing his honest opinion. However, the Athenians, both in council and those who stood without, were so angry when they heard it that they surrounded Lycidas and stoned him to death; Murychides they sent away unharmed. With all Salamis in turmoil over Lycidas, the Athenian women soon learned what had happened. Then, each urging on the other and gathering a crowd, of their own accord they rushed to Lycidas' house and stoned to death his wife and children.

With Attica again made barren, the Athenians began to lose all patience with Spartan leadership of the alliance. In a speech before the Spartan Ephors, Athenian ambassadors once again proclaimed their allegiance to the defense of Greece but hinted grimly that circumstances might force them to accept Xerxes' generous terms. Sparta now became genuinely terrified of Athenian medism and, at last, moved the allied army northward into central Greece. Leading the combined forces was the Spartan general Pausanias, who at the time was acting as regent for the underaged king, Pleistarchus.

Seeing the Greek army coming northward to challenge him, Mardonius moved out of Attica and returned to Thebes, where the ground was more suitable for cavalry operations. A major land confrontation now started to take shape near the city of Plataea, and Herodotus builds the tension with anecdotes like the one below.

[9.15–16] While the Persians were engaged in the fortification of Thebes, Attaginus, a Theban, after making great preparations invited Mardonius with fifty of the highest ranking Persians to a banquet. They accepted, and the banquet was held in Thebes. What now follows was told to me by Thersander, a native of Orchomenus, who was held in the highest esteem by his fellow citizens. He said that he was himself invited to the feast with fifty other Thebans; the seating arrangements did not separate the two nationalities, but a Persian and Theban sat side by side. During the drinking that followed the meal, the Persian who shared Thersander's couch spoke to him in Greek and asked him from what city he came. He replied that he came from

7. The "council" is the Athenian *boulē* of five hundred citizens who decided what matters to put up for a citywide debate.

Orchomenus, and then the Persian said: "Since you and I have eaten together at the same table and poured libation from the same cup, I should like to leave with you, in remembrance, this opinion that I hold, so that being forewarned you may take measure for your own good. Do you see these Persians dining here and the army that we left encamped by the river? In a little while you will see but few out of all these men left alive." While he spoke, the Persian shed abundant tears.[8]

Thersander, astonished at his words, said, "Ought you not to be saying this to Mardonius and the Persians next to him in authority?" "My friend," replied the other, "it is impossible for a human being to avert what the god has ordained. Even when the truth is spoken, no one is willing to believe. Many of the Persians know our danger, but we are constrained to follow our leader. The bitterest pain that can afflict men is this, to know much and to control nothing."

This is what I was told by Thersander of Orchomenus, and he also told me that he had related this incident to others before the battle of Plataea took place.

In the summer of 479 the Greek infantry forces gathered into a mass and moved north into Boeotia, where they took up position facing the Persian forces across the river Asopus. A long waiting game now commenced, in which each side hoped to lure the other into advancing across the Asopus— the north bank being favorable to the Persians' cavalry forces, the south favoring the Greeks. While waiting for a general engagement to begin, Mardonius experimentally sent a cavalry contingent to harass the Greek lines, to see how his expert horsemen would fare against armored Greek hoplites.

[9.20] Mardonius, seeing that the Greeks would not come down to the plain, sent all his cavalry against them under the command of Masistius, or Macistius, as the Greeks call him. He was a man of high repute among the Persians and rode a Nesaean horse[9] with a bridle of gold and other splendid adornments. Thereupon the cavalry, approaching the Greeks, attacked them in successive squadrons, inflicting considerable damage and insulting them by calling them women.

[9.21] It chanced that the Megarians occupied the most vulnerable section of the line, where the ground offered the easiest approach

---

8. This parallels a moment on the Hellespont where Xerxes had burst into tears (7.46) on the grounds that none of the vast Persian host would be alive in a hundred years. Their clock has by this time run quite a bit shorter.
9. This was a special breed reserved for the highest ranking Persians.

for cavalry. Being hard pressed, the Megarians sent a message to the Greek commanders, as follows: "Brothers in arms, we Megarians cannot withstand all alone the Persian cavalry, while still holding our original position. Until now we have held out with patience and courage, hard pressed as we are. But unless you send others to relieve us, know that we shall have to quit our post." Such was the message, and Pausanias called for volunteers among the Greeks to take up this position and provide relief for the Megarians. The others being unwilling, the Athenians accepted this task, with a body of three hundred picked men, commanded by Olympiodorus, son of Lampon. These were the men who, out of all the Greeks at Erythrae, volunteered for this task, taking the archers to accompany them.

[9.22] After the struggle had continued for some time, it came to an end in the following way. As the cavalry continued to charge in successive squadrons, Masistius' horse, being in advance of the others, was struck in the flank by an arrow, the pain of which caused it to rear and throw its rider. The Athenians at once rushed upon the fallen man, seized his horse, and slew Masistius in spite of his resistance. At first they could not succeed in doing this, being hindered by his armor. He was clad in a breastplate of golden scales, which he wore underneath a scarlet tunic. The blows they rained on the breastplate had no effect, but someone, seeing what was happening, struck him in the eye. Thus he fell and died. The other horsemen did not see him falling from his horse and dying, for this occurred as they were wheeling about for another charge. It was only when they came to a halt that they missed him, there being no one to give the word of command. Then they realized what had happened, and, urging one another on, the entire body of cavalry charged again, intending to recover the body.

[9.23] When the Athenians saw that the cavalry were attacking no longer in successive squadrons but in a mass, they called on the rest of the troops for assistance. While the infantry were still on the way to their aid, a fierce struggle developed around the body. As long as the three hundred were on their own, they had much the worse of the contest and had to give up the corpse; but when the other troops came to their assistance in full force, the enemy cavalry could no longer withstand them nor yet carry off the body, and they lost quite a number of their men in addition. Having withdrawn about a quarter of a mile, they deliberated as to their best course and decided that, being without a leader, they should return to Mardonius.

[9.24] When the cavalry reached the Persian camp, the entire army, including Mardonius, made deep lamentation for Masistius, shaving their heads and cutting the manes from their horses and pack

animals and wailing without end. The whole of Boeotia echoed with
their cries of grief, for they had lost a man whom the Persians and
their king esteemed as second only to Mardonius. Thus did the Persians in their own way pay honor to the dead Masistius.

[9.25] As for the Greeks, their morale was raised much higher,
for they had not only withstood the assaults of the cavalry but had
compelled them to retreat. They placed the body on a cart and pa-
raded it through the ranks. The body was a sight worth seeing, remarkable for its stature and its beauty. Indeed the troops had already
been leaving their ranks to gaze upon it; hence the decision to carry
it around for all to see.

*For almost two weeks, the opposing armies faced each other across the
Asopus, with neither willing to cross the river and attack on the enemy's
chosen ground. Diviners on both sides—Tisamenus for the Greeks, Hegesistratus for the Persians—gave religious sanction to the delay by continually
finding the auspices unfavorable to attack. During this time Mardonius con-
templated his next move.*

[9.41][10] On the eleventh day after they had moved to Plataea, with
the Greek forces receiving continual reinforcements, Mardonius
began to chafe at always sitting still. He called for a parley with
Artabazus, son of Pharnaces, a man who was respected by Xerxes as
few Persians were. From their council these opinions emerged:
Artabazus recommended breaking camp immediately and withdrawing inside the walls of Thebes, where food and horse fodder had been
stored up in abundance. There they could bide their time and eventually win out with this strategy: They had much gold with them, both
coined and uncoined, and much silver and precious drinking cups;
they should be unsparing in using these to bribe the Greeks, in particular the leading men in each city, and these would quickly surrender their own liberty without any risk on the part of the Persians. That
was Artabazus' opinion, and it coincided with that expressed earlier
by the Thebans,[11] proving the extent of the man's foresight.

But Mardonius' way of thinking was more forceful and heedless
of danger and utterly opposed to that of Artabazus. He thought that
his army was at that moment much stronger than that of the Greeks
and wanted an immediate battle to prevent the arrival of more Greek

reinforcements. Enough of Hegesistratus' auspices, he said; it was time to stop pressing for good omens. Follow the Persian way and attack. [9.42] No one dared to speak against Mardonius' opinion, for his authority was supreme; it was he, not Artabazus, who had been given command by Xerxes.

The unchallenged authority of Mardonius in the Persian camp is implicitly contrasted by Herodotus to the more frustrating task of Pausanias, the Spartan general trying to hold together the joint forces of the Greeks. The various Greek corps commanders held a parley with Pausanias after the Persians had succeeded in choking off a nearby water supply and inflicting numerous casualties with their cavalry raids. At this meeting, it was decided to move the Greek camp, under cover of darkness, to a better-protected place known as the Island. But in the actual maneuver, a number of contingents ignored those orders and moved instead to the town of Plataea, probably to get even farther out of range of the Persian horse. Worse yet, the Spartan forces, who held a vital wing position, got badly spread out as they decamped, for reasons described below.

[9.53] After watching the other regiments leave the encampment, Pausanias ordered the Spartans to pick up their weapons and follow the others (thinking that they were headed for the agreed-on place). All but one of the subcommanders were ready to obey. Amompharetus, son of Poliades, who led the Pitanate regiment, had not been at the council meeting earlier and was astonished at what he saw happening. He said he would never flee from the "foreigners"[12] nor see Sparta disgraced. Pausanias and Euryanax were dismayed at his refusal to obey orders but even more dismayed at the thought of leaving the Pitanate regiment behind; for if the Spartans followed the orders agreed to by the other Greeks, then Amompharetus and his men would be left to certain destruction. After reckoning up the risks, they ordered the rest of the camp to halt and set about trying to convince Amompharetus that he was wrong.

[9.54] While they attempted to persuade Amompharetus, the Athenians were standing their ground in their original position, knowing that the Spartans were apt to say one thing while intending something else. Finally, after all the encamped troops had started to move, they sent a man on horseback to see whether the Spartans were indeed setting out or whether they had no intention of moving at all,

12. A touch of dramatic realism; Amompharetus follows the peculiar Spartan habit of calling the Persians "foreigners" rather than "barbarians."

and to ask Pausanias what to do. When the messenger arrived, he saw
the men still in position and their leaders fallen out in a dispute. Pausanias and Euryanax were pleading with Amompharetus not to en-
danger himself by staying behind alone but had been unsuccessful;
and finally they had started shouting at one another, when the Athenian messenger rode up beside them. In the heat of the argument
Amompharetus picked up a rock with both hands and dropped it by
Pausanias' feet, saying, "Here's my vote: Not to run from foreigners!"[13] Pausanias called him a madman and a fool. Just then the
Athenian asked for instructions, to which Pausanias replied, "Tell
them how things stand here; ask them to move their forces over here
near us and move out as soon as we do." So the messenger went back
to the Athenians.

[9.56] Dawn found the Spartan commanders still arguing. At
last Pausanias, never dreaming that Amompharetus would let himself
be deserted by the other Lacedaemonians (though that did in fact
happen), gave the signal and led the rest of the troops away through
the foothills. The Tegeans followed as well. The Athenians went too
but followed a different route, as ordered. . . .

[9.57] As for Amompharetus, he had stood firm about remaining in position because he didn't believe that Pausanias would dare
leave him behind. But now that the men under Pausanias had gone
on ahead, he realized that they were abandoning him for good and all.
So he ordered his regiment to take up their weapons and march. . . .
Just as he caught up to the other Lacedaemonians, the Persian cavalry attacked in force. The horsemen were following their usual strategy, but when they saw the former Greek position empty, they rode
on and charged as soon as they found their target.

[9.58] When Mardonius saw that the Greeks had moved off during the night and left their camp empty, he summoned a Larisian
named Thorex and his two brothers, Eurypylus and Thrasydeius.
"Sons of Aleuas," he said, "What do you say now, seeing this empty
camp? You and your neighbors always said that the Lacedaemonians
never turn their backs on a fight; you said they were the finest soldiers
of all. But earlier, as you saw, they tried to shift out of their wing position,[14] and now, as we all see, they have taken to flight under cover
of darkness. No sooner were they faced with men of true excellence

13. The defiant gesture plays on the fact that many Greek citizens voted by
using pebbles as ballots.
14. The day before this, the Spartans had attempted to shift position so as to
place the Athenians, instead of themselves, opposite Mardonius and his Per-

than they showed themselves to be worthless, distinguished only for their prowess against other worthless Greeks. Oh, I can understand your mistake in praising their skills, since you know nothing of us Persians. But I'm truly amazed at Artabazus, who feared these Spartans and in his fear gave cowardly advice: to retreat within the walls of Thebes and withstand a siege. The king shall hear of it, I promise.

"But that's a tale for another day. Right now, these fugitives must not get away. We'll chase and catch them and make them pay the full price for what they've done to Persia."

[9.59–60] So speaking, Mardonius ordered the Persians to advance at the double across Asopus in pursuit of the Greeks, whom he thought to be in full flight. In fact, it was only the Lacedaemonians and Tegeans that he was pursuing, for he could not see the Athenians who were making for the plain by another way and were concealed by rising ground. When the commanders of the other divisions of his army saw the Persians hastening in pursuit of the Greeks, forthwith they all hoisted a signal and followed as fast as they could in great disorder and in no formation, a yelling mob, thinking that the Greeks would be easy prey. Pausanias, when the cavalry fell upon him, sent a horseman to the Athenians with the following message: "Men of Athens, a critical struggle lies before us, which will decide the freedom or slavery of Greece. We Lacedaemonians and Athenians have been deserted by our allies, who have fled during the night.[15] Now, therefore, our duty is clear; we must defend ourselves as best we can and assist one another. If the cavalry had attacked you first, it would have been right for us, together with the Tegeans who remain faithful to the Greek cause, to come to your assistance. But as the cavalry has attacked us in full force, it is right for you to give support to that section which is hardest pressed. If your situation is such that you find it impossible to come to our help, you will earn our gratitude if you send us your archers. We know that you have been the most eager combatants in this war, so that you will not refuse this request."

[9.61] When the Athenians received his message, they set off to aid the Spartans and defend them to the best of their ability. But they were on the march when they were attacked by those Greeks who were serving the Persian army, so they could no longer help, being exposed to these assaults. Thus the Lacedaemonians and the Tegeans—

---

sian troops. Mardonius had sent them a message taunting them bitterly for their cowardice.

15. Referring to the fact that most of the other Greek troops had retired to Plataea instead of the agreed-upon encampment.

who had not left their side—were left on their own. Including the light-armed, the Lacedaemonians amounted to 50,000, the Tegeans to 3,000. Being about to engage with Mardonius and his troops, they offered sacrifice; but the omens were unfavorable, and meanwhile many of their number fell and many more were wounded. For the Persians had made a barricade of their wicker shields, and from behind this they were discharging such a dense quantity of arrows that the Spartans were sore distressed. With the sacrifices being still unfavorable, Pausanias raised his eyes to the Plataean temple of Hera and called upon the goddess, beseeching her not to disappoint the Greeks of their hopes.[16]

[9.62–63] Then, when he was still at prayer, the Tegeans were the first to rush forward against the enemy, and a moment after Pausanias' prayer the sacrifices proved favorable for the Lacedaemonians. So at last they, too, rushed against the Persians, who left off shooting to receive their attack. At first the battle raged around the wicker shields. Then, when these fell, there was a bitter fight that lasted quite a long time alongside the temple of Demeter, and this developed into a hand-to-hand struggle, the Persians seizing hold of the Spartans' spears and breaking them. Indeed, in spirit and strength the Persians were not inferior, but they were without armor, untrained, and unequal to their opponents in tactics. Sometimes singly, sometimes in groups of ten, now in fewer, now in greater numbers, they rushed forward at the Spartans and perished. The Persians most pressed their opponents in that section where Mardonius fought on his white horse, surrounded by the thousand picked men, the flower of his army. As long as Mardonius was alive, they continued to resist, causing many casualties among the Spartans; but after Mardonius fell, and with him his bodyguard, the finest of their troops, then did the rest give ground to the Lacedaemonians and turn to flight. Their greatest disadvantage was their lack of body armor, for they were fighting without adequate protection against heavy-armed infantry.

[9.64] Thus, in accordance with the oracle, the slaying of Leonidas[17] was avenged for the Spartans in the person of Mardonius, and thus did Pausanius, son of Cleombrotus and grandson of Anaxan-

---

16. It may seem incredible to the reader, as it has to some modern historians, that the taking of auspices could dictate strategy at such a critical turning point in the fight. A possible alternative explanation is that Pausanias deliberately held back his troops to allow Mardonius to further overcommit himself, using the auspices as a pretext.

17. At the battle of Thermopylae the previous year.

drides, achieve the most splendid victory of any we know of. . . . Mardonius was slain by Arimnestus, a Spartan of distinction, who some time after the Persian war met his end in battle at Stenyclerus, along with his three hundred men, fighting against the entire force of Messenians.

[9.65] Being put to flight by the Lacedaemonians, the Persians fled in disorder and took refuge in their camp behind a wooden palisade they had erected in Theban territory. It is a marvel to me how it came about that, although the battle was fought near the sacred grove of Demeter, yet not a single Persian appears to have died in the holy precinct, or even to have set foot in it, whereas a large number died on the unconsecrated ground around the temple. My own opinion—if one may have an opinion on matters divine—is that the goddess herself would not admit them because they had burned her temple at Eleusis.

[9.66] Right from the outset, Artabazus had disapproved of Xerxes' strategy in leaving Mardonius behind and had consistently tried to dissuade Mardonius from committing himself to battle, with no effect.[18] His dissatisfaction with Mardonius led him to act as follows. He had a considerable force of 40,000 under his command; and when the battle began, well knowing the likely issue, he led his men forward in full battle equipment with orders to follow him at the pace he set. Having given these orders, he made as if to lead them into battle, but as he advanced he saw that the Persians were already in flight. No longer maintaining the same order, he wheeled about and beat a hasty retreat and fled not to the wooden palisade nor to the walls of Thebes but to Phocis, intending to reach the Hellespont with all possible speed.

[9.67–68] Whereas most of the Greeks on the king's side showed no enthusiasm for the fight, the Boeotians engaged in a long struggle with the Athenians. For those of the Thebans who espoused the Persian cause showed great keenness for the fight and were by no means slackers, with the result that three hundred of their best and bravest were slain by the Athenians. When they, too, were routed, they fled to Thebes, parting company with the Persians and the great mass of confederate troops who fled without striking a blow or doing anything of note. It seems obvious to me that the whole barbarian effort depended on the Persians, for the rest ran away before they could engage the enemy simply because they saw the Persians in flight. So they all fled except for the cavalry, the Boeotian cavalry in particular. These did good service to the troops in flight, keeping between them and

18. See 9.41 above.

the enemy and screening their own troops from the Greeks. But the victors pressed on, pursuing and slaying.

[9.69] Meanwhile, as the panic continued, those Greeks who were drawn up around the temple of Hera[19] and absent from the battle were informed that the battle was over and that Pausanius and his men were victorious. On hearing this, they rushed forward in a disorderly fashion, the Corinthians by the upper road across the slopes of Cithaeron and the hills leading straight to the temple of Demeter, the Megarians and Phliasians following the more level route across the plain. These latter had got close to the enemy when they were espied by the Theban cavalry who, seeing them hurrying in disarray, attacked them under the command of Asopodorus. They fell upon them, left six hundred of them dead, and pursued the rest to the shelter of Cithaeron. Thus did these perish ingloriously.

[9.70] The Persians and the mass of the troops fled to the wooden palisade[20] and succeeded in climbing up onto the towers before the Lacedaemonians came up; they at once proceeded to strengthen the defenses as best they could. When the Lacedaemonians arrived they were faced with a vigorous struggle at the defense works. As long as the Athenians were not on the scene, the Persians warded off their assailants and had much the better of it, the Lacedaemonians being unskilled in the art of attacking defensive works. With the arrival of the Athenians, there was a fierce and protracted contest. Finally, by their valor and perseverance, the Athenians gained the top barricade and made a breach through which the Greeks poured in.

First to enter were the Tegeans, and it was they who plundered Mardonius' tent, where among other booty they took the manger of his horses, all in bronze, a notable piece of work. This manger the Tegeans set up as an offering in the temple of Athena Alea, but all else they took they contributed to the common stock of Greek booty. When the barricade was broken down, the enemy no longer kept in close array, and not one of them gave any more thought to resistance; they were quite distraught, so many thousands of terrified men huddled together into a narrow space. So easily did the Greeks slaughter them that of the 300,000 men, minus the 40,000 who fled with Artabazus, scarcely 3,000 survived. Of the Spartans, the losses in the battle amounted to 91; the Tegeans lost 16, the Athenians 52.

19. That is, the Greeks who during the night had withdrawn to the town of Plataea, against orders.
20. In preparation for the battle, the Persians had constructed an enormous fort to serve as their refuge in case of defeat.

[9.71] On the enemy's side, of the infantry the Persians fought best, of the cavalry the Sacae, and of individuals it is said that Mardonius distinguished himself. Of the Greeks, the Tegeans and Athenians fought valiantly, but the Lacedaemonians surpassed all in courage. The only proof I have to show for this—for all the Greeks were victorious over the enemy stationed opposite them—is that the Lacedaemonians faced the strongest section of the enemy and conquered them. In my opinion, much the greatest courage was shown by Aristodemus, who, as the sole survivor of the Three Hundred of Thermopylae,[21] had to endure disgrace and opprobrium. Next to him, the most distinguished were three Spartans: Posidonius, Philocyon, and Amompharetus. However, when the question arose as to who had most distinguished himself, the Spartans who had taken part in the battle decided that Aristodemus, because of the accusation attaching to him, wishing to achieve a glorious death had rushed forward from his station like a madman and wrought valiant deeds, whereas Posidonius, with no wish to die, had behaved no less valiantly and was thereby the better man. Of course, it may be that envy was responsible for this view. All those I have recounted as dying in battle, except Aristodemus, received public honors; but Aristodemus, who courted death for the reason already explained, received no honors.

[9.72] These, then, were the men who most distinguished themselves at Plataea. Callicrates, the handsomest man not only among the Spartans but in the entire Greek army, was killed but not in the battle. As he was standing in the ranks while Pausanias was offering sacrifice, he was struck in the side by an arrow. While his comrades went into battle, he was borne out of the line, struggling against death. He did not grieve, he said to Arimnestus the Plataean, because he was dying for Greece, but because he had not lifted his arm against the enemy or done anything worthy of himself, for all his eagerness.

[9.73–74] The Athenian who is said to have gained most glory was Sophanes, son of Eutychides, of the deme Decelea. . . . Two stories are told of him; according to one, he carried an iron anchor fastened to the belt of his breastplate by a bronze chain. With this he would anchor himself whenever he drew near the enemy, so that when they made a charge the enemy would not be able to dislodge him from his post; then, when the enemy retreated, he would raise anchor and pursue them. The other story, differing from the former, relates that

21. See 7.229–32.

he did not have an iron anchor attached to his breastplate, but that on his shield he bore the device of an anchor, which he kept spinning around and around.

[9.77] The Mantineans arrived on the scene when all was over. Learning that they had come late for the fight, they were greatly distressed, declaring that they deserved to be punished. They were informed of the flight of the Medes with Artabazus and were all for pursuing them, but the Lacedaemonians refused to allow this. Returning home, they sent the leaders of their army into exile. After the Mantineans came the Eleans, and they too returned home in distress, which they also showed by sentencing their leaders to exile.

[9.78] Serving with the Aeginetans at Plataea was a man named Lampon, son of Pytheas, and of the first rank among the Aeginetans. This man made haste to approach Pausanias with a most unholy suggestion. "Son of Cleombrotus," he said, "what you have accomplished is great and glorious, and God has indeed granted to you to save Greece and gain the greatest renown of all men that we know of. Now finish this work so as to acquire even greater renown, so that no foreigner will in future venture to commit outrage against the Greeks. When Leonidas was slain at Thermopylae, Mardonius and Xerxes had his head struck off and impaled on a pike. If you now reply in kind, you will gain the approval of all Spartans and indeed of all the Greeks. Impale Mardonius' body, and then Leonidas, your father's brother, will be avenged."

[9.79] Thus spoke Lampon, thinking to gratify Pausanias, but the other replied: "My Aeginetan friend, I thank you for your goodwill and your regard for me, but your suggestion is far from acceptable. First you raise me to the skies, praising my country and my achievement, then you cast me into the dirt, urging me to insult the dead and thereby gain repute among men. What you suggest would be more fitting for barbarians than for Greeks, and even in barbarians it would be detestable. I seek not to please the Aeginetans by such means, nor any others who would approve such things. It is enough for me to gain the approval of the Spartans by righteous deeds and righteous words. Leonidas, whom you bid me to avenge, is already abundantly avenged. The price has been paid, both for him and for the others who fell at Thermopylae, by these countless lives that were taken. Come not to me again with such a suggestion, nor counsel me in this way, and be thankful that you go from me unpunished." Thus did Lampon, with this answer, go on his way.

[9.80] Pausanias then made a proclamation that no one should lay hands on the booty, and he ordered the helots to gather it all together in one place. So the helots went over all the ground where the enemy had been encamped and found there tents furnished with abundant gold and silver, couches adorned with these same precious metals, bowls, goblets, and drinking vessels all of gold, and wagons laden with sacks containing basins of gold and silver. From the bodies of the dead, they stripped bracelets and chains and scimitars with golden hilts, not even bothering with the richly embroidered garments. What the helots could not conceal they declared to the authorities, but many things they stole and sold thereafter to the Aeginetans, who thus laid the foundation of their great wealth by purchasing gold from the helots who apparently thought it was bronze.

[9.81] Once the booty was collected, a tenth was set aside for the god at Delphi, from which was made the golden tripod that stands on the bronze serpent with three heads, close to the altar. Portions were also allotted to the god at Olympia, from which was made a bronze Zeus ten cubits high, and also to the god at the Isthmus, from which was made a bronze Poseidon seven cubits high. The rest of the spoil— the Persians' concubines, the gold, the silver, other valuables, and the pack animals—was distributed among the troops, each according to his deserts. As to special awards for those who had won distinction at Plataea, I find no record, but I imagine that such awards were made. As for Pausanias, the portion set aside and granted him consisted of ten of everything—women, horses, talents, camels, and everything else.

[9.82] A story is also told that Xerxes in his flight from Greece had left behind his personal tent for Mardonius, and when Pausanias saw it, with its adornments of gold and silver and embroidered hangings, he gave orders to the bakers and cooks to prepare a meal such as they did for Mardonius. They did as bidden, and when Pausanias saw the couches of gold and silver beautifully bestrewn and the tables of gold and silver and the magnificent array of a banquet, he was astonished at the good things laid before him, and for a joke he ordered his own servants to prepare a Spartan meal. Seeing such a vast difference between the two meals, Pausanias laughed and sent for the Greek commanding officers. When they had gathered, he said, pointing to the two tables, "Fellow Greeks, I have brought you together to demonstrate to you the folly of the Mede, who, while enjoying this lifestyle, came to our country to rob us of our poverty." That's what Pausanias is said to have told the Greek commanders.[22]

22. Pausanias' observation here bears comparison with the words of his fellow Spartan king, Demaratus, on the native poverty of Greece (7.102); Sparta in particular cherished her lack of luxuries as a source of rigor and moral

[9.86] After the burial of the dead at Plataea, a council was held at which it was decided to proceed against Thebes and demand the surrender of those who had espoused the cause of the Medes, in particular Timagenides and Attaginus, the leaders of that faction. If the Thebans refused to surrender them, they would lay siege to the town until it fell. Accordingly, eleven days after the battle they besieged Thebes, demanding the surrender of the men. Meeting with a refusal, they laid waste the surrounding country and assaulted the walls.

[9.87] When the destruction had continued for twenty days, Timagenides addressed his countrymen thus: "Men of Thebes, since the Greeks are resolved to continue the siege until either they take the town or you surrender us to them, let not Boeotia suffer any longer for our sakes. If the demand for our surrender is merely a pretext and it is money that they really want,[23] then let us give them money from the treasury, for it was the state, and not we alone, that espoused the cause of the Medes. But if the purpose of the siege is really the surrender of our persons, we will give ourselves up to answer their charges." This proposal seemed right and met with approval, and forthwith the Thebans sent a message to Pausanias indicating that they were willing to surrender the men.

[9.88] As soon as agreement was reached, Attaginus made his escape from the town. His children were surrendered in his place, but Pausanias released them, declaring that children could not be considered guilty of their father's treachery. The rest of the men delivered up by the Thebans expected to be put on trial and hoped to secure acquittal by bribery. But Pausanias suspected this, and as soon as he took them into custody he dismissed the entire allied army, took the men to Corinth, and executed them.

That was what happened at Plataea and at Thebes.

---

virtue. In the mouth of Pausanias, however, this traditional Spartan sentiment carries an ironic twist. Only a few months after the end of the war, as we know from Thucydides (Herodotus alludes to the matter only cryptically), Pausanias lost all his Spartan self-discipline and began dressing and behaving like Persian royalty. Later, evidence came out that he was even conspiring with the Persian king to betray Greece to its old enemy, and he died trying to evade arrest by the Spartans.

23. Timagenides has good grounds for suspecting a mercenary motive, since both Miltiades and Themistocles had turned their hands to extortion following the victories they led at Marathon and Salamis.

[9.89]²⁴ Meanwhile Artabazus, who had fled the battlefield at Plataea, was making his way homeward. When he came to Thessaly, the inhabitants provided for his needs and asked him about the rest of the army; they knew nothing yet of the events at Plataea. Artabazus understood that if he told them the truth about the battle, the Thessalians might well attack him and he and his army would be destroyed. So weighing this risk, he had said nothing at all as he made his way through the Phocaeans, and now he spoke as follows to the Thessalians: "Men of Thessaly, you see how pressed and hurried I am on my march toward Thrace; I've been sent with these men to deal with matters there. You should expect Mardonius and his men to arrive here just after me. See to his needs and serve him well; he won't forget you later if you do." So saying, he marched his army straight through Thrace by way of Thessaly and Macedonia, "pressed and hurried" indeed; he kept to the inland route.²⁵ He arrived in Byzantium having lost many troops to Thracian raids and to hunger and exhaustion during the journey. From Byzantium he was ferried over to Asia.

The battle of Plataea had destroyed the Persian land army in Europe, just as Salamis the previous year had driven the Persian navy out of Greek waters. But the navy, unlike Mardonius' army, had not been destroyed. The ships that survived Salamis had made their way safely to the coast of Asia Minor, where they kept a close watch on the Greek cities of Ionia, protecting Xerxes' dominion over the region. This last remnant of the Persian threat still had to be dealt with if the mainland Greeks were to be assured of preserving their own freedom, or if the Ionians were to ever win theirs back.

In the summer of 479 the Greek fleet, under the leadership of a new admiral, the Spartan king Leotychides, set out for Ionia on a search and destroy mission. This time, though, the Persians were not willing to risk a battle at sea. They beached their ships on the mainland at a place called Mycale and built a barricade around themselves and their naval gear, hoping that the Greeks would not force a landing. But self-confidence was now running high in Leotychides' fleet. After sailing up and down the shore urging the Ionians to desert their masters, Leotychides landed his men and commenced an assault on the Persian barricade. The battle of Mycale, according to Herodotus, took place on the same day as the battle of Plataea and resulted in an equally definitive Greek victory: Persian weapons and tactics were no match for those of the Greek hoplites, and the barricade was breached,

24. This chapter was translated by the editor.
25. Thus avoiding the coastal Greek cities, where news from Plataea was more likely to have arrived before him.

leading to the total rout of the men inside. Those Persians who escaped the fighting were trapped and killed by the Ionian troops who had, up to that moment, been their allies. "Thus," proclaims Herodotus, "Ionia revolted from the Persians a second time"—finally winning freedom some two decades after the uprising of Aristagoras.

Whether Ionia could keep its freedom remained an open question, however, since the Persians still had ample resources with which to reconquer the region the instant the Greek fleet disbanded. The two leading states of the Greek alliance had very different views as to how to prevent this, as the following passage shows.

[9.106]²⁶ After the Greeks had finished off most of the enemy, both those who fought them and those who fled, they set fire to the Persian ships and to the barricade, having first removed the spoils and set them on the beach (including some chests of money they found there). Then they set sail, and when they got to Samos they held a council about the revolt of the Ionia. They thought it best to find a place to resettle the Ionians where the rest of the Greeks could protect them, and let the barbarian have the Asian coast; for it seemed impossible that they could maintain a presence in Ionia and safeguard its freedom forever, whereas if they didn't do this, there was scant hope that the the Persians would let the Ionians get off easy. The Peloponnesian commanders thought it best to seize the trading ports of those Greek cities that had fought on the Persian side, remove their populations, and then resettle the Ionians in these places. But the Athenians disliked the idea of removing the Ionians and also did not want the Peloponnesians making decisions about cities they had founded, and they pressed their case so urgently that the Peloponnesians gave in. And so they made a pact with the Samians, Chians, Lesbians, and other islanders who had fought with the fleet, exchanging oaths and swearing not to desert one another.

The pact referred to here looms far larger in post-war Greek history than Herodotus' brief mention of it suggests. For Athens had at this council meeting undertaken to lead a naval coalition in the eastern Aegean, and that coalition would become an empire. Without signaling explicitly the ramifications for the future, Herodotus shows here, and in the final stretch of his narrative below, how leadership of the Greek world passed from Sparta to Athens in the days after the defeat of the Persians. With its powerful navy, liberal democratic government, and enterprising spirit, Athens was willing

26. This chapter was translated by the editor.

to shoulder the responsibilities of a Panhellenic defense in perpetuity, whereas the Spartans preferred to withdraw into the fortress of the Peloponnese.

Before concluding the story of the Greek fight for freedom, however, Herodotus gives us one last, long, enigmatic look at Xerxes, who had remained in Sardis during the great Persian defeats of 479 B.C.E. Oddly, he shows us nothing of Xerxes' reaction to these catastrophes but instead recounts a lurid tale of illicit love, revenge, and rebellion. While in Sardis, Xerxes became infatuated first with the wife, then with the daughter of a Persian nobleman, Masistes; he began an affair with the daughter, Artaynte, even though she had by that time married his own son. When Xerxes' wife learned of her husband's infidelity, she took vengeance not on Artaynte but on the girl's mother, Masistes' wife, by mutilating her horribly. Masistes, who knew that Xerxes had colluded in the mutilation of his wife, set off for the province of Bactria to raise a revolt against the king, but Xerxes' men caught up with him on the road and killed him and all his sons and followers. The story forms a striking capstone to the saga of the Persian royal line that Herodotus has followed since the middle of the first book of the Histories; to many readers, it suggests a decline of Persian society from its martial origins, as predicted by the Lydian Sandanis at 1.71 and also as envisioned by Cyrus himself in the final anecdote of the text, 9.122 below.

Before reaching that endpoint, however, Herodotus focuses again on the leadership role assumed by Athens in the last stage of the war, with its unmistakable implications for the era of Athenian empire that was to follow—the more unmistakable in that Xanthippus, father of the great Pericles, was by that time in command of the Athenian fleet, replacing Themistocles.

[9.114–15][27] After leaving Mycale bound for the Hellespont, the Greeks . . . sailed to Abydus, where they found the Persian bridges already broken up.[28] They had expected to find them intact and, indeed, had come to the Hellespont on their account. So the Peloponnesians serving under Leotychides decided to sail home, whereas the Athenians, under the commander Xanthippus, stayed there to make sallies against places in the Chersonese.[29] So while the Peloponnesians sailed off home, the Athenians crossed from Abydus to the Chersonese and put the town of Sestus under siege. Since this town had the strongest walls of any in the region, people had streamed into

27. Chapters 115–22 were translated by the editor.
28. They had been destroyed by a storm some months earlier.
29. The Chersonese, today known as the Gallipoli peninsula, was of great strategic importance to Athens because it controlled the trade routes in and out of the Black Sea. Athens, with her large population and poor soil, relied on imported Black Sea grain for its food supplies.

it from all the other towns nearby as soon as they heard that the Greek fleet had arrived from the Hellespont. From Cardia had come a Persian named Oeobazus, seeking safety after having first stored the cables used in building the bridges. Native Aeolians were in possession of Sestus but there were lots of Persians and their allies inside with them.

[9.116] The ruler of this region was a Persian named Artayctes, whom Xerxes had appointed governor. He was a fearsome and high-handed fellow. During Xerxes' march on Athens, he had stolen the wealth belonging to the hero Protesilaus[30] from out of his shrine at Elaeus. . . . For in Elaeus, in the Chersonese, there is a tomb of Protesilaus and around it a sanctuary, containing lots of money, gold and silver drinking cups, bronze, clothing, and other offerings; all this Artayctes had plundered. . . . Now he was under siege by the Athenians, without having made adequate provisions (for he did not expect the Greek attack; they had taken him by surprise).

[9.117] The siege went on until autumn, and the Athenians began to chafe at being away from home and at failing to break through the wall. They asked their commanders to give up and go back, but the response was that first either the city must be taken or the Athenian government must issue orders for their recall. So they made the best of their circumstances.

[9.118] Meanwhile, inside the walls, the holdouts had reached the final extremes of hardship, such that they were boiling and eating the leather straps from their bed frames. When even these were gone, the Persians, including Oeobazus and Artayctes, made an escape at night by lowering themselves down the wall at a point where the besiegers were fewest. When dawn arrived, the local population signaled to the Athenians what had happened, and opened the gates. Many of the troops went off in pursuit of the runaways, while others took control of Sestus.

[9.119] Oeobazus made it to Thrace, where the Thracian tribe called Apsinoi caught him and sacrificed him to their god Pleistorus, as is their custom; those accompanying him were killed in some other way. Artayctes and his group had set out later from Sestus and were caught a little ways beyond Aegospotami. They fought off their pursuers for a long time and many were killed, but others were taken

---

30. Protesilaus, significantly enough, was the mythic Greek hero who was the first to die in the war on Troy. Thus at the endpoint of the text we are reminded of the opening chapters, in which Herodotus reported the Persian belief that Euro-Asian warfare had begun with the Trojan War.

alive. The Greeks tied them up and brought them to Sestus, Artayctes and his son among them.

[9.120–21] And while one of the guards was frying dried fish, the following marvel occurred, according to the inhabitants of the Chersonese: The fish suddenly jumped and wriggled above the fire as though they had just been caught. And when Artayctes saw this, he said to the man frying the fish, "Don't fear this marvel, my Athenian friend; it is not meant for you, but to me it signifies that Protesilaus, the hero of Elaeus, though dead and dried out like these fish, still has power from the gods to punish wrongdoers. I wish now to make reparations for the money I took from the shrine. I will offer a hundred talents to the god in compensation, and I will give two hundred more to you Athenians for my own life and the life of my son." But Xanthippus, the Athenian commander, would not accept. The people of Elaeus wanted Artayctes killed in retribution for Protesilaus, and Xanthippus' own feelings tended the same way.

So, taking him to the headland where Xerxes had built his bridge (some say rather the hill above Madytus), they nailed him alive to a plank and set it upright; then they stoned his son to death before his eyes. After that, they sailed back to Greece, bringing with them many spoils and, in particular, the cables from the bridges, which they intended to dedicate as offerings in their temples. And in that year nothing more transpired.

[9.122] This Artayctes who was hung on the plank had an ancestor named Artembares, who once made a proposal to the Persians to which they gave serious consideration. They brought the matter before Cyrus, saying as follows: "Since Zeus has given empire to the Persians and to you, Cyrus, by way of your conquest of Astyages, let us leave this paltry and rocky land we live in and get other, better territory. Right here next door, and further beyond that, lie many lands, any one of which would make us far more splendid than we are. It's the fitting thing for an imperial race to do, and when shall we have a better opportunity than now, when we rule many peoples and have conquered all of Asia?"

Cyrus heard them out but did not admire their reasoning. He told them to go ahead and do what they proposed, but also to prepare themselves to be ruled rather than rule others; for, he said, soft lands produce soft men; no single land could produce both rich harvests and men skilled in war.

The Persians agreed with his reasoning and went away, bested by the judgment of Cyrus. They chose to live in a harsh land and rule, rather than farm the level plains and be slaves to others.

*   *   *   *   *   *   *   *   *

Historical Epilogue

The events recorded by Herodotus form the first act of a great three-act historical drama unfolding over more than two centuries, roughly from 550 to 330 B.C.E. During all this time, the Greeks confronted the aggressive, expansionist Achaemenid Persian empire to their east, the only power on the world stage that could challenge their growing domination of the eastern Mediterranean. Herodotus chronicles how this Persian state established itself, became master of Asia and North Africa, began to threaten the peoples of Europe, and finally encountered a Greek counterthrust that ended its European ambitions forever. But the story of Greco-Persian conflict did not end there.

Because Xerxes and many of his forces had escaped destruction in 480 and 479, Persian power remained largely intact, still a threat to the freedom of the Asian Greeks and a check on the expansion of the Greek world generally. To safeguard the cities of Ionia and keep the Persians out of the Aegean, Athens formed the Delian League, a coalition of cities and islands dedicated to Greek autonomy even on the Asian mainland. A joint naval force was formed out of contributions, of either ships or money, from the member states; with Athenian commanders at its head, this coalition made important sallies against the Persians in Asia and defeated them decisively in 469 at the river Eurymedon in southern Turkey. Some years later, Athens, acting alone this time, sent a large naval expedition to free Egypt from Persian control, but this force met with reverses and was entirely destroyed. Sometime around 450, Athens and Persia seem to have signed an armistice in which Athens ended hostilities in return for a Persian guarantee that it would leave the Ionians unmolested.

However, in the second act of this geopolitical drama, the Persians slowly crept back toward the Aegean, using their huge cash resources to buy what their armies could not win on the battlefield. Athens and Sparta, divided by the disastrous Peloponnesian War of the late fifth century, actually competed with one another to win the favor, and the financial backing, of the Persian king. By playing off the two superpowers against one another, the Persians weakened both and soon insinuated themselves back into the affairs of Ionia. By 387 B.C.E., the tide had turned enough that Artaxerxes II was able to end the autonomy of the Asian Greek cities, the prize for which the mainland Greeks had fought so zealously a century earlier.

But with the rise of Alexander the Great and the forging of a forced but enduring unity among the Greek cities, the tide turned once again. Proclaiming a war of retribution for the Persian invasions of Europe in 490 and 480, Alexander led the Greeks and Macedonians into Asia, smashing Persian forces at the battle of Gaugamela (331 B.C.E.) and ending the Achaemenid state forever.

Main Characters and Places

Aegina: An island off the coast of Attica, frequently at war with Sparta, Athens, or both.

Alcmaeonids: "Descendants of Alcmaeon"; a wealthy family whose members (including Cleisthenes) exerted great political influence at Athens.

Alexander: King of Macedon at the time of Xerxes' invasion of Greece, when he generally supported the Persians; ancestor of Alexander III, "the Great."

Amasis: Became king of Egypt in 570 after a rebellion against Apries; ruled successfully until 525.

Aristagoras: Son-in-law to Histiaeus of Miletus and ruler in his stead at the time of the Ionian revolt (499); leader of rebel forces in the initial phase of the revolt.

Artabanus: Persian noble, brother to Darius and uncle to Xerxes; depicted by Herodotus as an elder sage.

Artaphernes: (1) Persian noble and governor of Sardis, brother to Darius, and (2) his son of the same name, a general who (with Datis) co-led the naval invasion of Greece in 490.

Artemisia: A Carian queen who ruled Halicarnassus for the Persians and accompanied Xerxes on his invasion of Greece.

Astyages: Last king of the Medes, overthrown by Cyrus of Persia in 549.

Athens: Most populous and wealthiest of the Greek cities of the mainland; ruled by the Pisistratid tyrants from 560 to 510; a limited democracy beginning in 508, under which regime it contributed ships to the Ionian revolt of 499 and thereafter became the principal target of the Persian invasions.

Athos: Headland jutting into the northern Aegean at the tip of the Acte peninsula; site of a Persian shipwreck in 492; thereafter cut by Xerxes' canal.

Atossa: Daughter of Cyrus who became Persian queen, wife of Darius, and mother of Xerxes.

Attica: Region of Greece in which Athens is located.

Babylon: Seat of a powerful and ancient Mesopotamian empire, conquered by Cyrus in 539 and again by Darius after a revolt.

Boeotia: Region of Greece centered around Thebes; base of operations for Mardonius' army in 480 and 479.

Bosporus: Straits that form the entrance to the Black Sea; bridged by Darius at the outset of his invasion of Scythia (c. 517).

Cambyses: (1) Persian nobleman, chosen by Astyages to marry his daughter and who thus became father of Cyrus the Great; (2) his grandson of the same name, son of Cyrus, who ruled Persia briefly (530–22); conqueror of Egypt.

Candaules: Last king of the Heraclid dynasty in Lydia; overthrown by Gyges.

Chersonese: Long peninsula in the eastern Aegean today known as Gallipoli; largely dominated by Athens starting in the mid-sixth century; ruled by Miltiades (the younger) before his escape to Athens.

Cleisthenes: Alcmaeonid politician who spearheaded a democratic reform of the Athenian constitution in 508.

Cleomenes: Powerful Spartan king who dominated Spartan affairs, including its interventions into Athenian politics, during the period 520–490; refused aid to the Ionian revolt.

Corinth: Greek city located near the isthmus where the Peloponnese joins Greece proper.

Croesus: King of Lydia 560–46, who extended his rule over the Greek cities of Ionia; brother-in-law of Astyages the Mede; defeated by Cyrus and (according to Herodotus) made into a Persian royal counselor.

Cypselus: Tyrant at Corinth c. 655–25 and father of the more famous tyrant Periander.

Cyrus: Dubbed "the Great"; Persian nobleman who overthrew the Medes and established the Persian empire c. 550; conqueror of Lydia (546) and Babylon (539); killed (according to Herodotus) in a failed attack on the Massagetae.

Darius: Persian noble who joined with six others to overthrow the Magi usurpers in 522 and thereafter became king himself until his death in 486; invaded Europe by way of the Bosporus c. 517, where he was repulsed from Scythia but conquered Thrace; dispatched invasions of Greece in 492 (under Mardonius) and 490 (under Datis and Artaphernes) to punish Athens and Eretria for their part in the Ionian revolt.

Datis: Persian general who (with Artaphernes) co-led the invasion of Greece in 490.

Deioces: Mede who founded the Median monarchy.

Delos: Sacred Greek island at the center of the Aegean, supposedly Apollo's birthplace.

Delphi: Greek oracular shrine where the Priestess of Apollo, known as the Pythia, answered questions about the future; repository of vast wealth.

Demaratus: Spartan king exiled in 491 after a protracted power struggle with his coregent, Cleomenes; fled to Persia and later (according to Herodotus) accompanied Xerxes on his invasion of Greece.

Democedes: Greek physician who fell into Persian hands and became doctor to Darius and his family.

Elephantine: The "Ivory City," a trading post on the Nile at the southern limit of Egypt.

Ephialtes: Greek traitor who informed the Persians of a path that led to the rear of the Greek position at Thermopylae.

Eretria: Greek city in western Euboea that joined Athens in contributing ships to the Ionian rebellion in 499; subsequently destroyed by Persia.

Getae: A primitive, non-Greek people inhabiting Thrace.

Gyges: First Lydian king of the Mermnad dynasty; usurper of Candaules.

Halicarnassus: Greek and Carian city on the coast of Asia Minor; home city of Herodotus.

Halys: River crossed by Croesus in his invasion of Persian territory, 546.

Harpagus: Median noble; general serving first under Astyages, later under Cyrus.

Hellas: The Greeks' name for their own territory, referring principally to mainland Greece or the Balkan peninsula.

Hellespont: Straits at the western entrance of the Sea of Marmara, today known as the Dardanelles; bridged by Xerxes in his invasion of Greece.

Heracles: Greek mythic hero; son of Zeus who was later deified.

Hippias: Son of Pisistratus who inherited his father's tyranny at Athens in 528; driven out of the city by a Spartan army in 510, took refuge in Persia, and (according to Herodotus) guided the Persians to Marathon in 490.

Histiaeus: Persian-sponsored puppet ruler of Miletus in the late sixth century; helped to foment the revolt of the Ionians from Persia; according to Herodotus, safeguarded the Persian retreat from Scythia.

Ionia: A term usually used by Herodotus to refer to the Greek-populated coast of Asia Minor, but sometimes only the middle portion of that coast is meant (i.e., the portion settled by Ionic-speaking Greeks).

Lacedaemon: The south-central region of the Peloponnese, centered around and politically dominated by Sparta.

Leonidas: Spartan king 489–80, who led the Greek forces at Thermopylae and died there.

Leotychides: Spartan king who replaced Demaratus on the throne after conspiring with Cleomenes to oust him (491).

Lydia: Non-Greek kingdom in western Anatolia; imperial master of various Ionian Greek cities starting in the early sixth century.

Macedonia: Partly hellenized kingdom situated north of mainland Greece; at first resistant to, but later a collaborator with, Persian rule.

Marathon: Coastal plain lying about twenty-five miles northeast of the city of Athens.

Mardonius: Persian noble who commanded the land army of Darius in the first invasion of Greece (492) and then again in the invasion of Xerxes (480–79).

Medes: An Asian people who became powerful starting in the seventh century, participating in the defeat of the Assyrians at Nineveh in 612, thereafter masters of the northern and eastern segments of the Assyrian empire; subjugated by the Persians in 550, they became integrated into Persian society, such that Herodotus often calls the Persians "Medes."

Memphis: Egyptian city visited by Herodotus.

Miletus: Ionian Greek city located on the coast of Asia Minor; intellectual and economic capital of the Asian Greeks prior to its destruction by Persia in 494.

Miltiades (the younger): Athenian nobleman who ruled the Chersonese on behalf of Athens in the late sixth century and early fifth; escaped Persian pursuit and arrived at Athens in time to serve as one of ten generals at the battle of Marathon.

Mycale: Naval station near Miletus, on the coast of Asia Minor.

Peloponnese: Peninsula comprising the southern half of mainland Greece; dominated militarily and politically by Sparta.

Periander: Ruler of Corinth, c. 625–585.

Persia: Originally a province of the Median empire; home to the race who overthrew the Medes to establish the Persian empire.

Phoenicians: A Semitic people famous for seafaring and trade, based in the cities of the Levant but spread widely throughout the Mediterranean; provided the principal naval forces of the Persian empire.

Piraeus: A port on the west coast of Attica; after 493, the harbor serving Athens.

Pisistratus: Ruler of Athens starting around 560, ejected and returned to power numerous times; died in 527, leaving power to his sons.

Plataea: Greek city on the border between Attica and Boeotia.

Polycrates: Ruler of Samos c. 546–22; imperial ruler who built a navy that dominated much of the Aegean; killed by Oroetes, a Persian governor.

Pythia: Greek term for the Priestess through whose mouth the oracular responses were given at Delphi.

Scythia: Territory east and north of the Danube River and north of the Black Sea; invaded by the Persians under Darius c. 517.

Solon: Athenian sage and lawgiver, whose political leadership commenced in 594; died perhaps c. 560.

Sparta: Dorian Greek city in south-central Peloponnese; military superpower of Greece throughout the archaic period.

Susa: Main capital of the Persian empire.

Thebes: Greek city in Boeotia, supportive of the Persians after the fall of Thermopylae in 480; home base for Mardonius' army in 479.

Themistocles: Athenian political leader and naval commander; leader of Athenian contingent of the Greek fleet at the battle of Salamis.

Thrace: Barbarian land situated north of the Aegean.

Xerxes: Son of Darius by Atossa, and king of Persia starting in 486; leader of the great invasion of Greece in 480; died in 465.

Index of Proper Names

Abydus, 128–31, 188
Achaemenes (son of Darius), 120
Adeimantus, 153–4
Adrastus, 12, 14–5
Aeschylus, xv, 157 *n.*
Aegina, 99–100, 138, 139, 152, 190
Agariste, 116–7
Alcmaeon, 115 f.; Alcmaeonids, 93, 114, 115–8, 190
Alexander (son of Amyntas), 88, 165–7, 190
Alexander the Great, xiii, 125 *n.*, 188–9
Alyattes, 6–7, 9, 18
Amasis, xx–xxi, 9, 55–6, 64–6, 190
Ameinias, 157
Ameinocles, 142
Ammon, 15, 59–60
Amompharetus, 173–4, 179
Amphiaraus, 15
Amyntas, 88–9
Anacharsis, 82
Anacreon, 73
Anagyrus, 160
Apries, 54–5
Arabia, 70–2
Araxes River, 46–9
Argeia, 100–1
Argos, 1–2, 10, 21, 77, 139
Ariabignes, 159
Arimaspians, 72
Arion, 8–9
Aristagoras, 90–3, 94–6, 97–8, 121, 184, 190
Aristides, 156–7
Aristodemus, 100
Ariston, 101–4
Artabanus, xvi, xvii, 83, 123–8, 131–3, 190
Artabazus, 172–3, 177, 183

Artaphernes (half-brother of Darius), 90, 94, 95, 97, 190
Artaphernes (nephew of Darius), 107, 121, 123, 190
Artaxerxes, 108, 109
Artayctes, 128, 186–7
Artembares (Mede), 33
Artembares (Persian), 187
Artemisia, xiv, 158, 160
Artemisium, 139, 151
Assyria, ix–x, xx–xxi, 28, 30, 39, 43
Astrabacus, 104
Astyages, 15, 17–8, 26, 120, 190; overthrown by Cyrus, 30–9
Athens, xv, 190; development of, xii, xvi–xvii, xx–xxi, 93–5; supports Ionian revolt, 95–6; chief target of Persian aggression, 96, 107, 121–2, 161; fights off Persians at Marathon, 109–15; becomes a naval power, 138–9; chiefly responsible for Greek victory, 136–7; evacuation of, 152, 168; sought as ally by Xerxes, 165–9; safeguards Ionian freedom, 184–7, 188. *See also* Attica, Miltiades, Salamis, Solon, Themistocles
Athos, 107, 190
Atossa, 76, 120 *n.*, 190
Attaginus, 169–70
Attica, 77, 105, 109, 115, 123, 124, 138, 152–3, 163, 169, 190
Atys, 12–5

Babylon, x, xiv, xx, xxi, 18–9, 191; conquered by Cyrus, 43–5; by Darius, 79–82; customs of, 45–6
Biton, 10
Boeotia, 45, 139, 142, 151–2, 172, 177, 191; Spartan army sent to, 168, 170

Boreas, 141
Bosporus, bridged by Darius, 77 *n.*, 83, 123, 191
Brygi tribe, 107
Bubares, 89
Byzantium, 183

Cabiri, 63
Callatian Indians, 63
Callicrates, 179
Callimachus, 112
Cambyses (father of Cyrus), 31, 36, 191
Cambyses (son of Cyrus), 48, 72–3, 120, 127, 191; conquers Egypt, 51, 56; attacks the Ethiopians, 57, 59–60; goes insane, 60–3; death of, 66–7
Candaules, 4–6, 25, 191
Carystians, 164
Chaldaeans, 43
Chersonese, 85, 185 *n.*, 191
Choaspes, 44, 92
Cimon (father of Miltiades), 109–10
Cleisthenes (of Athens), 93, 118, 191
Cleisthenes (of Sicyon), 116–8
Cleobis, 10
Cleomenes, 99–100, 191; rejects pleas by Aristagoras, 91–3; ousts Demaratus, 101–4; madness of, 105–6
Cobon, 103
Coes, 91
Colchis, 2
Corinth, 7–8, 77, 153 *n.*, 160, 178, 191; isthmus of, 139, 152
Crete, 139
Crius, 100, 105
Croesus, 4, 63 *n.*, 191; converses with Solon, 9–12; loses his son Atys, 12–5; tests the oracles, 15–6; makes war on Cyrus, 17–23; advises Cyrus, 24–5, 42, 47–8, 62; advises Cambyses, 61–3

Cyaxares, 15, 30
Cybebe, 96
Cynegirus, 114
Cyno, 32, 36
Cypselus, 8
Cyrus, x–xi, xxi, 15, 17–8, 61–2, 69, 82, 120–1, 187, 191; attacked by Croesus, 19–23; advised by Croesus, 24–5, 42, 47–8, 62; birth and accession of, 30–9; relations with Greeks, 40–1; conquers Babylon, 43–6, 79; attacks Massagetae, 46–50

Darius, 39, 43, 48–9, 63, 78, 91, 125, 191; advocates monarchy, 69; cured by Democedes, 75–7; reconquers Babylon, 78–82; invades Scythia, 83–5, 123, 127; plans attack on Athens, 96–7, 107–9, 121; death of, 119–20
Datis, 107–8, 121, 192
Deioces, 28–9, 192
Delos, 108, 192
Delphi, oracle of, xvii, 6, 7,15–6, 25, 103–4, 115, 137–8, 192; dedications to, 10, 181; attacked by Persians, 151–2
Demaratus, 100–5, 106, 120, 192; converses with Xerxes, 134–6, 144–5
Democedes, 74, 75–8, 192
Demophilus, 148
Dorieus, 143

Ecbatana, 29
Egypt, viii, xx–xxi, 51–6, 60–1, 120–1,188. *See also* Amasis, Nile River, Psammetichus
Elaeus, 186
Elephantine, 54, 57, 192
Eleusis, 9, 102, 106 *n.*, 177
Ephialtes, 146–7, 192
Epizelus, 115
Erechtheus, 141

Eretria, 95, 109, 192
Eridanus, 71
Eualcides, 96
Europa, 2
Eurybiades, 152–6, 162
Eurypylus, 174

Getae, 87, 192
Gobryas, 84
Gordias, 12
Gorgo, 93
Greece, xi–xiii, 2–3; customs of, 40, 41, 63–4, 122, 168. *See also* Athens, Corinth, Ionian Greeks, Sparta, Thebes
Gygaea, 89
Gyges, viii, 5–6, 25, 192
Gyndes River, 44

Halicarnassus, xiv, 1, 192
Halys River, 4, 18–9, 30, 38, 192
Harpagus, 20, 31–8, 42, 192
Hecataeus, ix
Hellespont, 131, 134, 193; bridged by Xerxes, 121, 128–30; as line of retreat, 123, 161–3, 185
Heracles, 4, 193
Hermophantus, 95
Herodotus, vii, xiv–xviii, xxi, 1, notes passim
Hippias, xii, 93, 94, 109, 111, 193
Hippocleides, 116
Histiaeus, 85–6, 90–1, 96–7, 193
Hydarnes, 145–7
Hyperanthes, 148
Hystaspes, 48–9

India, 70
Io, 1
Ionian Greeks, 42, 122, 133, 159–60, 193; side with Croesus against Cyrus, 19, 40–1; help Darius retreat from Scythia, 84–6; revolt from Persia, 91, 95–8, 184; urged to desert Persia, 151, 183

Jews, x

Lacedaemon, 4 *n.*, 193. *See also* Sparta
Lacrines, 41
Leonidas, 143–51, 180, 193
Leotychides, 102–5, 183
Lydia, 26–7, 193; rise of, 4–9; conquered by Cyrus, 19–20, 22–4; revolt of, 41–2. *See also* Croesus, Sardis

Macedonia, 86, 122, 183, 193
Magi, 30, 66–7
Mandane, 30–1, 36
Marathon, 193; battle of, 109–15
Mardonius, xv, 106–7, 119, 161, 170, 193; supports invasion of Greece, 120–2; makes overtures to Athens, 165–9; leads Persian army at battle of Plataea, 170–80
Massagetae, 46–50, 127
Medea, 2
Medes, ix–x, xx, 16–8, 193–4; rise of, 28–30; conquered by Persians, 36–9, 67, 69, 120. *See also* Persians
Megabates, 90
Megabyzus, 68
Megacles, 115–8
Megistias, 147
Melanthius, 95
Memphis, 51, 52 *n.*, 194
Mermnads, 4
Midas, 12
Miletus, 6–7, 41, 90, 98, 193
Milo, 78
Miltiades (the younger), xvi, 85, 109–14, 194
Minos, 73
Mitradates, 31, 36
Mitrobates, 72
Mnesiphilus, 153
Murychides, 168
Mycale, 183, 194

Naxos, 90, 107
Neocles, 138
Nile River, viii, 51, 53, 54
Nineveh, x, xx, 30, 43
Nitocris, 43–4

Oasis, 60
Oeobazus, 83
Oreithyia, 141
Oroetes, 72–5
Otanes, 68

Pactyes, 41–2
Paeonians, 88
Panaetius, 157
Panites, 160
Pantagnotus, 64
Paris, 2
Pasargadae, 37
Patarbemis, 55
Pausanias, 169, 180–2, 181 *n.*; leads
   at battle of Plataea, 173–7
Peloponnese, 194; defense of,
   136–7, 144, 152, 153, 155, 185;
   Spartan fears for, 166; Xerxes'
   designs on, 121
Pelops, 121
Percalus, 162
Perialla, 103
Periander, 7, 8–9, 194
Pericles, xxi, 118
Persians, ix–xi, xxi, 188–9, 194;
   customs of, 39–41, 69, 120–1,
   133, 181; overthrow Medes,
   37–9; send spies into Greece,
   77–8; debate invasion of Greece,
   119–25; valor of, 135, 145, 174–5,
   187; poverty or wealth of, 17,
   69–70, 75, 181, 187. *See also*
   Cambyses, Cyrus, Darius, Xerxes
Phalerum, 115
Philippides, 110–1
Phoenicians, 1, 3, 128, 194;
   admirals at Salamis, 159–60
Phraortes, 30

Phratagune, 148
Phylacus, 158
Pierians, 140
Pindar, 63
Piraeus, 158, 194
Pisistratus, 109, 194
Plataea, 169, 194; battle of, 173–82
Polycrates, 64–6, 72–4, 194
Prexaspes, 61–2
Priam, 2
Procles, 101
Protesilaus, 128, 186–7
Psammetichus, xx, 51–2
Pteria, 19
Pylae, *see* Thermopylae
Pythagoras, 98
Pythermus, 41
Pythius, 130

Sacae, 41, 114, 122, 140, 179
Salamis, 137–8, 152–6, 168; battle
   of, 157–61
Samos, xiv, xxi, 60, 64–6, 72–4, 78–9
Sandanis, 17
Sardinia, 97
Sardis, 7, 9, 41–2; siege of, 19–23;
   Greek sack of, 95–6. *See also*
   Croesus, Lydia
Sciton, 75
Scythians, 30, 39, 82–3; Persian war
   against, 77, 83–6, 123, 127
Sestus, 128; siege of, 125–7
Sicinnus, 155, 163
Smerdis (brother of Cambyses),
   58 *n.*, 66–7
Smerdis (pretender to Persian
   throne), 66–7, 67 *n.*, 68
Socrates, xvii
Solon, xx, 194; wisdom of, 9–12, 23
Sophanes, 179
Sophocles, xv
Spargapises, 49
Sparta, xiii, xx, 195; fails to relieve
   Croesus, 21–2; scorned by Cyrus,
   41; refuses to aid Aristagoras,

91–3, 95, 166; power struggles at, 99–106; fails to help Athens at Marathon, 111, 115; targeted by Xerxes, 121; military code of, 134–6, 144–5, 145 *n.*, 149–50, 173–5, 180; poverty of, 134, 181; balks at defending Attica, 152, 155, 168–9; fears Athenian medism, 166–7, 169; leads at battle of Plataea, 173–9; advises Greek abandonment of Ionia, 184. *See also* Cleomenes, Demaratus, Leonidas, Pausanias
Stesagoras, 110
Stesilaus, 114
Susa, 44, 195
Syennesis, 18
Syloson, 64, 79

Tabalus, 41
Tellus, 10
Thales, 18, 19
Thebes (in Egypt), 52
Thebes (in Greece), 139, 150 *n.*, 195; held in suspicion by Leonidas, 143, 147–8; medism of, 150, 151, 177; used as Persian base, 165, 169; Greek siege of, 182
Themistocles, 138–9, 138 *n.*, 151,

162–3, 163 *n.*, 195; forces Greek navy to fight at Salamis, 153–7; besieges Andros, xvi, 163–4
Theodorus, 65
Theomestor, 158
Thermopylae, 139; battle of, 142–9
Thersander, 169
Thrace, 86, 87, 98, 107, 183, 186, 195
Thrasybulus, 7
Tomyris, 47–50

Xanthippus, 118
Xerxes, xi, xv, xx–xxi, 108–9, 195; accession of, 119 *n.;* plans invasion of Greece, 120–8; bridges Hellespont, 128–34; converses with Artabanus, 125, 126–8, 131–3; with Demaratus, 134–6, 144–5; leads at battle of Thermopylae, 142–9, 151; at Salamis, 158–60; retreats from Greece, 160–2; offers alliance to Athens, 165–8; falls in love with Artaynte, 185

Zacynthus, 104
Zopyrus, 79–82
Zoster, 161